Wrong Wa

About the author

Lorna Hendry worked in graphic design for many years until she unplugged herself from her computer to travel around Australia with her husband and their two young sons. On their return to Melbourne she changed careers and is now a freelance writer, editor and proof-reader, and teaches Professional Writing and Editing at RMIT University in Melbourne. She lives in Fitzroy, but is still homesick for the Kimberley.

Wrong Way Round

by Lorna Hendry

EXPLORE
AUSTRALIA

Explore Australia Publishing Pty Ltd
Ground Floor, Building 1, 658 Church Street,
Richmond, VIC 3121

Explore Australia Publishing Pty Ltd is a division of Hardie Grant Publishing Pty Ltd

hardie grant publishing

Published by Explore Australia Publishing Pty Ltd, 2015

Maps and design © Explore Australia Publishing Pty Ltd, 2015
Text and photos © Lorna Hendry, 2015

A Cataloguing-in-Publication entry is available from the catalogue of the National
Library of Australia at www.nla.gov.au

ISBN-13 9781741174793

10 9 8 7 6 5 4 3 2 1

All rights reserved. Without limiting the rights under copyright reserved above, no part
of this publication may be reproduced, stored in or introduced into a retrieval system,
or transmitted in any form or by any means (electronic, mechanical, photocopying,
recording or otherwise) without the prior written permission of both the copyright
owners and the above publisher of this book.

The maps in this publication incorporate data © Commonwealth of Australia
(Geoscience Australia), 2006. Geoscience Australia has not evaluated the data as altered
and incorporated within this publication, and therefore gives no warranty regarding
accuracy, completeness, currency or suitability for any particular purpose.

Printed and bound in China by Everbest Printing Co Ltd

Cover design by Josh Durham, Design by Committee
Commissioned by Melissa Kayser
Project managed by Lauren Whybrow
Edited by Martine Lleonart
Proofread by Emma Schwarcz
Cartography by Emily Maffei and Bruce McGurty
Layout and typesetting by Megan Ellis

For James, Oscar and Dylan

Contents

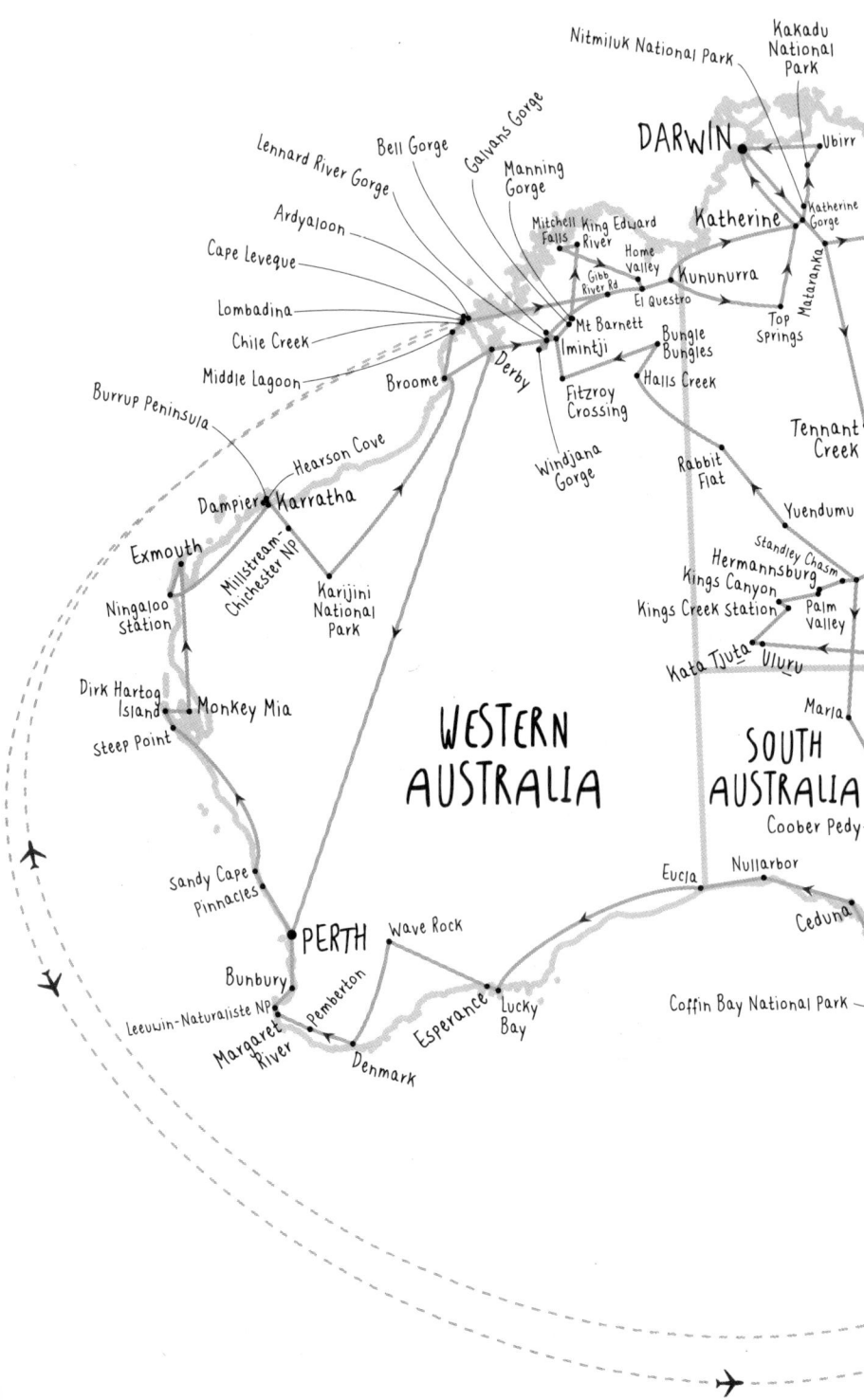

Nitmiluk National Park

Kakadu National Park

Bell Gorge

Galvans Gorge

Manning Gorge

DARWIN

Ubirr

Lennard River Gorge

Katherine

Ardyaloon

Mitchell Falls

King Edward River

Katherine Gorge

Cape Leveque

Home Valley

Kununurra

Gibb River Rd

Lombadina

El Questro

Top Springs

Chile Creek

Mt Barnett

Bungle Bungles

Mataranka

Middle Lagoon

Imintji

Tennant Creek

Broome

Derby

Halls Creek

Burrup Peninsula

Fitzroy Crossing

Hearson Cove

Windjana Gorge

Rabbit Flat

Dampier

Karratha

Yuendumu

Standley Chasm

Hermannsburg

Exmouth

Millstream-Chichester NP

Karijini National Park

Kings Canyon

Kings Creek Station

Palm Valley

Ningaloo Station

Kata Tjuta

Uluru

Dirk Hartog Island

Monkey Mia

Maria

Steep Point

WESTERN AUSTRALIA

SOUTH AUSTRALIA

Coober Pedy

Sandy Cape

Pinnacles

Nullarbor

Eucla

PERTH

Wave Rock

Ceduna

Bunbury

Coffin Bay National Park

Leeuwin-Naturaliste NP

Pemberton

Esperance

Lucky Bay

Margaret River

Denmark

Thursday Island
New Mapoon
Cape York
Bamaga
Jardine River
Eliot Falls
Gunshot Crossing
Bramwell Junction
Weipa
Lockhart River
Butterfly Springs
Lorella Springs
Archer River
Roper Bar
King Ash Bay
Musgrave Roadhouse
Cooktown
Borroloola
Mitchell River
Cape Tribulation
Mission Beach
Cape Crawford
Hells Gate Roadhouse
Dunbar Station
Port Douglas
Wongaling Beach
Robinson River
Karumba
Tully
Dunk Island
Adels Grove
Gregory Downs
South Mission Beach

NORTHERN TERRITORY
Townsville
Richmond
Harts Range
Boulia
Winton
Muttaburra
Alice Springs
Longreach
Rubyvale
Barcaldine
Lambert Gravitational Centre
Mount Dare
Dalhousie Springs
Oodnadatta
Halligan Bay (Lake Eyre)
QUEENSLAND
William Creek
Muloorina
Coolum Beach
Coward Springs
Arkaroola
BRISBANE
Iga Warta
Gold Coast
Byron Bay
Wilpena Pound
NEW SOUTH WALES
Broken Head
Port Augusta
Whyalla
Nambucca Heads
Myall Lakes
Blue Mountains
Innes National Park
Point Turton
Corny Point
ADELAIDE
Burralow Swamp
Wagga Wagga
SYDNEY
Port Willunga
VICTORIA
CANBERRA
Robe
Mount Kosciuszko
Port Fairy
Princess Margaret Rose Caves
MELBOURNE
Port Campbell
(HOME)
Launceston
Devonport
Freycinet National Park
Coles Bay
Wineglass Bay
HOBART
+ Hazards Beach
TASMANIA
Cockle Creek
Port Arthur

Bruce Highway

Chapter One

'This is the most important thing we have', said James, waving a small piece of black plastic in my face. It was a 12-volt triple adaptor. One end had a plug designed to fit into the battery of our brand-new camper trailer, the other end had three outlets. Six months before I hadn't known such a thing existed. Now I was nearly as excited about it as he was.

'We can put the fridge in the kitchen and run two lights off the battery at the same time', James said. 'That way we don't have to leave the fridge in the back of the car all the time. Like this.'

He plugged in the camping lights. They flickered, then shone a weak yellow light into the afternoon sun. He plugged the fridge in and we listened for the hum as it started up. Nothing happened. James peered at the plug and tugged on it. It refused to budge. He pulled harder and it broke off in his hand, the business end of the plug firmly wedged in the adaptor.

We ended up hauling the fully stocked fridge into the back of the car, and James spent fifteen minutes prying the plug out with a screwdriver.

It was an early lesson that when you are camping things often don't go to plan.

We were on our first day of a trip around Australia with our two sons, Oscar, eight, and Dylan, six. We had quit our jobs, rented out our house, enrolled the kids in Distance Education and left home to have an adventure.

It wasn't the first time we had been camping. It was the second. We had done a practice run at Hanging Rock with a borrowed tent a few months earlier. Just before dusk, after the rangers had locked the gates behind the last of the day visitors, we set up the tent, laid out our mattresses and sleeping bags, and settled in for a night under the stars. We drank wine around a fire with the rest of the campers and went on a guided bushwalk in the dark to look for owls, most of whom had sensibly deserted their usual spots before we tramped down the track with forty overexcited kids. The whole experience would have been better if we had taken pillows, torches, a gas bottle that actually fitted our stove and some bottles of drinking water. As a training run, though, it did the job.

When we left home for real, we had an 80-litre water tank, self-inflating mattresses, a two-burner stove with a gas bottle that fitted and a stove-top coffee maker. We also had a laptop; a fold-up toilet seat; four packs of cards; an axe; four books of maps; a logbook to record our mileage and fuel consumption; an iPod with 6000 songs, a complete set of Spanish lessons and six Harry Potter books read by Stephen Fry loaded onto it; a 20-metre extension cord; a barbecue plate; a bottle of vodka in an unbreakable container; and a kitchen sink.

That first day we had driven 233 kilometres from Melbourne to Port Campbell on the Great Ocean Road. Not a huge distance, but we weren't in a hurry; we had a whole year to make our way around the country. That day we spent more time putting up our tent than we had spent in the car, even including an unscheduled stop at the base of the West Gate Bridge. We had to pull up to calm Dylan down, who was sobbing loudly in the back. The reality of our trip only hit him when he saw the bridge and realised we were about to drive out of Melbourne and not come back. James and I had spent three years planning this, but it wasn't until that moment that it dawned on Dylan that he wouldn't see any of his friends for a year.

To cheer him up, James let both boys climb onto the roof rack and ride on top of the car while he drove it slowly around the car park of the petrol station. I was pretty sure that was illegal but I didn't want to have an argument with James in the first half-hour. I fussed around on the ground, terrified that they would fall off and our trip would begin with a day at the hospital having broken legs set in plaster. But they held on tight and Dylan completely forgot to be sad about what he was leaving behind. I bundled them back into the car and when we reached the top of the West Gate all four of us cheered the start of our adventure.

Setting up the camper trailer wasn't as easy as we had expected. Despite being given a demonstration when we bought it, and having a practice go before we left, our first argument was about which way we should park the trailer on the site. We tried to keep our voices down and the swearing to a minimum, but the elderly couple camped opposite us vanished into their van as we bickered. I stopped arguing when I worked out that I had no idea which way the tent would be facing once it was set up.

After unfolding the canvas from the trailer, we realised that we had lost the sheet of paper with the set-up instructions. James disappeared into the tent and, after half an hour of swearing and clanging of poles, he emerged – sweaty and flushed – and we had a fairly square tent. We laid out the beds, swung out the kitchen unit on the trailer's tailgate, connected the gas, put out the tables and chairs and looked around for someone to show off to.

No other campers were around. Neither were Oscar and Dylan.

In celebration of our new freedom, we had told the boys to 'go and play' while we set up. Taking advantage of this unusually relaxed parenting, they had climbed to the top of the cliff at the end of the beach. Now they were standing on the edge, 80 metres above the crashing waves, waving frantically at us.

'Help! Help!'

James and I raced up the old wooden stairs as fast as we could. I couldn't believe that we had been so stupid. Just one day out of the city, and we had forgotten how dangerous the world could be.

'Look at us! Look how high we are! Did we scare you?'

The boys – who were, of course, perfectly safe – laughed as we fell at their feet, heaving for breath, too tired and relieved to even swipe at them.

That night I wrote in my brand-new diary that the boys had played tennis and football, jumped waves, dug holes in the sand, climbed cliffs, rode their pushbikes fast over speed humps, walked to the shop for milk by themselves, written a letter home, shared chocolate and found a dead penguin washed up on the beach. James recorded that we ate spaghetti bolognaise for dinner. Exhausted, we all fell into bed at the same time.

The next morning I woke up slowly and peacefully. For the first time in years I hadn't been jolted awake by an alarm, a crying baby or the boys' demands for breakfast. The light coming in through the canvas was soft and gentle, I was warm and comfortable, and I had absolutely nothing to get up for. The boys were both curled up on their sides, reading. Dylan looked up and smiled at me, then went back to his book.

I climbed down from the bed, put on the same clothes I had worn the day before, and went outside. The sun had just risen. The sky was clear and the air was crisp and cool. As the kettle boiled noisily on the stove, I opened up the big box that held all our kitchen supplies to find the tea.

The entire box was crawling with tiny black ants.

'I'm going home', I said.

But, of course, I couldn't. Our home belonged to a family from Canada for the next year. They had seen our ad on the internet and decided our house was exactly what they wanted. Their daughters were the same age as our sons, they would rent our family car, and they were happy to look after the cat.

When the Canadians found us, it was obvious that we were actually going to go through with this crazy idea of taking a year off to go camping. We'd been talking for years about the frustrations of juggling work commitments and not being able to spend enough time with the boys. Our lives had become a mad cycle of spending money more quickly than we could earn it. There was nothing to look forward to except a few weeks of holidays that we had to share out between us to cover the long summer break when school and child care were closed.

'Well, what do you want to do?' I'd asked James one night after we had put the boys, then aged two and four, to bed. 'If we're going to work this hard, let's make it be for a reason.'

'You know what?' he said. 'I've always thought it would be great to take the boys around Australia.'

This wasn't entirely unexpected. After being asked to leave his private school in Year 11, James found a job, with the help of his father, as a jackaroo on a cattle station near the Northern Territory border. James was sixteen years old when he got off the bus in Mount Isa with his hair dyed jet black. The ringers on the station took one look at him and decided he was a wanker. But he learned to ride a horse, and the horse taught him to muster cattle, and after a few years of wandering the country he had come back to Melbourne with a love of the outback.

To me, this part of James's life was just something that made him different from most other people I knew. But as he talked about it again that night, in the context of taking our children to see those massive empty spaces, I realised that he had never stopped thinking about those years. He hated the idea of his sons growing up in the inner city, where the biggest outdoor space they knew was the Melbourne Cricket Ground.

I was a city girl. My family had migrated from Scotland in the mid-70s when I was seven. I had never really felt at home in the suburbs where we had lived for all my school years, but I had fallen in love with Fitzroy the first day I set foot in it. That was in 1984. James and I now lived next door to the terrace house that I had shared with friends more than twenty years before. But my mother, Nannette, lived in Darwin, so I knew a little bit about northern Australia from visiting her. I had driven from Alice Springs to Darwin, I'd been to Uluru and Kakadu and seen the Devils Marbles. And I wasn't a complete camping novice: I'd been on a school trip to the Flinders Ranges when I was fourteen.

That night we decided we would travel for at least a year. We agreed we needed to quit our jobs and not have a definite return date. We wanted to feel free to wander the country and act on whims. It seemed sensible to wait a few years, so Dylan could finish his first year of school before we went. He would have basic reading and writing skills that we could build on during a year of homeschooling.

We also needed time to save money. We would have to spend a lot on equipment and a car. James was adamant that we would be bush camping. Back then I let that slide, deciding it was a minor detail that we could negotiate at a later date. I wasn't naive enough to think we could stay in hotels the whole way around the country, but living in a tent wasn't going to happen. I planned to talk him round to something more suitable closer to the time.

At the end of that night I made James promise not to tell anyone about our plans. In case we didn't do it. In case we got too scared to throw in our jobs and run away. In case we started thinking like sensible grown-ups instead of impulsive teenagers heading to Europe with $1000 and a backpack.

I don't know why I was worried. James had recently gone out at four o'clock on a rainy, cold Melbourne dawn to strip naked and lie on the wet bank of the Yarra with hundreds of other people for a photo shoot by the American photographer Spencer Tunick. Exhilarated, he had been talking about the shoot later that day over a coffee at our local cafe.

'I thought about doing that', said our neighbour. His wife shot him a withering look.

'That's the difference between you and James', she said. 'You thought about it but he actually got out of bed and did it.'

Although she might have been a bit harsh on her husband, she did have a point. Once there is an idea lodged in his head, James can be guaranteed to follow it through. It might not be perfectly well thought out or planned – that's my job – but he'll get it done.

This wasn't the first time we had run away from our jobs and home. Seven years earlier, James had been working for a courier company. He spent his days sitting in a glass alcove the size of a phone box and his nights dreaming of radio calls and missed deliveries, but what he really wanted to do was work in theatre.

'Do some research', I said one day. 'If that's what you really want, at least spend a few hours finding out how to make it happen.'

The next year he was accepted into the National Institute of Dramatic Art (NIDA) and we moved to Sydney. Three months later, I was pregnant with Oscar.

I can't remember when I slept, but I still have vivid memories of long afternoons lying on the grass in parks, hours spent pushing the pram up and down Sydney's hills, and taking turns with another new mother to swim laps in the local pool. I remember James arriving home to our tiny flat on his motorbike for an hour of feeding and bathing the baby before tearing off again for an evening performance.

When he had got through the second year at NIDA and we had survived our first year of being parents, we decided we were so good at it that we should do it again. Dylan was born a few weeks after we returned to Melbourne. For me, that year was a nightmare of sleep deprivation and borderline madness. James had launched himself into the world of theatre. He was never out of work and hardly ever home. Dylan wouldn't sleep for more than two hours at a time, regularly waking three or four times every night. He and I even spent a week in a special hospital ward, where they put him in a sealed soundproof room at night and made me go to group sessions with other exhausted and depressed mothers.

After one particularly bad night, I drove across town to take Oscar to a Wiggles concert. I was so tired that I couldn't remember which way to turn the steering wheel as I reversed, and I scraped the side of another woman's car as I tried to get out of the parking spot. As she shouted at me from high up in her shining 4WD, I clenched my fists and cried.

The years passed. Dylan learned to sleep, Oscar started school and I was offered a full-time job. The money was too good to refuse but the juggling got harder. The more we earned, the more we spent. The weekend that I sat down and drew up a timetable for the month ahead to make sure there was someone – not always one of us – to pick up the boys every afternoon, feed them, bath them and put them to bed, I knew it had all gone wrong somewhere.

Looking back, it's not surprising that all it took was one crazy idea to get us planning our escape. Three years was a long time to wait, but we started putting money away each fortnight. Once a month we'd have a planning night, which usually just involved eating chocolate while we browsed the internet, reading about places we wanted to visit.

We bought a map of Australia and started to think about what route we would take. We drew a route on the map in pink highlighter and stuck it on the kitchen wall to remind us that we were really going. We broke the news to the boys even though they had no concept of the distance and time we were talking about. And, despite our vow of secrecy, within a month we had told everyone we knew. We tried not to talk about it too much but, as everyone around us started renovating their crumbling inner-city homes and spent entire evenings discussing tiles and taps, we found ourselves launching into monologues that started, 'Well, when we go on our trip ...'

We didn't do much research. We avoided having too much information in case it turned out that this was a stupid idea and we should resign ourselves to going to work every day, like everyone else. One day a friend asked me what we were taking: a tent or a campervan?

We were still a bit stuck on that. I had assumed we would have a campervan with beds that folded out of either end. This idea was based entirely on the drawings in a children's book we had bought the boys to get them excited about the trip. James thought campervans were nothing more than tricked-up caravans. He was determined that this was going to be a camping trip, not a caravanning one. We would have tents so we could go anywhere we wanted, no matter how rough the roads were. We were at an impasse. My friend's husband rang a few days later and said that what we needed was an off-road camper trailer.

I didn't know what that was, so that night I looked them up on the internet. Basically, a camper trailer is a tent that is permanently attached to a heavy-duty trailer. The inside of the trailer could be used for storage and a kitchen was usually attached to the tailgate. When the tent was unfolded, a queen-size mattress would fit on the top of the trailer, and two single mattresses could go on the floor of the tent. We made a trip to a couple of showrooms the next weekend and a few weeks later we ordered our camper trailer from the first place we visited.

Before it could be built, we had to buy a car. The trailers were custom-made to match the car's width and clearance. Ideally, they would also have the same wheels so the spares could be used for both the car and the trailer.

We had a car in mind, but it already had an owner. One of our best friends had a LandCruiser that he had driven all around the country for a year of birdwatching. He was back in Melbourne, so we decided he didn't need it anymore. His new girlfriend agreed with us. His car had already been to most of the places we wanted to go and had survived. We wouldn't need to drive around second-hand car yards and we wouldn't need to pretend we knew anything about 4WDs. It would be a lot easier for everyone if our friend sold his 4WD to us. He eventually gave in, on the condition that he would get the first option to buy it back when we came home.

We told the camper trailer company about our car and gave them a list of the extra features we wanted: a larger cover so we could heap all our bedding on top of the queen-size mattress when we packed it up and still get the cover over everything; a two-burner stove so we could cook pasta and sauce at the same time; an awning with side walls to protect the kitchen area from wind; an 80-litre water tank in case we got stranded in the desert; a tool box and a stone guard, just because the salesman said we needed one; a Treg hitch instead of a tow ball so we could throw the trailer around on the rough dirt roads we would be driving on; and electric brakes because the whole thing was going to be really, really heavy.

People starting saying, 'Are you really going?'

We painted the worst walls in the house, ripped up the stained carpet, polished the floorboards and threw out an entire skip full of junk from the back of the kitchen cupboards. We enrolled the kids with Distance Education Victoria and then had to find space for the two big boxes of coursework they gave us.

After pestering the very patient men at our local camping shop for advice, we went and looked at cheaper products at the bigger chain stores, then went back and bought their high-quality, well-chosen stock instead. When they found out that we were planning to go all the way around the country, they recommended we buy their national parks guidebook. I hesitated, thinking of the five books I already had, and the man sighed and said, 'I'm just going to give it to you'. He even marked some good spots in it when he realised we didn't know anything at all about where we were going.

Our route was planned in more detail, this time using a blue highlighter on the map. I handed in my notice at work.

Finally, we did a budget. It was a bit late, but we were scared if we did it too early we'd realise we couldn't afford to go.

We realised we couldn't afford to go, so we extended our mortgage.

Our camper trailer was ready just before Christmas and we invited our friends to watch us put it up in the playground of the local school. We loved it, sometimes going outside just to stand and look at it. We couldn't wait to leave.

But here I was, eight weeks later, looking at an infestation of ants in the kitchen box. I swore and clanged and bashed things around as I emptied the box, item by item, and brushed the ants off. The containers we had bought for the dried food had done their job and the ants hadn't been able to get into any of them.

I killed them anyway, sprayed the outside of the box with heavy-duty surface repellent, repacked all the food, and our first day of freedom finally got underway.

Chapter Two

The caravan park was full of retirees. We had been warned that we would meet lots of grey nomads, but I didn't have a problem with that. People who travelled were now my kind of people, I reasoned, regardless of their age. We impressed some of them by telling them we were on a year-long trip – until they asked how long we had been away and we said this was our second day. They smiled and went back to talking about fishing.

I didn't know that James was keen on fishing. In the eighteen years we had spent together, he had been fishing exactly once. Yet here he was, chatting away in the Port Campbell caravan park about bait and lures and rigs and sinkers and floats with the same enthusiasm he had previously saved for the Collingwood Football Club.

'Eric, the guy in the tent next to us, says that salmon are running at Gibson Steps, next to the Twelve Apostles.' I didn't even know what that meant. 'I thought I'd go and give it a try tonight, when you and the kids are in bed.'

I probably should have taken more notice. At the time, I thought it just a bit of a stage he was going through, brought on by the euphoria of not having to go to work. A new passion that he would chuck in a few weeks, like the unicycling craze of 1990. Or the time he was convinced that his destiny was to be a professional golfer and convinced me that he had to take six months off work to give it a go. He said he didn't want to spend the rest of his life wondering if he could have made it as a golf pro. For six months, he played golf a couple of times a week and spent the rest of his time lying around imagining what it might be like to be a highly paid international sporting star. For six months, I wondered what the hell he was doing all day and got grumpy if the bathroom was dirty and the fridge was empty. Eventually he agreed that it probably wasn't going to happen and went back to his old job.

It didn't occur to me that, like supporting Collingwood and playing golf, fishing was yet another pastime that involved spending a lot of time out of the house with other men and drinking beer.

He bought a set of heavy-duty sinkers for fishing in the surf. Later that night he headed off with his new gear, his bought-for-the-trip tackle bag, an esky filled with ice, beer and bait, and a camp chair.

At Gibson Steps he lugged everything down 300 steps to the base of the cliffs. After carefully setting up his chair and the esky, he strode to the water and made his first cast. The sinkers flew out in a long graceful arc and the carefully baited hooks followed. As the whole lot splashed into the surf, he realised that he only had 15 metres of line on his reel. His brand-new gear disappeared into the water, trailing nothing but empty line.

Half an hour later, after respooling his reel and rigging up a new line with sinkers and hooks, he was ready to start again. In the meantime, two fishermen and their girlfriends had arrived and set up further along the beach. Twenty minutes later it started to get dark and he thought perhaps he should have brought a torch.

An hour passed. The surf brought in phosphorescence that glowed in the sand for a few seconds after each wave and the silhouettes of the Apostles loomed out of the ocean. This time last week he was probably sitting inside watching television. Further up the beach, the men caught something. He watched by their torchlight as they pulled in something large. He felt a strong jerk on his line. It was a struggle to reel his line in but, eventually, the rod bending and straining, his catch rolled out of the surf.

He wasn't completely sure what it was, so he picked it up by the tail and staggered over to the other fishermen to borrow their light. It was a gummy shark, they said. And he had caught it without the aid of bait. There was one hook in its tail fin, another in its dorsal fin and a metre of line wrapped around its body. Their girlfriends told him how to decapitate it and bleed it out to make sure the flesh was free of blood. He did that, then packed his things and headed back up the 300 steps to the car park. He had less beer to carry now, but was weighed down with a shark that was too big to go in the esky.

I woke up to hear him hissing at me. 'Lorns! Come and look at what I caught!'

I climbed down from the bed and out of the tent. When I saw him holding up the bleeding torso of a huge shark, I was staggered. 'What are you going to do with it?'

'I'm not sure', he said, a bit hysterically.

Just then Oscar crawled out of the tent, not properly awake. When he saw the headless shark he gasped and took a wide berth around us on his way to the toilets.

I followed James to the designated fish-cleaning area behind the toilet block and watched as he turned what was left of the shark into two kilos of prime fresh flake fillets and ten kilos of stinking mushy mess that we dumped in the fish bin.

The next day, after spending the morning picking strawberries at a berry farm, we found the town of Timboon and a small row of shops. One sold cheap runners, and the other sold hot chips. Oscar had already lost his shoes, so we bought him another pair, then cooked the flake on the barbecue in the local park and got a bag of chips to go with it. It was delicious and it was free and we loved every bite.

At the seaside town of Port Fairy, the dream home of bookish retirees, summer and the school holidays were over but the caravan park was full. I couldn't work out why, until I saw the big striped tents going up in the paddock alongside the park.

'Is there a circus coming to town?' I asked the lady in the office.

'There's a music festival here next weekend', she explained, speaking slowly and carefully, as if to a complete idiot. Which was exactly how I felt. The Port Fairy Folk Festival is an institution. Every year, on the Labour Day long weekend in March, over 400 musicians perform to more than 10,000 people – many of whom were already setting up their campsite.

'You were lucky to get a site at all. I could only fit you in because you wanted two nights.'

This time we set up the tent in slightly over half an hour. Just as we finished, an elderly couple came over to have a good look at our camper trailer. They were thinking of getting one themselves and, unlike us, had been doing their research. James showed them around and they were very impressed. We felt quite proud of ourselves until an old man shuffled out of his caravan to let us know that we had attached the springs to our tent ropes upside down.

That evening we walked across the causeway to Griffiths Island, a small rocky outcrop of low scrub and dark rocks that was separated from the mainland by the Moyne River and pounded on the other side by cold Southern Ocean waves. We were going to watch the mutton birds arrive home at dusk after a hard day of fishing for their chicks. Mutton birds, or short-tailed shearwaters, are designed for flight. They travel extraordinary distances – their annual migration around the Pacific Ocean is a round trip of 30,000 kilometres. But they aren't designed to land. When they come in, they look and sound like someone is throwing winged legs of lamb out of the sky. They crash violently into the scrub and their momentum hurls them forward into the bushes while they flap their wings madly trying to stop.

I laughed as the boys ducked and squealed while the birds fell to earth around them. I thought the birds knew what they were doing, that – despite the awkward landing – they must have a highly sophisticated navigational system that was more than capable of avoiding people standing on a raised boardwalk. Later a park ranger told me about a young girl who had been knocked to the ground by a bird that crashed into the side of her head.

'It's really – watch out! – quite common.'

The next day, we knew we had to start doing some schooling, so after breakfast we dragged the boxes of coursework out of the back of the trailer. We had a year's supply of handbooks and resource materials that were guaranteed to give our boys a structured curriculum. We were confident that they would come back from our year of travelling well-rounded and bursting with life experience, with all of their Grade 1 and Grade 3 skills under their belts too.

I was secretly looking forward to it. I imagined the world opening up for them as their natural curiosity and enthusiasm expanded, fed by the amazing experiences we were going to give them. The freedom of life on the road would let the four of us approach their education as another adventure. James and I would adapt the curriculum material to the places we were travelling through. Australian explorers? We would live it as we crossed the Nullarbor in the footsteps of Edward John Eyre and followed the route of the Old Telegraph Track up Cape York. Food production? We would drive through diverse farming land all over the country, past some of the largest cattle stations in the world and see coastal fishing ports that processed tonnes of seafood each day. Ethics of nuclear testing? Maralinga – here we come!

For each of them, we had a large A4 booklet that held two weeks' work. Every fortnight had a theme: 'My Family', 'Animals', 'The Human Body'. The booklets were divided into ten days. Every day had exercises devoted to handwriting, reading, mathematics and general activities around the theme. There were also art and craft projects and a physical education section. We had maths tool books with cardboard clocks, hexagonal spinners to use as dice, and paper versions of blocks, rods and cubes.

A smaller booklet was just for us: the parent-teacher. Dylan's Grade 1 teacher's guide had scripts for each day that told us exactly what to say and when to say it. Oscar's Grade 3 teacher's guide was less prescriptive but just as detailed. There was also a handbook on the official Victorian method of handwriting that showed exactly how letters should be formed and described correct pencil grip and posture.

As instructed, we had filled pencil cases with 2B pencils, sharpeners, erasers, coloured pencils, textas, crayons, glue sticks, pens, scissors, paper clips, a stapler and staples. Both boys had a clipboard to hold their work. We had been given special paper lined in dotted thirds to help the boys form their letters at the right size. There was a CD with audio tracks for each lesson. We had access to library books that could be posted out to us. There were even classes held live over the internet and the boys could be in email contact with their teachers at any time.

Each school day, we were to work through one day's work in the booklet. At the end of the fortnight, we would send back the booklets in prepaid, addressed envelopes. The teachers would check and assess them, then return them to us with feedback. We had arranged for Astrid, a friend in Melbourne, to get our mail and post it to us in batches. We were planning to ring her every week and let her know where we were going to be.

It was all so well planned that it came as a terrible shock when it fell apart completely on the first attempt.

It was a very windy day, so everything was flapping about and we couldn't keep our places in the handbooks. We moved the table and chairs into the tent, creating a small and claustrophobic space for four people to work in.

We had already decided that we should both pitch in with the teaching, as neither of us could work out how to manage both boys and all the books at the same time. I took Dylan and James worked with Oscar.

Despite having just one booklet each – the boys with their workbooks and us with our instruction manual – within minutes there was complete chaos inside the tent. There was paper everywhere. Our legs were too long, the chairs were uncomfortable and the table was too small.

I carefully read the prepared script from Day One, Week One of Dylan's handbook. 'Trace the letters without lifting your pencil from the page. Then copy the letters on the lines below.'

He gave me a blank look. 'I don't get it.'

I read it again. He held his pencil as if it was a dagger, twisted his body around on the bench until he was sitting at right angles to his page, and jabbed at the paper.

'Not like that, honey. Sit up straight.'

'I CAN'T. There's no ROOM.'

'Yes there is, darling. You just have to sit on the seat properly.'

'Well, I'm TRYING!'

I pushed his legs under the table and straightened him up. Then I took his hand in mine and tried to sit the pencil in the approved grip. 'Like this.'

'That feels funny. I can't write that way.' He did the absolute worst 's' he could manage. 'Why can't I just hold it the way I like to?'

'Because you can't. Look, the book says so.' I had a surge of dismay that it had only taken me three minutes to resort to the authority of the handbook.

'You're being mean!' he wailed. His eyes were shiny with tears and I wondered how his Prep teacher had ever taught him to read.

On the other side of the table, James was discovering that Oscar had a concentration span of about fourteen seconds. Every time James took his complete attention off him, Oscar would revert to doodling Pokémon figures at the edges of his workbook. Unlike Dylan, he wasn't belligerent about doing the work, he was just quietly distracted. When James prodded him to get back to it, he smiled happily at him, did one more sum and then went back to what really interested him.

'Oscar! Stop drawing bloody Pokémon. Just do the maths!'

'James!' I said. 'Don't be nasty. You need to have some patience.'

He sank his head into his hands. 'I can't. He's driving me mad.'

'I'll do him then. You take Dylan.'

James looked over at Dylan, who was sniffing and shaking as he laboriously traced a row of 's' letters that were almost as twisted on the page as he was on his seat.

'No, you do him. You're better at it than me.'

An hour and a half later we were all exhausted. My head pounded as I looked around the tent and wondered how my beautifully organised box of work had turned into this explosion of paper. We had barely got through the maths and handwriting section of the first day's work.

'It's okay', I assured James. 'It was our first day. I'm not too worried about the reading we missed. They're both reading in the car.

I'd rather they read for pleasure than turn it into a task anyway. And we don't need to do sport and art at the moment.'

I had just dismissed half of the curriculum.

He hauled himself up and looked around at the disaster zone. 'Can you deal with this? You've got a system. You know where everything goes. I'll go and kick the footy with them.'

After lunch all the evidence of our failure was stuffed back into the trailer and I took the boys back to Griffiths Island for a walk to the lighthouse. It was still windy, but the sky was bright blue and the sandy track was lined with yellow wildflowers. The kids ambled ahead of me, side by side, deep in conversation. A wallaby bounced across the track ahead of us. I called out, and they looked back at me as I jogged to catch up with them.

'Did you see the wallaby?'

This was what it was really all about. Not sums or perfectly formed letters, but nature, wildlife, being out in the fresh air and experiencing life.

'No', said Oscar and they returned to their conversation.

'Charizard is the *third* evolvement of Charmander. Not Charmeleon. That's only the second. It doesn't have the same powers.'

Chapter Three

When we arrived at the Princess Margaret Rose Caves campground in the Lower Glenelg National Park on the Victoria–South Australia border, the managers told us we were the only people there. I didn't believe them – we had just been kicked out of Port Fairy because there was a long weekend coming. But there really was no sign of anyone else around at all. It was very much just us, in the bush, all alone.

Our site was a small clearing in the bush. It had its own fireplace with a blackened metal barbecue plate and a rusty tap with a 'Not for Drinking' sign on it. This felt like *real* camping. We had no power, no drinking water and nowhere to do any emergency shopping.

After we got the tent up, James took the boys over to the nearby pine plantation to collect wood and I had a look around. I was relieved to find a wooden toilet and shower block but, as I wandered around the deserted campground, the only sounds were my feet crunching on the gravel, birds chirping and an occasional rustle in the grass. I hadn't been alone like this for a very long time. On the rare times that I was at home on my own, I usually had the radio on and there were always people walking past outside.

I couldn't remember when I had become so used to having company. As an only child, I had spent a lot of time alone. It had never bothered me at all. One of my strongest memories was of coming home from a school camp overwhelmed by a week of constantly having other people around. I had gone for a walk in the suburban streets, perched on a low brick wall and sat there for an hour until the tumult inside me settled down and I felt like myself again.

Now being on my own in the bush was spooking me, so I went to find the boys. It was easy; I just followed the sound of the axe. James had decided to cut down a dead tree on the edge of the plantation. The boys were ecstatic. They were running around, finding other trees and begging him to chop those down too. We took turns dragging the butchered tree back to our site and built our first camp-fire of the trip.

It was a big fire, ridiculously big for cooking a few sausages. But for James, this was a symbol of our new freedom. A fire was what camping was all about, he told us. We slumped back in our chairs after dinner, the soles of our filthy runners melting in the heat, toasting marshmallows and watching satellites spin across the sky.

That night there was a heavy blanket of silence hanging over us. It would have pushed me down into a deep sleep if it hadn't been punctuated by the sounds of scampering wildlife and the faint roar of logging trucks. It was unsettling. And very different from the sounds of the city, muffled by walls and curtains, that had lulled me to sleep in our old life. I tried very hard not to imagine a crazed logger stalking down the track from the pine forest, trailing his chainsaw, seeking revenge for the theft of a tree.

Early in the morning I was woken by the scratchy sound of tiny scuttling feet. A shadow play of morning greetings was being acted out on the roof of our tent by a family of tiny birds. As I watched them hopping about on the canvas above me I felt faintly ridiculous about being scared the night before. We were only about 300 kilometres from Melbourne, not exactly the heart of Deliverance country. I resolved to toughen up.

I caught my first fish that day. It was a tiny little bream that I wasn't able to touch. Some instinct deep inside my brain wouldn't let my hands make contact with it. It was just like the time I had accidentally let the chickens out of their coop at the childcare centre. After chasing them around the garden and cornering them, I had been confused to find that I was physically unable to pick them up. Now when I tried to grab the fish, something more primitive was again overriding the order.

This time, James was there to deal with the fish for me. He twisted its slick thrashing body around as he worked the hook out of its cheek, then held it in the water until it wriggled out of his grip and swam off. Oscar turned out to have a knack for casting but was squeamish about using bait. Dylan was happy to stick worms on his hook and took great delight in stabbing the one fish we decided to keep for dinner.

When we got tired of fishing we went on a tour of Princess Margaret Rose Cave. The limestone formations were beautiful. It was amazing to think that underneath the ground was this huge chasm full of twisted pillars and globular mounds. In the yellow light, the rocks looked like the Mateus bottles dripping with melted wax that my mother used to drag out for dinner parties in the '70s.

The guide told us about the young man who found the cave in 1936. He had lowered himself down a shaft to explore it, with only a candle, a box of matches and a ball of string to help him find his way back out of the darkness. Later, he and his friends carted down kegs of beer and threw parties where they played spoons on the stalactites.

Over the next few days we settled into a routine of lazy breakfasts, half-hearted attempts at school, then a few hours of canoeing or fishing followed by illegal tree felling and bonfire building. James taught us to play spotlight. The boys loved skulking around the bush in the dark but I hated standing on my own at dark, waiting for them to sneak up behind my back and shout in my ear. I was too freaked out to enjoy it and begged for the game to stop after a few rounds.

The nights were bitter. Every morning we woke up to find our blankets wet and cold. Water vapour from our breath had spent the night collecting on the canvas above us, condensing in the freezing air and then dripping back down onto our bedding. The days were getting warmer, though. It was so hot that the boys overcame their nervousness about brown water and threw themselves off the old wooden jetty and into the murky Glenelg River.

When the long weekend arrived it brought more campers with their boats, generators, late-night drinking sessions and, curiously, a plague of flies that droned and buzzed around our heads. We discovered that flies really like being inside tents. If they couldn't get in, they would hang out under the roof of the awning. Shouting at them, snapping tea towels and bashing the canvas awning with brooms didn't bother them at all.

When night fell, they did a quick handover to the mosquitoes. 'Four humans. Two big, two small. The small ones have exposed legs and ears. The big ones use repellent, but you can usually get a nip in on their hands while they're doing the dishes.' Then they went to sleep under the awning. That's when we could flick them and move them on, buying ourselves half an hour of fly-free time in the morning.

We decided it was time to kick the footy over our first state border. It took a while to find a sign that declared we were driving out of Victoria and into South Australia, but when we did we all had a go at booting the ball from one state to the other and decided to make it a tradition. Our next stop was Robe on South Australia's Limestone Coast, a popular holiday destination famous for its 12-kilometre beach, fresh seafood and excellent local wine. We knew all that, but we didn't know about the prevailing winds and we had booked a site right above the beach. James and I battled violent gusts for an hour to get the tent up, shouting at each other and the boys the whole time. When it was finally secured, we had to leave the caravan park just to get out of the gale.

I decided we should treat ourselves to some local crayfish. We asked for directions at the caravan park office and walked for an hour in the tearing wind. When we made it to the warehouse in the back blocks of Robe's industrial estate, it was closed.

When we got back, the tent had blown down. James put it back up, cursing the wind as it hurled sand into his eyes and mouth and hair. It was too windy to cook. The gas stove wouldn't stay alight and, even when I hunched over the pot with a towel over it and my head to shield it from the wind, the water refused to boil.

That night our beds were full of sand, the tent poles creaked and groaned as they bent in the gale and the canvas flapped noisily, but the next morning was calm and peaceful. The sea glistened under the clear blue sky. I shook the sand out of the sheets and we spent the next four days in paradise. James fished off the rocks every night and caught four more sharks. The kids and I didn't bother to get out of bed to have a look; we just mumbled vague congratulations through the flywire and went back to sleep. We worked out when the warehouse was open and ate fresh crayfish two nights in a row.

One day we drove out along the Old Coorong Road. All I knew about the Coorong was that one of my favourite movies when I was a kid, *Storm Boy*, had been filmed there. I was expecting wetlands and pelicans but instead there were only salt lakes that stretched for miles, bordered by sand dunes on one side and stubby scrub on the other. There was no sign of any birdlife. Long years of drought had transformed the region. Once there must have been mudflats teeming with life, but now everything around us was dry and quiet and still. We stopped and walked out onto one of the lakes. The boys didn't believe that they were walking on salt until we made them taste it.

James wanted to test out the car on the dunes. I didn't really see the point. We knew what was on the other side. The road had already taken us within metres of the ocean at a spot where the dunes were smaller and further apart. Huge waves pounded into shore with such power that I banned any idea of swimming. The stories of shipwrecks I had been reading out loud from our guidebooks came alive for us as the sand shuddered under our feet with each breaking wave.

But there was a track over a dune and James wanted to see what our car could do. I shuffled through the mess of books and maps and paper at my feet, looking for the notes from the 4WD course I had gone on before we left.

'I can't find them. But I think I remember most of it. You need to have low tyre pressure so the weight of the car is spread over a bigger surface area. Drive in existing tracks, where the sand is compacted and firmer. Go straight up, not on an angle, and don't change gears as you go. You have to keep the momentum going, that's what gets you up the dune. And you're meant to have a flag at the front of the car so people coming the other way can see you.'

James pointed out that we had only seen one other vehicle since we had turned off onto the dirt road. He thought a flag was unnecessary. I thought the whole idea was silly and pointless. He argued that it was important to see what the car was capable of before we got into more remote areas. He got cross, I got upset, and the kids sat in the back reading their books. I started to panic about the fact that we had no spare drinking water or food. James took this as proof that I was being hysterical and off we went, up the dune.

Halfway up, anyway. The wheels dug into the sand and the car shuddered and stalled. He reversed down and got out to let down the tyres. On the second attempt we made it up the dune to whoops of delight from the kids and a triumphant grin from James.

From the top we could see that this was just one in a series of sandhills before the beach. There was very little flat ground between the dunes – it was like a miniature roller-coaster made of sand. The boys were in heaven. Suddenly the car was fun.

We made it over four dunes but we couldn't get up the fifth. When we trudged over the last hump on foot and slid down to the beach, we saw that we had been lucky. There wasn't enough room between the final dune and the sea to turn the car around. I wandered along the edge of the water for a while, but James was fidgety and on edge. The boys had taken off down the beach and he shouted at them to get back immediately.

'What's your problem? They have to run off a bit of steam after all that. I think we scared them a bit.'

He confessed that, going down one of the dunes, it had seemed much steeper than the rest. When we didn't make it up the last hill, he realised we might not be able to get back up the steep one. We gathered up the boys. After inching the car round and round in the dip between the sandhills until it faced the other direction, we took stock.

'I've got no mobile coverage,' I said, checking my phone. James's phone was usually more reliable than mine but he hadn't brought it with him today. 'If we get stuck in the sand, we'll just dig under the wheels and put down those planks of wood we've got and drive over them.'

'I forgot to put the wood and the shovel in the back before we left the campground.'

We had no recovery gear and no way to contact anyone if we got stuck. We had no food, very little water and we had only seen one car out here all day. It was 40 kilometres to the road and it was already early afternoon. The boys had no warm clothes. We did have an EPIRB (Emergency Position-Indicating Radio Beacon), but I didn't think this was a good enough reason to summon the armed forces. The EPIRB was a bit like Susan's horn in Narnia: only to be used in times of desperate need or Aslan might get really, really cross.

'We better not get stuck then.'

James gunned the engine and it screamed in protest as the car powered up the dune. The boys screeched with delight as they bounced around in the back. I gripped the dashboard and leaned forward. I felt as if I was pushing us up the hill with all the psychic power I could muster.

The tyres slipped on the sand and my heart dropped into my gut but the car recovered and we reached the crest and were up and over the dune. The next hill was smaller and the next one was firmer and the last one, the tricky first one, turned out to be easy and we were back on the dirt, laughing.

I apologised to James for freaking out and he promised to put all the recovery gear on the roof of the car. We pumped up the tyres and drove back to Robe where we watched a pod of dolphins and ate crayfish for dinner again.

We had been on the road for more than two weeks, but we had only gone a little over 500 kilometres. At this rate, it would take us years to get around the country. A friend in Melbourne, after learning of our itinerary, had taken James aside for a quiet word.

'Mate, I reckon you're going about this all wrong. For the first month, you're only going to be a day's drive from Melbourne. If it was me, I'd get her across the Nullarbor quick smart so she can't nick off home.'

We had a date, though. We were meeting my aunt, Jane, and Nannette at Port Willunga on the Fleurieu Peninsula, that point of the coastline south of Adelaide that kicks towards Kangaroo Island. We were celebrating our year of turning forty, fifty and sixty. Nannette was flying down from Darwin and getting a lift with Jane and her daughter to the house we had rented for the weekend. When we arrived in Port Willunga there was no sign of them. I rang Jane's mobile.

'Where are you?' Hysterical laughter rang out from the phone.

'We're not exactly sure', said Nannette when she could speak. 'Jane got lost.' There was more laughter in the background. 'We followed the signs to Willunga, but I think that's a different place.'

'Bloody hell', said James. 'You and your family. Honestly.'

I glared at him, but he was completely right. None of us can read a map without twisting it around until it faces the direction we are going and we are all perfectly capable of getting lost on roads we have driven for years.

'I think we're nearly there. We can see the water.'

'Give me the phone', said James. He guided them in. 'The sea should be on your left now. That's the side the passenger sits on.'

The car pulled up and they fell out, clutching their sides and doubling over as the giggles got the better of them.

'At least my family can laugh about it', I said to James, who was watching with raised eyebrows. 'Yours would be all grumpy and arguing about whose fault it was and the whole weekend would be stuffed.'

Our weekend wasn't stuffed. We slept in proper beds for the first time in weeks, shared a bottle of Grange Hermitage that had been bouncing around in the back of our car, argued constantly and laughed about nothing, as families do.

In Adelaide the boys discovered the joy of the BIG4 caravan park chain. This one had two swimming pools, a jumping pillow and a games room. It was so good, Jane said, that a friend of hers booked in for a week every school holidays, even though she only lived a few blocks away. I felt like I could have stayed a week too, but so far this trip had been too tame. We were up for adventure and the outback was calling.

Chapter Four

Before we headed into the Red Centre, James had a bit more fishing to do. The east coast of the Yorke Peninsula was said to be a holiday paradise. We weren't on holiday, we were having an adventure, so we drove down the west coast instead.

Point Turton is one of the best fishing spots in South Australia so it wasn't really surprising that the caravan park was packed. The sign on the office door said 'Back in ten minutes' so we wandered around the park to check it out. This was a new tactic we had adopted after realising that caravan park managers liked to put us very close to toilet blocks and very far away from swimming pools, playgrounds and other families. Given the chance, they also liked to give us sites with lots of concrete and very little grass, even though we always told them that we had to peg the tent down. We couldn't work it out. Perhaps it was because our camper trailer was still so clean, or maybe we had an invisible sign over our heads saying 'city folk'. It had turned us into more assertive caravan parkers, though. Whenever we could, we drove around and picked out our preferred spot before checking in. If that wasn't an option, we would park on the allocated site and then look at the alternatives. Often we would go back to the office and say, 'Do you reckon we could go on 23A instead?' This time the only available spot seemed to be squeezed between the toilets and a fibro shack.

The manager, who was wearing a very short towelling bathrobe and plastic thongs, spotted us and wandered over to tell us the park was fully booked. I fought hard to pay attention and keep my gaze from straying below the loosely tied belt on his robe as he suggested we try the next caravan park along the coast.

Forty kilometres of unsealed road later we got to Corny Point. A sign on the fence of the property next to the caravan park warned 'Keep Out. Trespassers will be shot.' There was no beach in sight. Even the kids, looking up briefly from their books, were worried.

'Are we staying here?' Dylan asked nervously.

'No way', said James.

I hunted at my feet for the map. 'We're about 50 kilometres from Innes National Park. It says "Spectacular coastal landscapes, a diversity of wildlife habitats and a wide range of recreational opportunities."'

'Sounds good', said James. 'Let's go.'

We were starting to identify regular patterns in our routine. On pack-up days we got up early. While the kids and I were still eating breakfast, James would start shouting at us. He needed the dishes done and put away so he could wrestle our huge kitchen box into the trailer. Our clothes had to be packed and taken out of the tent so he could stack the bedding. All the chairs and tables needed to be folded up so they could go in the back of the car. And we had to GET OFF the groundsheet so it could be shaken out, folded and put on top of the trailer.

In his haste, he would sometimes remove the poles holding up the annexe roof and the heavy canvas would fall on my head while I was doing the dishes. At some point he would disappear into the tent and start cursing as he undid the poles and the whole thing collapsed on him. Sometimes he would forget to roll down the windows first, so the boys and I would rummage around in the floppy canvas and do that from the outside.

My job was to pack up the kitchen, but I also had to make lunch and snacks for the day's drive. Then I'd remember I had to organise dinner, especially if we were going to be driving all day. I would fossick around in the freezer to find something to defrost on the dashboard, which we had christened 'nature's microwave'.

James would emerge from the collapsed tent and I would be surrounded by a disaster of food and drinks and cut-up fruit and plastic containers and half-washed dishes.

I always said, 'I don't know what your hurry is'.

He always replied, 'I don't want to be setting up the tent in the middle of night'.

It was a jerky, disjointed dance we had devised, and I knew it was horrible to watch. We alternated between giving the kids jobs, then shouting at them to work faster, and telling them to get out of the way until it was all done. If we weren't in a hurry I would take the kids away to do schoolwork and James would pack up by himself. This was the most harmonious option but it took about three hours so we didn't do it often.

By the time we were in the car everyone would be in a foul mood and it would take ages before we remembered that this was supposed to be fun. I'd find a spot for my feet between the bag of food and snacks, the bottles of water and the box of maps and guidebooks. Just as I got comfortable the call would come from the back: 'Is there a snack?'

James always drove. I tried to research the spots ahead as we went. I couldn't read for the first half-hour of the drive without getting carsick but after that I could look at maps and plan our day without a problem. The boys weren't bothered by motion sickness and could disappear into their books for hours at a time. I had been exactly the same when I was that age, but until now I'd never been sure that my sons knew the joy of losing themselves in a story. Their choice of reading material might be very different to mine – *Captain Underpants*, not *Narnia* – but the result was the same.

Dylan had developed the habit of racing through a new book as fast as he could, reading only as much as he needed to work out the basic plot. When he reached the last page, he immediately went back to the beginning and started all over again. This time, he read more slowly, giggling as he got jokes he had missed the first time. Only by the third or fourth reading would he ask questions about what particular words or phrases meant.

This led to some renegotiation of one of our new rules. James and I had decided that all the books belonged to everyone, but that the person who had chosen the book had the right to read it first. To Dylan, this seemed very unfair. He didn't want to give up a new book after he'd only read it once. For Oscar, waiting impatiently to start a new story, the sight of Dylan getting to the end only to start again straight away was intolerable. And me? Even in the midst of teary fights about whose turn it was to read the latest R.L. Stine *Goosebumps*, I was in heaven: they were arguing about books.

When we got to our new campsite, the boys would burst out of the car and go on the hunt for other kids. James and I would climb down slowly, stiff from hours of sitting still, and check out the spot. He would walk around for a bit, then stand with his legs planted solidly on the ground and stretch his arms out in front of him.

'I think we'll set it up here so we're looking at the fireplace [or bush or creek] with our back to the toilet block [or neighbours or footpath].'

I'd consider this and then ask which way the kitchen would face.

'The same way it always does.'

I had to close my eyes and perform a tiny pantomime, which unfortunately was not always in my head. If the trailer was turned around *that* way, then the *back* of it would be here, and it opened *this* way, so the kitchen would be *here*.

When the trailer was in the right spot, we would check the spirit levels that we had glued onto the steel frame. The legs were adjustable, but if the ground was very uneven James would have to dig a hole under one of the trailer wheels until the whole thing was sitting flat. I helped unhook the waterproof cover over the trailer, then we slid off the groundsheets, unfolded the tent, stretched it out and pegged it down.

James would then disappear inside the mound of tent to do some swearing and muttering, his body pushing the canvas up in strange bulges as he wrestled with the poles. I would potter around outside, unzipping the windows to let in light and air.

When the tent was up, the boys' mattresses went on the floor, all our clothes bags were dumped on our beds and we would start creating our outside room. A heavy rubber mat went down on the ground to stop us walking dirt into the tent. The awning was secured with more poles and ropes. The tailgate of the trailer swung open to reveal a two-burner stove and a cupboard. A metal frame that hooked onto the side of the stove held the plastic bucket that was the kitchen sink. A tap beside the stove pumped drinking water from the tank under the trailer. When the gas bottle was hooked up to the stove, the kitchen was done.

When the boys got back, we'd get them to set up the chairs and tables as we dragged all our boxes out of the trailer. The big grey kitchen box held all the pots and pans, dry food and cans. A smaller black box was filled entirely with shoes. Into the tent would go the library box with all our books, the backpack of school stuff and a big bag of Lego. Another tub containing even more food was opened and wedged in the open end of the trailer in case we ran out of canned tomatoes. If we had a powered site, we would pull the fridge out of the car and plug it in. The lights went up last and finally we were finished.

It did sometimes feel like hard work, but it was really the only work we had to do.

When we finally drove into the flat, scrubby campground at Pondalowie Bay in Innes National Park it was cold and windy. What was meant to be an easy day's drive had finished with us racing to get the tent up and dinner ready before dark. Most of the sites were vacant, so we chose one that was close – but not too close – to the toilet block and backed the trailer into the generous space defined by a fence made of thick pine logs. When I climbed out of the car I could smell the salt from the sea and, under the whistling of the wind, I thought I heard waves crashing on a beach. It was rugged and a bit deserted, but as a kangaroo bounced past I was glad to be here.

James had just unfolded the canvas from the trailer when one of the boys said, 'There's heaps of big ants around here.' A seething mass of bull ants were furious because James had just dumped a tent on their home. Unlike the ants that had invaded the kitchen box on our first morning at Port Campbell, these weren't to be messed with or easily exterminated. They were fierce and surprisingly fast and we gave in immediately.

I left James to pack the tent back onto the trailer and wandered around looking for a better site. When I found one that looked insect-free, I waved him over. 'The ground looks pretty hard', he said.

He put a metal tent peg on the ground and hit it with the mallet. The peg jumped about on the rock and I could see the reverberations run up his arm to his shoulder.

'No, not here.'

All the sites seemed to be the same. There were only a couple taken and they had vans on them. Caravans suddenly seemed to be an incredibly sensible option. You could just drive in, park, and put the kettle on.

'I'll just tie the bloody thing down.'

We tied ropes to the top corners of the tent and lashed them to the wooden bollards that edged each site. The boys collected stones and we put them at each corner of the tent, inside and out. The tent wasn't very square, but then it never was. We ate a hurried meal of curry and rice and got inside just as the wind picked up and the rain started.

It was still raining the next morning. I wanted to pack up and leave, but James was still exhausted from the previous day of driving and the tent was soaking wet. It was a good day to catch up on schoolwork. It was too cold and windy to work outside, so the boys sat on their beds and tried to work on their laps. The wind howled around us, flapping the sagging canvas walls. Every gust made us flinch.

A flock of galahs were holed up in the branches of a dead tree, squabbling and flapping and fighting for the best spots. The white undersides of their wings shone out against the dark sky. Suddenly I couldn't bear it anymore: the cold and the rain were making everyone miserable. The galahs were the only ones having fun.

'Let's go out for lunch.'

We drove for an hour to the nearest town to buy hot chips and burgers and milkshakes and on the way back I decided that a change in attitude was needed. We would put on all our warm clothes and our raincoats and explore the beach. It would be fun, I promised, and after that we would have hot showers, then snuggle up inside the tent to eat spaghetti bolognaise, drink warm Milo and play cards. Despite a sideways look from James that told me that he knew what I was up to and believed it was doomed to failure, the boys got excited.

Positive thinking did work, I thought, as I huddled in the rain on the beach watching Oscar and Dylan do cartwheels on the wet sand. Even when the showers didn't provide more than a tepid dribble of strange-smelling water and we discovered that all our warm clothes were damp and sandy, things didn't seem all that bad. After all, we had months of warm weather to look forward to. Our clothes would dry. We would have showers at some point. By the time night fell we were all squashed on a mattress in the tent playing an exuberant round of Shithead, and I wouldn't have been anywhere else.

Two days later we packed up our wet tent and drove north up the Yorke Peninsula towards the top of the Spencer Gulf. The sky cleared in front of us. It felt as if we were leaving behind the grey clouds and rain forever. On the side of the Augusta Highway, in front of a tiny blue shack just out of Port Pirie, we saw a sandwich board advertising freshly shucked oysters. We stopped and sat on the plastic chairs by the side of the road and ordered a dozen each. James bought a lemon too, cut it in half with his fishing knife and squeezed the juice into the polystyrene container. I'd never tasted anything so good in my life.

At that moment I felt a rush of absolute joy. I couldn't remember ever feeling that relaxed and happy in my whole life. We had a year of exploration in front of us. Our only job was to make sure the kids kept up with their schoolwork (although even that was sliding down our list of priorities) and to see and do as much as we could. We were sitting on the side of a road eating oysters and the only decision we had to make was where to camp that night.

We chose Wilpena Pound, arriving at the busy campground just before dusk. We were lucky to get a spot. The campground is only one section of the resort in the heart of the Flinders Ranges National Park. Tourists can also choose from 'luxury' camping and a motel that boasts a restaurant, a bar and a swimming pool. The resort sits just outside Wilpena Gap on the eastern side of the Pound. The Gap is the only place where it's possible to walk directly into the Pound – Wilpena Creek trickles out through a gorge cut into the walls of the Pound as you walk in.

The Pound itself is a ring of rugged mountains, a natural amphitheatre that circles a huge area of grassland and scrub, 17 kilometres long and 8 kilometres wide. Indigenous stories explain the creation of the Pound walls from the bodies of two giant serpents. From above it looks like a giant crater. To the early white settlers who named it, it looked like a giant natural cattle-pound. Predictably, they tried to use it for farming, but periods of drought and the difficulty of clearing the thick scrub in the interior of the Pound defeated them. The final attempt by the Hill family came to an abrupt end in 1914 when a flood destroyed the road that had been built through the Gap. Many of the buildings from the old station are still standing, including the Hill family's stone homestead.

The campground was neatly laid out with straight, tree-lined tracks leading to sensibly numbered powered campsites. Each site had its own safe campfire pit and was in close proximity to one of three clean, modern toilet blocks. I suspected, though, that the vast area inside the high rock walls of the Pound was still as untamed as ever.

As we put the tent up, stars began to appear. The clear sky released all the heat of the day and a damp chill set in, but the pegs slid easily into the red dirt and we had hot showers for the first time in four days. That night, we all slept long and hard.

In the morning a family of kangaroos had moved into the kitchen area of our tent and a joey was hiding under the table. The roos were everywhere and the tourists loved them. Some were a bit too fascinated – despite the signs asking people not to feed the native animals, we saw some German tourists tempting a group of kangaroos to come closer for a photo by holding out open bars of chocolate.

After breakfast we wandered into the heart of the Pound, past Old Wilpena Station and the homestead, and an old memory surfaced. 'I came on a school camp here.' No-one was particularly interested. 'We climbed one of these mountains. St Mary Peak, I think. They told us it was the highest mountain in the Flinders Ranges. It was really beautiful up there, you could see all the way down into the Pound. Then we walked back through the Pound to the campsite. It took all day. I must have been about fourteen.'

'Can we do that?' asked Oscar.

'I'm not sure. It might be a bit far.'

'We can walk further than you two', said Dylan.

'Yeah', said Oscar. 'Can we?'

The trail brochure classified the St Mary Peak walk as 'difficult'. It recommended allowing eight hours and carrying 4 litres of water for each person. We mentally knocked a couple of hours off the walk time and thought that we could carry 10 litres of water between us. That should be plenty.

At eight o'clock the next morning, after I had made lunches and we had cleaned up and hidden all our food from the crows and kangaroos and made sure everyone had sunscreen on and told the people on the site next door what our plans were and when to call in the cavalry, we set off.

The start of the track wound around the outside wall of the Pound. For the first hour we walked in the shade of the gum trees and the track rose up so gradually we hardly noticed it. We played 'Animal, Vegetable, Mineral', a variation of 'Twenty Questions', as we went. It got a bit tricky when the kids were sketchy on the classifications – 'What about the sky? Is that a mineral?' – but it passed the time. When that got boring, I told them about my high school hike.

I had been so grumpy about having to do the bushwalk that I had trudged along with my head down, watching my feet and refusing to look at the 'scenery' the teachers were going on about. Something slammed hard into my forehead and when I came around I was lying flat on my back on the gravel path. I was convinced someone had thrown a boulder at me. It was a few minutes before my Maths teacher could stop laughing for long enough to tell me I'd walked into a fallen tree that was lying across the track at head height. In the 1980s, minor concussion was no reason to stop someone completing a 20-kilometre hike. He helped me up and told me to pay more attention.

Later in the day, when we were climbing up to the summit, another teacher asked what was jingling in my pockets.

'Money for the machine.'

I should have known from the look on her face to stop talking right there.

'What machine?'

'The drink machine on top of the mountain. Mr Scott told me. I've got twenty-cent pieces to get a cold can.'

My embarrassing stories kept us all going until things started to get a bit tougher. The track headed steeply up the outside of the Pound wall. We had to clamber over boulders and pull ourselves up, getting a knee onto the next rock and hauling our bodies up after it. I didn't remember this part of the walk.

Dylan made the mistake of looking down. He froze and we had to coax and bully him to keep him going. I was having trouble keeping a solid footing on the loose rocks. As we climbed higher and left the shade from the trees behind, it got hotter. We had to stop in the rare patches of shade to catch our breath and have a drink.

At the top, James and I took stock. From here the signs pointed right to St Mary Peak, a three-kilometre return distance with a lot of climbing. Left was the visitor centre back at the resort, a 12-kilometre walk through the Pound.

'We should go back the way we came', he said. 'It's a lot shorter.'

'I don't think I can get back down that way. It's too steep. And Dylan will freak out when he sees how high up it is. I think we have to go the long way back, through the Pound. But I remember it. It's an easy walk, lots of shade and flat the whole way.'

James and Oscar decided to do the extra walk up to the top of St Mary Peak but Dylan didn't want to go with them. James and I checked the trail notes.

'It says there's a campsite about 4 kilometres away. We'll stop there and wait for you', I said.

We split up what was left of our water. I took the first-aid box and the toilet paper and gave James half the Tim Tams. When I went to give him the camera so he could take a photo of himself and Oscar at the peak, I didn't have it. We had left it back at the camp. I was gutted. We'd done all that hard walking and wouldn't even have a photo afterwards to remind us. We'd have to rely on our memories.

When Dylan and I started walking again, I knew immediately that either my own memory was faulty or something about this path had changed. We were hiking along a ridge in the side of the hill. Under our feet, pebbles the size of golf balls slid and quivered as we stood on them. The track sloped slightly downwards, and every few minutes I'd gasp as my feet slipped out from underneath me. We inched along slowly, holding on to tree trunks where we could.

At one point I lost track of the trail markers. I sat Dylan in a patch of shade under a small shrub and told him to stay there, then hunted around for one of the orange triangles. It took ten minutes to find one. The temperature was in the thirties, Dylan and I were rapidly running out of water and there was no-one else walking out here.

I had promised Dylan that when we reached the campsite we would have a rest under a tree and get a drink of water. But when we got there it was an empty dust bowl with no shade and no water. It was so exposed that we couldn't afford to wait there for the others. Heat stroke was becoming a real possibility.

We opened up the first-aid kit and left a message in bandaids on the sign pointing from the main track to the camp. We fashioned an 'L' and a 'D' and an arrow going straight ahead, in an unconscious echo of the carvings on the Burke and Wills Dig Tree. Those markings, carved into a coolabah tree on the banks of the Cooper Creek, indicated where vital supplies had been buried in case Burke, Wills and King, presumed to be dead, somehow managed to return. Which they did, just nine hours after the depot party had departed for Adelaide. Only King survived.

As we walked, resting at each shady place and then bracing ourselves for the long hot stretches in between, Dylan started chatting. He had plenty to discuss. How much would a bowler hat cost? How could a hippopotamus eat a person? What *could* a kangaroo kill? What do flies eat? I knew he was trying to distract himself from the heat and his sore legs, but he was keeping my mind off it too and I was very grateful.

On and on we went, dragged forwards by the trail markers every 200 metres. Finally we arrived at the homestead. Dylan collapsed on a picnic bench in the shade and I stumbled to the tap to fill our water bottles. My feet and my head throbbed in unison. Half an hour later, James and Oscar came limping along the track. They were in worse shape than us. They had run out of water and James was half-crippled by his new hiking shoes that he now knew were half a size too small.

After a rest and a drink we hauled ourselves up and made it through the Gap. The boys had a sudden burst of energy and bounded ahead, climbing rocks on the side of the track and shouting at us to hurry up because they were hungry. We got back to camp eight hours after we set out, just as the neighbours were starting to get worried about us.

That night, despite my exhaustion, I was kept awake by terrible thoughts of what could have happened. I felt foolish and irresponsible, and horribly guilty because it had all been my idea. A cool change arrived and the wind and rain muffled the sounds I made as I cried into my pillow. The next day, James and I set an upper limit of 10 kilometres on all future bush walks and he threw his new boots in the bin.

But when Oscar tried to clamber out of his sleeping bag in the morning, he had bigger concerns. 'What's happened to my legs?'

Chapter Five

The campground at Arkaroola in the northern Flinders Ranges was a desolate, rocky site high on a ridge. We chose a spot that looked across the gravel plain towards bare red hills that glowed at sunset. When the sun went down that night, the flies disappeared but no mosquitoes came to take their place. Millions of stars shone down on us as we slept and the sun woke us the next morning.

We were here to tackle Arkaroola's self-drive 4WD tour. James wanted to see what conditions the car could cope with. The trek notes said the tour was only for experienced and advanced 4WD drivers, but James felt that my one-day course more than qualified us. We collected a map from the office and signed ourselves out. The woman at reception said that if we weren't back in six hours someone would come and find us.

Ten minutes later we stopped at the bottom of a rocky hill that was so steep it would have been a struggle to walk up. I checked the map. 'It says to be in low range and first gear.' James looked sceptical.

'I drove up a hill like this on the course', I said. It was unusual for me to know something about cars that James didn't, but this time I was confident. 'Put it in first gear and then don't touch the accelerator once it's going. The car will just chug its way up. Don't try to steer, it'll find its own path. And don't put your foot anywhere near the clutch.'

He followed my instructions and the car rumbled up the hill like a tank, teetered on the crest and then eased down the other side. The kids were shrieking in the back and James looked slightly pale.

'It's like being on the back of an elephant', he said.

For the next four hours, our elephant carried us through rocky dry river beds, it crept down inclines that were so steep that we couldn't even see the bottom as we descended, and it dragged us through patches of deep sand. Midway through the drive we remembered that our recovery gear was still in the trailer.

On the way back, the boys were giddy with excitement. They were throwing things at each other in the back of the car, singing silly songs and bickering over which of them had got the best snacks. I was exhausted and they were driving me mad. I kicked Oscar out of the car and told him to walk back to camp.

We drove slowly behind him for a few minutes, watching him have a lovely time on the side of the road. He was ambling along, stopping to look at rocks, and bobbing his head as he sang out loud. I decided he was having too much fun, so I put him back into the car. Back at camp I tried to hide in the tent, but within minutes both the boys were in there with me. Dylan put on my sunglasses and flounced around, whirling his arms in giant circles.

'I am your MOTHER! You are VERY silly. Get out of the car and WALK!'

I couldn't sulk and laugh at the same time, so I went outside and watched James teach them to play bocce by throwing rocks around on the flat dirt plain.

I wanted to visit Iga Warta on our way out of Arkaroola. I had trawled the internet before we left home, looking for Indigenous communities that welcomed visitors. Iga Warta had cultural tours, accommodation and camping and we were going to be driving right past. I thought we could stay there for a night, sign up for a tour and learn a little about Indigenous culture from real people instead of reading about it in brochures or booklets. From Arkaroola, it was only an hour's drive.

'Can't we just keep going?' said James when we got there.

'But we wanted to do this. I think it's important.'

'It's only eleven o'clock. I don't think we need to stop for another day. Besides, it's weird. This is their home. We'll be wandering around looking at people like they're animals in a zoo.'

'But they want visitors. It's what they *do*. It's their business.'

'Yeah …' His voice trailed off.

'Let's at least go in and have a look.'

We parked the car and I went into the office while James and the boys hung around outside. I smiled at the woman behind the desk, but I wasn't quite sure what to say. My plan of booking a campsite and a tour was looking like it might not work out. I picked up a couple of brochures and mumbled something about having a chat with my husband. Although James and I had never bothered to get married, whenever I used the word 'partner' outside the inner city, I could feel my own eyes rolling. On this trip, James was quickly becoming my 'husband'.

'The campground looks nice,' I said, showing James the picture. 'We can go on a bushwalk today and then do this campfire thing tonight.'

He looked at the brochure. 'It's a lot of money to go for a walk and sit around a fire. I can make us a fire for nothing.'

'It's not about that, though, is it? It's about meeting people and hearing them tell their stories.'

He squirmed. 'I don't know. I really don't want to do this. Maybe when we get a bit further north. You know, near Alice Springs, or in Western Australia.' He shuffled his feet in the dirt as he spoke and I realised he was seriously uncomfortable. This had been important to me, but I didn't think I would be able to change his mood and have enough energy to make it fun for all four of us.

I looked back down at the brochures in my hand. One was for Chile Creek, a small community north of Broome. I promised myself that we would go to Chile Creek, or somewhere like it. I would find a way to at least meet some Indigenous people who wanted to teach us a little about their culture. But it wasn't going to happen today. We drove off without even going back into the office to tell them we weren't staying.

Only a few hours later, we were looking at the Oodnadatta Track. The dirt road stretched ahead of us, smooth and wide and featureless, just like the landscape around it. It curved gently to the left, following the arc of the embankment that held what remained of the train tracks that used to run from Adelaide to Alice Springs. The old railway itself traced the route taken in 1861 by the explorer John McDouall Stuart when he led the first expedition party to trek across Australia from south to north – and make it back. It took fourteen months. Stuart, almost blind and in great pain, was carried nearly 1000 kilometres of the return trip on a litter between two horses. He died four years later, aged fifty-one. The same trip from Adelaide to Darwin on the Stuart Highway, which is named after him, can now be done in thirty-six hours.

Work on the Central Australian Railway began just sixteen years after Stuart's successful expedition, but the first train to travel all the way to Alice didn't run until 1929. It was called the *Ghan*, in honour of the Afghan camel drivers who had made the whole scheme possible. After decades of damage from flash floods, extreme heat and termites, the railway was abandoned in 1980. The new line, built with termite-proof concrete sleepers, is further to the west and now goes all the way to Darwin.

On the outskirts of Marree, at the southern end of the Oodnadatta Track, we saw our first outback road conditions sign. Under a red strip that warned of severe penalties for travelling on closed roads, bright green panels fastened with brass padlocks gave us the go-ahead. Marree to Bopeechee: OPEN. Bopeechee to William Creek: OPEN. William Creek to Oodnadatta: OPEN. Oodnadatta to Marla: OPEN. Feeling very intrepid, we climbed back into the car and drove onto the track. We were on our way.

Two kilometres later we turned off down a side track. We had decided to camp at Muloorina Station, a privately owned 400,000 square hectare cattle station 54 kilometres west of Marree. It had a very cheap campground and, more importantly, vehicle access to the shore of Lake Eyre. Heavy rains in Queensland were rumoured to have caused water to flow into Lake Eyre. Depending on whom you talked to, the lake was either awash with yachts and catamarans or bone dry and likely to remain that way for at least another decade. We knew that a small part of Lake Eyre would be visible from the Oodnadatta Track, but we were keen to see more of it – especially if there was a chance of seeing it as it started to fill.

The campground was large and spacious, dotted with gnarly gum trees and a few tents set up at generously spaced intervals. 'Nice', I thought, as we drove in.

Within seconds of getting out of the car we were bombarded by more flies than I had ever encountered in my life. If I could have collected every single fly I had ever seen or heard and put them all in one big box, there would be fewer in that box than there were swarming around our heads at that moment. I swatted at them, swearing and freaking out as they crawled all over me, even climbing inside my clothes and getting stuck in my hair. I choked as they hurtled into my mouth and dive-bombed down my throat. We set the tent up as fast as we could then retreated back to the car. A hundred more flies came with us but we rolled down the windows as we drove and bashed them with maps and books until they were squashed flat or sucked outside.

When we got our first glimpse of the southern arm of Lake Eyre there was water. We trudged through silvery, slippy mud to verify it wasn't a mirage. We were stunned. It didn't seem possible that water could have reached the driest, most southern areas of the lake without us hearing about it.

Excited, we continued on to Lake Eyre North. It was completely dry. What we had seen was only a puddle left over from recent rain. Now the surface of the lake was crunchy under our boots. Dylan knelt down, picked up a handful of the lumpy grey crystals, tasted it and was delighted to find it salty. He ran back to the car for an empty bottle as the rest of us wrote our names in the salt and wondered why there were no flies.

It took thirteen minutes. One fly cruised around my head and I assumed it was lost, perhaps a hitchhiker from our car. Within ten seconds there were twenty. A minute later they were swarming around us. We raced back to the car, wondering how they had found us.

Back at our dusty campsite at Muloorina I had to accept that the flies weren't going anywhere. There was no point organising dinner until they went to sleep at dusk so James and the boys played cricket while I hid in the car, pretending to consult maps until darkness brought some peace.

When we sat down to eat, a couple of ants crawled past my plate. I brushed them onto the ground. A minute later I noticed a few more. I swept them away again and checked the food containers on the table. They weren't coming from there. Something crawled on my head. I ran my fingers through my hair expecting to find a fly. As I searched, tiny legs crawled down my back and inside my shirt. I leapt up and shook myself, hair flapping, spinning around and hitting myself in the back.

'They're everywhere', said James. The table was covered in roaming ants.

'Where are they coming from?' I said. I looked up into the canopy of the gum tree above us. A convoy of ants were dive-bombing us from a branch above our table, marching up the branch from their nest and dropping, one by one, onto us.

That night I only woke once, when a herd of wild horses thundered through the campground on their way to the waterhole. They called to each other as their hooves pounded past the tent, so close that I could hear their breath snorting as they galloped through the moonlight to the waterhole.

We left the campground at Muloorina Station early and were back on the Oodnadatta Track by eight o'clock in the morning. The first car we overtook, after driving for nearly two hours, was also towing a dusty campervan. Its roof was loaded with surfboards and a tinny rested upside down on the van, and as we went past the two kids in the back and the adults in the front waved and gave us big smiles.

We had been surprised by the absence of other families since the start of our trip. Before we left, every second person we talked to had a story about someone they knew who had done the same thing. For a while we wondered if there were thousands of families driving around the country.

But so far we hadn't met any. We had met families living in caravan parks, but they were on a completely different journey. Sometimes we met people camping with their kids on weekends. We had started keeping track of the days, trying to time our Saturday stops at places where there might be families. The April school holidays had just started in Victoria and South Australia, but the Oodnadatta Track was a long way for anyone to come for a fortnight's holiday.

These people had looked like us – a bit feral, a bit dirty, and way too relaxed to be a family on a mini-break. They were also cruising through the dry heart of Australia with surfboards and a boat – not something you see a weekend traveller doing. Perhaps there were other families on the road after all.

A few hours later, at an old railway bridge just south of William Creek, we checked our map. We were already only 205 kilometres from Oodnadatta but it seemed silly to dash all the way up the Track in just two days. After our standard lunch of warm ham and salad rolls washed down with orange Tang, we stretched our legs and explored the abandoned train tracks.

What was left of the original wooden sleepers lay broken and scattered alongside the red dirt road. In some places they had been positioned along the slight rise of the old tracks to spell out words. Baz Woz Ere. Jack 4 Me. Ireland Forever. 'Don't believe that crap about there being no wood on the Track', we had already been told. 'It's everywhere.' We collected some and put it on the roof of the car to use as firewood. I felt bad about taking it but, looking around, it was obvious that there wasn't any other firewood – probably for hundreds of kilometres.

As we burned those sleepers over the next week – and they were made of hardwood that burned hot and long – they left behind six-inch nails that still bore the marks of the blacksmith's hammer.

Millions of nails, crafted by hand, must have been pounded into the wooden beams to build that 1500-kilometre railway. That day Oscar and Dylan also picked up handfuls of those old blackened nails from where they lay beside the remains of the steel tracks. Those nails jingled on the floor of the car for months.

William Creek was the first town since Marree, if you can call a place with a population of six a town. There was one pub and one general store, which faced off across the dusty road like feuding relatives. Both establishments had campgrounds, but neither of them seemed like a nice place to spend the night. The store looked cleaner and brighter than the pub, but it had all the character of a truck stop. We chose the pub. Inside, it was dark and dusty and the walls and ceilings were groaning under the weight of the detritus of drunken tourists. Foreign bank notes, fading student cards, postcards, torn t-shirts and even lacy bras lined every surface, but at least the air was cool.

We sat in the dim lounge bar and nursed our icy drinks. The boys were zoned out in front of a huge plasma screen showing the Disney Channel when the family we had passed on the road came in. The kids made a beeline for the cartoons and their parents looked at us and rolled their eyes.

Sue and Tim were from Queensland. Like us, they were on the road, homeschooling their kids, Troy and Kirralee, who were a bit older than our boys, and cruising around without much of a plan. They had camped the night before at Coward Springs, an old telegraph station that had been turned into Oodnadatta Track's version of an outback playground, about a hundred kilometres back down the road. We had considered camping there but dismissed it as too touristy, instead spending the night with swarms of flies, mosquitoes and ants at Muloorina Station. But Tim and Sue had loved Coward Springs. It was named for its thermal pools, part of the chain of permanent water sources that spring from the Great Artesian Basin and make life possible in this hot, dry region. They had swum in the mineralised water that bubbled out of the ground, and at night the manager lit a fire under a steel drum to heat water for showers.

I asked them where they were planning to camp tonight, knowing without even looking at James that, whatever their answer, we would say, 'Us too!'

'Coober Pedy', said Sue. Damn. Coober Pedy was pretty much in the opposite direction to where we were going. 'We want to get into an underground camping place. I'm going to ring them from here and see if we can book in.'

Deflated, we discussed the dismal prospect of camping at William Creek. Tim chimed in and said he had read about a camping spot on the edge of Lake Eyre. We checked our maps. Halligan Bay, in Lake Eyre National Park, was accessible by a 70-kilometre 4WD-only track that started just a few kilometres south. Tim was keen on the idea but their kids had their hearts set on opals and caves.

We asked the woman behind the bar about Halligan Bay. 'People go out there all the time. It's a bit of a rough road, though. I've never been. There's nothing out there.' She warned us the drive would take a few hours.

Aware of how quickly darkness would come, we dragged the kids away from Disney and got moving. Tim and Sue wished us luck as we waved goodbye.

One kilometre along the Halligan Bay road we passed a registration booth. You were meant to fill in a form stating your car registration, the date and the number of nights you planned to stay, then put your money in the envelope and put it in the box. As I did all that, James complained that it was a ridiculous system. He said local kids probably raided the box for loose change to spend on pots at the pub. I ignored him and read the signs posted at the booth that warned of the extremely rough condition of the track and the complete absence of water at the campground.

As we drove I read up on Lake Eyre in the increasingly dirty and torn guidebooks that lived at my feet. Kati Thanda–Lake Eyre (as it has been known since 2012) is 144 kilometres long, 77 kilometres wide and covers nearly 10,000 square kilometres. At 15 metres below sea level, it is the lowest point of Australia. When it fills, which it only does about four times every century, it is the largest lake in Australia.

In the aftermath of monsoons, floodwaters flow south from waterways right across Queensland's Channel Country. The water makes its way first into Lake Eyre North, reaching depths of up to five metres and swelling the numbers of native fish that have managed to survive for years in small, isolated pools. As the water spreads south, birds arrive in their millions. Pelicans first, then silver gulls, grebes, ducks, falcons and eagles. No-one can explain how the birds know when the lake has water, especially as this happens so infrequently. The birds breed and feed on the fish or prey on smaller birds until the lake disappears as quickly as it appeared.

When the lake is dry, which it usually is, life is scarce. The salt crust can be 50 centimetres deep in places. One hardy fish species has evolved to survive in water fifteen times saltier than the ocean, and there is a local lizard that lives in the mud underneath the salt.

It is not a hospitable place for humans.

The track to Halligan Bay deteriorated quickly. The car rumbled along, bouncing over rocks that were so numerous that James gave up trying to steer around them. After a long, slow hour, during which we had seen no other vehicles, we passed a small white cross on the side of the track. 'Caroline Grossmueller. 11 Dec 1998. PERISHED.'

I flicked through my books for an explanation, but found nothing.

Around us, the landscape was a wasteland of black rock. Giant slabs sloped away, colliding with each other and shearing off, leaving edges as clean as a knife blade. There were no trees in sight and, even in April, it was hot. I couldn't imagine what it would be like in December. A rush of nausea flooded through me and dried my mouth. I had a sip of warm Tang and did a quick mental count of how many litres of water we were carrying.

'Can we stop and ride our bikes?' said Oscar.

'No.'

We drove on.

I imagined arriving at the campground to see a few tents, or maybe even another camper trailer with a couple of kids. We would sit around a fire with other people later that night, share a drink and congratulate ourselves for being so far from the city.

When we arrived, there was one elevated toilet block, a few information signs and no signs of life. We were the only people there. We might have been the only people in the world. I felt a tiny worm of fear uncoiling in my gut, stretching out and spreading through my body, and I strode off up a sand dune in an attempt to outrun it.

White salt spread out in front of me as far as I could see. At the shore, where the patchy scrub gave up its attempt to spread onto the lake's inhospitable surface, the salt was grimy and grey, but further out it shone as if it was illuminated from below. As I looked out onto its vast expanse, I had to fight to stop myself checking over my shoulder. It was the silence, I realised. There were no birds calling, no tiny creatures rustling in the bush, no lizards scuttling under the rocks. I swiped at my face. But there were flies. There were always flies.

A national park sign repeated information about the lake that I had already discovered in my books, with the addition of a sketch of a species of lice that lived in the salt crust. The sign also quoted, with a disarming honesty that I suspected must have escaped the notice of the park's marketing team, Edward John Eyre's report from one of his failed expeditions into the centre of Australia in search of an inland sea: 'The whole was barren and arid-looking in the extreme, and as I gazed on the dismal scene before me I felt assured I had approached the vast and dreary desert of the interior'.

I knew exactly how he felt, and I'd only travelled a few hours to get to the lake. The first white man to see Lake Eyre had come across the massive salt lake on his third attempt to find a route into the interior of Australia. After weeks of slogging north from Adelaide through dry and inhospitable country, he found his path blocked by the dry lake that would later bear his name and knew that his goal was impossible. In his journal, he wrote about his overwhelming despair at seeing the expanse of salt that lay in front of him: 'cheerless and hopeless indeed was the prospect before us … I had now a view before me that would have damped the ardour of the most enthusiastic …'

The kids had successfully nagged James into untying their bikes and they rode past me and out onto the salt. Despite signs forbidding the driving of cars on the lake, tyre tracks showed that someone had been doing circle work. But not recently. No rain had fallen out here for a long time. The salt held the imprints of all its visitors for an age. People had gouged their names into the crust and the lake was criss-crossed with footprints.

I looked at the light shimmering on the horizon. I could see what looked like water and mountains rising out of the lake. I shook my head, blinked and looked again. There was nothing there.

I turned my back on the lake and its disconcerting illusions and went back to the tent, where I rushed around preparing dinner. I had to keep moving; when I stopped, I could feel the fear rising and sending tendrils of ice into my limbs. As I cooked, the sun dropped over the horizon. The lake glowed with soft shades of purple and a full moon rose in a lavender sky. I have never seen anything so beautiful in my life, before or since. Yet, even if I live to be 100, I don't think I will ever feel so alone as I did that evening.

The moon was so bright that we didn't need our lights, but I couldn't eat more than a few mouthfuls. I whisked away the plates as soon as everyone was finished and did the washing-up quickly. I raced to bed, hoping that sleep would shut down my imagination until the morning. Sunlight would surely bring a saner perspective.

Things didn't get any better after I went to bed. I felt completely out of place, so wrong and so unwelcome. In the darkness, my imagination took over. Maybe empty space is a vacuum that beckons to the imagination. Mine obliged, filling the void with images of cars approaching in the night, carrying men with ill intent in mind. The silence hummed in my head, masking the sound of the vehicles I knew were coming.

Twice I felt the gorge rise in my throat. The only thing that stopped me from vomiting was the fear of having to go outside the tent to do it. I lay completely still, because the rustling of any tossing and turning would stop me hearing the footsteps of anyone approaching the tent.

A beam of moonlight tracked a path across the canvas walls of the tent. I watched it for hours as it passed over the foot of my bed, across the wall and touched for a while the sleeping faces of our sons.

In the depth of the night I said, 'James, I am absolutely crapping myself.'

'Me too', he said. His voice was so clear that I knew he had been lying wide awake for hours too. 'I've got the axe under the mattress.'

I forgot I had to be quiet. 'Why? No-one knows we're out here.'

His theory, developed over several hours of listening to his heart thumping in his ears, had two parts. One was that the people at the pub had told the local serial killer that we were out here. This was just a reworking of a movie plot, so I ignored it. His second theory was that by registering at the turn-off, I had placed us on the psychopath's menu. The murderer only needed to check the box to find out that two adults and two children were camping alone on the edge of the lake. This was harder to dismiss, particularly as it contained the twist that my insistence on following the rules had sentenced us to death.

My stomach churned. 'That's ridiculous.'

In that moment I realised that when you are in the grips of a mindless fear, the knowledge that you are not alone in your imaginings makes it ten times worse. If it's just you thinking the unthinkable, your fears are silly and groundless. If two of you think it, you can't help but wonder if some basic survival instinct is at work.

It took me an age to work out that the night was over. There were no birds to herald the sunrise with song, so the dawn arrived in complete silence. After the longest and slowest sunrise I have ever endured, it was finally light. I had imagined this moment all night. The sun would come up and everything would be okay. My fears would shrivel and vanish in the brightness of a new day.

I crept out of the tent and stumbled to the toilet block. My legs were weak and uncooperative. Cramps gripped my bowels.

When I heard steps approaching, my guts turned to ice. For one terrible moment, I knew that in the brief time I had been shaking on the toilet, my family had been slaughtered and I was next.

'Mum? Are you finished in there?'

For months afterwards, I couldn't stop thinking about those 15 hours we spent alone on the edge of Lake Eyre. I needed to understand why we were so scared. One friend, bemused at why it had terrified us so much, said, 'But there's nothing out there'.

'Exactly', I replied.

Later that year, when I finally had both time on my hands and internet access, a quick Google search turned up a coroner's report explaining what had happened to Caroline Grossmueller.

Caroline and Karl Goeschka, Austrian tourists with no experience of 4WD vehicles, had wanted to see Lake Eyre. Following the instructions in their guidebook, they told the barman at William Creek their plan. He wrote their names and the date in a notebook, telling them if they weren't back the next day he would 'hit the panic button'. At the Halligan Bay campground, they drove into soft sand and bogged their vehicle. Despite letting air out of their tyres and digging around the wheels, they were unable to free the car. After two days, when no-one had come to rescue them, they decided to walk back to the Oodnadatta Track, a distance of 67 kilometres. They left at night, when it was a little cooler, but Karl became ill and had to return to the campground.

Three days later, Caroline's body was found 30 kilometres from the road. She was still carrying more than six litres of water. There was a note in her rucksack: 'HELP! Had to leave boyfriend alone due to health problems with less water … Myself still trying to get out of this hell heading towards William Creek, which 2 inhabitants simply forgot us. Please try to find us!'

The police found Karl, still alive, at Halligan Bay. He too had written a series of notes in anticipation of his death. A police officer deflated the vehicle's tyres, spent ten minutes digging out the wheels and drove the car out of the sand.

The coroner's report into Caroline's death included recommendations about compulsory training sessions for tourists hiring 4WDs and mandatory communication and recovery equipment in all rental vehicles. The coroner also ruled that the people at William Creek were not to blame. However, in his evidence, the man they had spoken to admitted that he had indeed forgotten all about them.

I also discovered that I wasn't alone in seeing mountains rising from what looked like water in the lake. Lake Eyre is famous for its hallucinatory qualities. Navigational equipment goes haywire too. In the days before GPS you couldn't even rely on your compass. Nor can you trust your ears. One research team accurately recounted conversations that they had overheard quite clearly across several kilometres of salt. More bizarrely, they reported seeing one of their shore-based colleagues riding towards them on a penny farthing.

I think now that what I felt that night at Halligan Bay was not just about being alone. It was also that, after forty years of city life, I was surrounded for the very first time by a landscape that made no concessions at all to the requirements of human life. I had spent my entire life priding myself on my independence, when only a few days' drive from home there were places where my urban resourcefulness was totally inadequate.

Chapter Six

'This is great', I said, as I wandered around the Pink Roadhouse.

I loved Oodnadatta. I loved the noticeboard papered with clippings about the roadhouse's crazy owner, Adam Plate. Adam was so well known that people from all over the world rang him when they were planning their outback holiday. For hundreds of kilometres, he had planted pink metal signs to point out interesting landmarks, give directions at the intersection of unmarked dirt roads and tell you how much further you still had to drive.

Although James wanted to keep driving, he knew there was no chance of getting me out of a town that night, even one as shitty as Oodnadatta. We set up in the campground behind the pub. It was eerily reminiscent of the one in William Creek that, just twenty-four hours before, we had spurned in order to spend a terrifying night on the edge of Lake Eyre.

Oscar and Dylan spent the afternoon hurtling down an old metal slide that had been precariously placed on the edge of the swimming pool. On the other side of the fence, road trains loaded with two layers of cattle rumbled into the service station, but not even the smell of the cows and their mournful lowing could put a dent in my celebratory mood. I felt like having a drink.

James went to the store, returning with beer and a six-pack of premixed cans. 'It's all they had. I'm not paying $40 for a bottle of bad wine that you won't even finish.'

My tolerance for alcohol had taken a beating on this trip, probably because I was so dehydrated the whole time. Just one glass of wine squeezed every drop of moisture out of my body and replaced it with an instant headache. I had struggled to get any enjoyment out of drinking. Nausea and pounding temples came well before any lightening of my mood and stifled any urges to tell mildly inappropriate stories to strangers around a campfire.

I cracked the icy can and took a sip. It was cold. Bubbly, but not too fizzy. Sweet, but in a tangy kind of way. Not like lemonade. I sipped again. Ten minutes later, the can was empty. I put it down in mild shock. James grinned at me. 'That went down pretty fast.'

I reached for another one. 'There's nothing much to it. It's like a soft drink, really.'

After two cans, I decided to get dinner organised before I lost the will to move. I stumbled back to the tent and managed to cook pasta and slop some tins of tuna and tomatoes over the top. I knocked off another can as I worked, and finished a fourth as we ate.

At four o'clock in the morning I was wide awake. So much heat was pouring off my body that I couldn't believe James was sleeping through it. My skin was tight and dry, rasping painfully wherever my limbs were touching. My cheek on the pillowcase felt dangerously hot. I rolled over to find a cooler patch but the movement triggered a sludgy wave of nausea that I couldn't ignore.

Five minutes later, as I vomited in the portable toilets on the edge of the caravan park, I felt my spirits lift. I knew that, despite what James was going to say about how much alcohol I had drunk, I was purging the fear that I had been carrying for the last twenty-four hours. The next morning, feeling much better than I deserved to, I regained my camping mojo and agreed to go to Dalhousie Springs, on the edge of the Simpson Desert.

The track across the Simpson wasn't on our itinerary. We knew about it, though; it was an iconic desert crossing and one of the things that people on the road used to work out who was a serious traveller and who wasn't. More than once we'd been asked, 'Are you doin' the Simpson?' We weren't. For one thing, it went in the wrong direction for us. It would take us east, past Poeppels Corner where the borders of South Australia, the Northern Territory and Queensland collide, all the way to Birdsville. From there, the only way out was back across the desert, or south down the Birdsville Track. Also, as far as I could tell, the track was pretty much 600 kilometres of sand dunes. Sand dunes weren't our strong suit so far. Plus, all the recommendations about the crossing included strongly worded statements about carrying lots of fuel, water and spare parts, travelling in a group, and being prepared for at least six days on the track. It wasn't the kind of trip you did on the spur of the moment, no matter how free and spontaneous you felt.

It did look beautiful, though. The pictures I had seen showed sand dunes rolling for miles under a bright cloudless sky. Tiny white wildflowers somehow managed to grow amongst the ripples of the bright red sand, and lizards left tracks that scuttled across the face of the dunes and disappeared into clumps of pale spinifex. One solitary track carved out a straight line between the dunes and then went up and over each one, as if a child had pushed a toy car from point A to point B with a single-minded disregard for the terrain. But it also looked very lonely. And lonely was not a place I was eager to return to in a hurry.

Dylan wanted to send the salt he had collected at Lake Eyre back to his classmates. As James packed up the tent, the boys and I went to the roadhouse, which doubled as the post office. Oscar stayed outside to kick dirt and Dylan and I went inside.

A group of campers came in, bursting with enthusiasm for shopping. I watched as they scanned the souvenirs and examined the prices on the boxes of Barbecue Shapes. As they raced around, looking for something to buy, they reminded me very strongly of home. I decided to test my theory.

When Dylan asked how long the package would take to arrive, I answered a fraction too loudly. 'Maybe two or three days to Adelaide, then one to the post office in Melbourne, then another day to get to FITZROY.'

A head snapped around. The woman examined Dylan and me, then looked outside at Oscar, who was trailing a stick in the dirt.

'Is that Oscar?'

I was shocked by my powers. But I had been right: these were my people.

'He went to kindergarten with my twins. That's them over there. Bill and Ted. Remember?'

I did, vaguely, but out here casual acquaintances were practically family. A vague memory was more than enough. Within ten minutes I was back at the tent.

'James, you'll never guess who I met in the shop. Bill and Ted's mum. Remember them? Of course you do. Those twins from kinder, the blond ones. Anyway, they're travelling with a group' – I had to rush through this part, James had developed the lone travellers' disdain for tour groups – 'but it's just them and some friends and a man who knows the area. They're going to Dalhousie today. Won't it be nice for the boys to have kids to play with!'

James glanced up at me and continued to roll up the tent ropes. 'I'm not barging in on a tour group.'

'It's not really a *tour* group. And we were going there anyway so it just means we'll have people to talk to tonight.' I was developing a flounce. 'For a change. Besides, they said that last night they met another family who were doing a trip like us and they might turn up as well.'

As we bounced along the road to Dalhousie Springs, my spirits were as jaunty as the car. The road was a barely discernible imprint of two tyre tracks running through a field of gibber rocks the size of baseballs. James said the only thing distinguishing the track from the landscape around it was that the rocks were marginally smaller.

Dalhousie is famous for its thermal springs. Water seeps underground somewhere in Queensland, travels slowly down through layers of earth and is warmed by the heat from the earth's core. Millions of years later, it emerges back through the crust. When it comes out, it can be as hot as 40°C. Driving through a field of rocks, it was impossible to imagine there was any water out here until we passed a grove of palm trees. The Afghani men who had helped to build the first railway line had planted date palms wherever they found water.

Dalhousie Springs turned out to be a beautifully maintained campground with running water, showers and a brand-new toilet block.

'Flush!' reported Dylan happily.

We raced for the river and hit the million-year-old hot brown water with shouts of delight. Within seconds, I could see the boys' faces turning bright pink and felt a deep lethargy leaching into my legs. I knew we should get out and drink some water – this heat was the very last thing we needed – but it was so nice in there. If I stayed very still the water around me seemed to cool slightly. It was only when I moved that my arms and legs tracked through warmer water and beads of sweat formed on my forehead.

Soon the water was full of bodies. Kids with floaties strapped to their arms splashed happily. Adolescent boys discovered the thick black mud on the riverbed and painted their arms and faces with it. Bearded men reclined in inflated inner tubes, balancing cold tinnies on the dusty black rubber. Pudgy women slid quickly out of their sarongs and into the murky water.

'What do you reckon the rich folk are doing?' someone said.

We all laughed. We were all four days of solid driving on terrible roads away from any major city. This was our reward and it was priceless.

Wandering back to our tent we saw a car drive in, loaded up with surfboards and towing a van and a boat. We waved casually to Sue and Tim, trying not to show how excited we were at the prospect of finally making some friends on this trip. We gestured towards our campsite and let them know that we had no problem if they felt like camping next to us and pretended not to care as they slowly circled the campground and then made their way back to where we had set up.

When I worked out that they were the family that the other people had met, I was a bit disappointed. I had thought maybe there were more families out here. Sue agreed; they had expected to meet more people as well.

It was actually so rare that when we did meet another family, the conversation inevitably came around to the topic of why we were out here doing this, and why no-one else was. So far, there seemed to be one common factor: just about everyone had experienced the early death of a parent.

Between us, James and I had lost three parents in the space of seven years. James's father had died from cancer when James was nineteen. When I was twenty-five, my father collapsed in his office during an asthma attack and died at his colleagues' feet. My maternal grandmother died the same day on the other side of the world, and later that year my father's mother had a heart attack. Two years later, James's mother was gone, also from cancer. James and I had always known that we couldn't count on being around to see our sons grow up to become adults.

I floated my theory with Sue. She saw my point, but their reasons for travelling were different. When she and Tim were in their early twenties, years away from even thinking about children, they had met European backpackers in Darwin who had told them about places like Wave Rock and Ningaloo Reef and the Kimberley. They had vowed that, if they ever did have kids, they'd make sure they saw their own country before they started travelling overseas. This trip was the culmination of that promise.

'Are you homeschooling?' I asked her.

Tim, out of sight under his van, snorted loudly and muttered something about a complete bloody nightmare. The four kids looked at each other and did a synchronised eye roll. They were in telepathic agreement that school was bad enough but school with your parents was worse.

We swapped stories all afternoon. The kids' words tumbled over each other as they argued about who had the right to tell particular tales and who had climbed the highest mountain or swum in the coldest water or endured the longest day's drive. Our paths had criss-crossed for weeks. Sometimes we had camped in the same places just days apart. By the time the Fitzroy group rolled in with their tour leader, we didn't even feel a pang of rejection as they set up on the other side of the campground.

'They're on a tour', Sue said. 'They're nice, but real city folk. Not like you', she added politely. My heart swelled.

When the flies crawling on every inch of our exposed skin became unbearable, we went to join the other people in the hot springs. Sue and I were bobbing lethargically in the water when Tim came striding down the path with a huge grin on his face. He was dressed in boardies, dusty boots and had a green fly net draped over his face, and he was carrying a surfboard. He launched himself into the water with a whoop of joy and soon had kids climbing all over him.

Later, I went to examine the toilet block, which was an elegant building with curved corrugated iron walls. As well as flush toilets and showers it had a laundry sink. It was being put to good use by a woman scrubbing out a sleeping bag.

'Spew', she said wearily.

She told me she was travelling with her husband and their three kids, his two brothers, and their wives and kids. The men made an annual trek across the Simpson Desert and had decided to bring the families along for the ride this year. They had driven non-stop for three days to get here and were heading onto the desert at first light the next day.

I mentioned that we had been out to Lake Eyre.

'We thought about doing that', she said. 'We started down the Halligan Bay track, but we had to turn back. It was too rough.'

We spent two days at Dalhousie, hanging out with the other families. The kids swapped books, taught each other new card games and ate their body weight in toasted marshmallows by the fire at night. James and Tim talked about cars and pored over maps, comparing routes to Western Australia. They had a different plan to us. They were heading straight to Alice Springs and then out past Uluṟu to drive to Western Australia on the Central Desert Road. We were going to Uluṟu next, and then making our way back down to cross the continent on the Nullarbor Plain. We all swallowed several flies a day, but it didn't seem so bad when there were people around to laugh every time your sentence was cut short and you doubled over, choking and gagging.

We told the Fitzroy group the best stories of our trip, and encouraged them to pass them on to everyone at home. Oscar and Dylan quickly realised that their adventures were deeply impressing the other kids.

On the third day we drove out to Mount Dare Hotel, the last fuel stop for vehicles travelling across the desert to Queensland. We filled up, paying the highest price so far for our fuel. Inside the hotel, the kids huddled round a tiny laptop in disbelief that they had internet access. The men were just as incredulous about cold beer. Although it was technically still morning, stubbies were ordered.

When James overheard someone complaining about the prices he gave a short lecture on the need for travellers to support these remote businesses so they could continue to provide a valuable service. He made his point by buying a slab of beer that cost even more than the diesel.

That afternoon we said goodbye to Tim and Sue and the tour group and were soon kicking the footy from South Australia into the Northern Territory. As we drove I caught a glimpse of a small sign pointing to the Lambert Centre. Bored, I checked my books to see what it was. 'The geographical centre of Australia', they informed me.

We had no idea what that meant, but it sounded suspiciously like a landmark. We had already decided that we would visit the western, northern, eastern and southern tips of the country. Lake Eyre was the lowest point and we were considering adding 'climbing Mount Kosciuszko' to our to-do list. Had we known there was an official centre as well, that would definitely have been on our agenda. We did a U-turn.

The Lambert Centre, we decided half an hour later, was quite possibly the silliest monument in the country. It consisted of a flag-pole that was a replica of the spire on top of Parliament House in Canberra, flying a tattered Australian flag. The pole was surrounded by a single length of light metal chain that was hung at knee height and supported by short metal poles that had been concreted into the ground. Inside the fence was a plaque, on which were engraved the exact latitude and longitude of Australia's gravitational centre of gravity. Apparently if you balanced Australia on a pin at exactly this point it wouldn't wobble.

We stared at the plaque, failing to imagine the entire continent suspended on a pin, and then spotted an old radiator nailed to a wooden stump nearby. Inside it was a visitors book donated by the Victorian 4WD Club and a red pen. We echoed the comments already made.

'Very cool. Stoked to be here. Lorna, James, Oscar and Dylan from Fitzroy.'

Back on the main road, the smooth dirt track stretched out in front of us. Silver shimmered on the horizon. I blinked and shook my head but it was still there. I couldn't watch it. It kept shifting under my gaze. I looked across to the bare plain beside us instead. When I turned back, it was still there. I looked across at James. He was hunched forward in the driver's seat, squinting.

'Can you see that too?' he said.

'Yes. Do you think it's the highway?'

'No, that's at least 40 kilometres away.'

Within minutes we worked it out. 'Boys, look! It's the *Ghan*!' The new passenger train from Adelaide to Darwin was stopped across the road.

We slowed down, stopping just metres from the train, and got out of the car. James and I sat on the bonnet and waved at the people inside. They couldn't get off, but being stationary was enough of a diversion that they had lined up along the heavily tinted windows of the carriages to look out at us. They seemed happy to be trapped. I imagined the cool, clean air they must be breathing inside their metal box. Two little girls in pretty dresses stood with their father in his short-sleeved collared shirt and waved back at me. All these people were on an adventure to the Red Centre too. They were just bringing a little more city with them than we were.

I was confused when I realised that the passengers were taking pictures of us. What was there to photograph? James had walked off to talk to the smartly uniformed man who had emerged from a secret door and was walking along the tracks. Dylan was clambering around on the roof of the car and Oscar was wandering along beside the train in bare feet, kicking stones. We were scruffy and dusty and dressed in our uniform of dirty shorts and baggy T-shirts. As I looked at us, through their eyes, I realised for the first time that my family had become ever so slightly feral.

Chapter Seven

Yulara, Uluṟu's tourist precinct, had a supermarket and pubs, the internet had been magically switched on, drinking water flowed from a tap next to our tent and for the first time in weeks there were no flies.

It was also packed. There were tourists in five-star hotels, a campground full of school groups, European backpackers in beaten-up old cars, grey nomads in lace-curtained caravans, families in shiny white rental campers and young couples in brightly coloured kombi vans.

We went to Uluṟu to watch the sunrise. At the first spot we found, the boys got upset when people around us ignored the signs asking everyone to stay off the vegetation. We had been getting Dylan to read national park signage out loud for practice. Even at six he understood the rules. But in their search for the perfect vantage point to photograph the sunrise, people were leaving the sealed road and trampling all over the plants. Feeling cross and strangely protective of the country the four of us had been driving and walking through for six weeks, we packed up and drove further along the road, forsaking a good view for peace and privacy. Five minutes later, as we were eating our breakfast on the bonnet of the car, a bus pulled up and disgorged a hundred tourists beside us.

The sun rose to a muted and slightly disappointed welcome from the crowd. Within minutes the car park was empty. Many of the buses were on their way back to Alice Springs. Their passengers had booked an overnight trip into which they had squeezed an afternoon at Uluṟu with the option of climbing, a quick trip to Kata Tjuṯa and a viewing of the sun setting behind Uluṟu, then this sunrise stop on the way out. No wonder they looked exhausted.

At least they had some idea of the landscape around them. In the supermarket, an American man straight off the plane from Sydney had ignored me when I suggested that one 600ml bottle of water might not be enough, given his plan to climb Uluṟu that afternoon with his eight-year-old daughter.

'It's really hot out there', I said.

He raised his eyebrows. In the heart of the resort, every building was fiercely air-conditioned and, even outside, kilometres of shade cloth held back the desert heat. He had been picked up from the local airport by a climate-controlled bus and dropped at a cool hotel lobby. This trip to the shop was his first venture outside and he had probably found it quite pleasant.

He had no idea yet how quickly the hot breeze carried away every drop of moisture from your skin. Sometimes it was hard to drink enough water to replace what you were losing. We were flavouring bottles of water with cordial so that we could stomach drinking 4 litres a day. On a long driving day, the water would be hot by the afternoon, so we tried to drink the flavoured bottles first. To start with I'd been a bit stingy with the sugary flavouring, but weak warm orange cordial tasted and looked disturbingly like urine.

Stories abounded of tourists being caught out in the heat at Uluṟu. We heard about an Irish man who had decided to climb in plastic sandals. They had melted onto his feet and he had to be airlifted off the rock, along with his seven-year-old son. It was rumoured that an extraordinary number of older tourists died quietly in their hotel beds a few hours after climbing. The theory was that the exertion of a strenuous climb in the midday heat, often after years of inactivity, was too much for their hearts. These incidents were hushed up, the story went, and the deaths were put down to natural causes.

James and I had talked to the boys about the issues around climbing Uluṟu. It was a tricky one. Both of us had climbed on a previous trip, more than ten years earlier. We couldn't pretend that we weren't aware of the traditional owners' opposition to the practice back then: we had known and we had climbed anyway. We told Oscar and Dylan it was up to them, but said we wanted to go on the ranger tour first and walk around the base of Uluṟu before they made any decisions.

The ranger was an Aboriginal man who found it hard to conceal his impatience with the tour group. 'This is the Mala Walk. Does anyone know what "mala" means?'

There was a long excruciating pause while twenty people gazed at their feet. He sighed. 'It's a small marsupial that used to live around here. They were pretty much wiped out but we're reintroducing them.' He looked around. 'It's called the *Mala* Walk. Didn't any of you wonder what that meant?' He sighed again and launched into his rehearsed spiel.

We walked behind him, humbled and slightly ashamed. Someone braver than us asked about climbing Uluṟu. The ranger explained that for the local Anangu people, the climb was a path of spiritual significance. It was only done by Aboriginal men for special ceremonies. The Anangu would prefer tourists didn't climb, for several reasons, but mostly because so many people had been hurt or died. Then he paused, and added something I had never heard before.

'You know, the Anangu people, they have a huge respect for tradition and culture. And when all these white people started coming out here and climbing the rock, they saw it was really important for you lot. They think, "Those whitefellas, it's strong in their culture that they climb." They would prefer you don't do it, but they aren't going to say, "No, you are not allowed." It's not their way.'

I felt a twinge of shame about climbing a decade ago. Back then I had been determined to prove to James that I could do it. It had been a decision based on pride and vanity and at the top, surrounded by exultant white people, some of whom were pissing on that sacred rock, I had already felt the sting of regret.

The ranger finished his talk with a few words about snakes. Snakes mostly avoided people, he said. Anyone who was bitten by a snake was either very unlucky or very stupid. The vast majority of snake bites were on the hand, from people bending down to get a close-up with their camera.

We left the group behind to walk the 10-kilometre track around the base of Uluṟu. By now it was mid-morning and it was already hot and dry. When we emerged from the shadow of the rock, the only respite from the heat came from the intermittent stands of skinny trees. We huddled in tiny patches of shade to drink warm cordial and eat stale biscuits before dashing out into the sun again.

Towards the end of the walk, the boys had stopped running ahead to explore the path and we were all trudging along silently in single file. Our feet crunched on the gravel path and my heartbeat pounded in my ears. It was a sign I recognised as an early warning of dehydration and mild heat exhaustion.

'Snake!' shouted Dylan.

Everyone froze.

James's foot stopped in mid-air and hovered over a two-metre king brown that was sliding across the path towards the sandstone slope of Uluṟu.

Shaken, we took a break on a large rock between the car park and the base of the climb and watched people slip on the smooth rock face as they clambered on their hands and knees up to where the chain link fence started. As we ate the last of our biscuits, I wished I was sitting there with a clear conscience instead of this lingering feeling of guilt. I decided to spare the kids from having the same experience as adults.

'You know what?' I said. 'I've changed my mind. You boys can't climb.'

James agreed. 'It's too hot and too dangerous. I don't want to go with you and you can't go on your own. When you're eighteen, you can come back and decide for yourselves, but right now we're saying no.'

Oscar made a few noises about it not being fair but I could tell they were both relieved that the decision had been taken out of their hands.

It was now after midday and the temperature was in the mid-thirties. Drops of sweat slid out from under my hat and trickled down my sunscreen-slick cheeks, leaving trails of pale freckled skin in the film of red dirt that covered me. A young woman started up the slope, dragging two small children along behind her. She was wearing a flimsy dress and lightweight sandals. Her foot slipped and as she crashed down on one knee, pulling one of the small children down too, we saw that she also had a baby in a sling strapped to her chest.

'That lady's an idiot', said Oscar. No-one disagreed.

At the visitor centre the boys bought postcards that declared 'I respected the wishes of the Anangu and did not climb Uluṟu' and pointed out loudly that James and I couldn't say the same.

Back at the campground, rehydrating with icy poles and a swim in the cold resort pool, the boys worked out it was Easter Saturday. I distracted them from obsessing about chocolate by talking to them about the meaning of Easter, trying to be even-handed about other people's religious beliefs.

James was less diplomatic. 'It's all just bullshit stories.'

Dylan looked up at us, balancing the need to respect his father's views with a desire to eat his body weight in chocolate the next day.

'So God and Jesus are just made up', he said carefully, 'but the Easter Bunny and Santa exist. Right?'

The next day, when the Easter Bunny dropped far too many chocolate eggs in the red dirt and the sugar levels rose in the campground, I decided to take advantage of the wireless internet in the five-star hotel lobby and update our website. As I lingered with an icy cold soda water and watched the progress bar on the web loader fail to move, the airport shuttle bus deposited a family arriving for their three days and two nights stay. Tidy blond children wearing freshly ironed white T-shirts, crisp shorts and spanking new sandals stood patiently in the lobby as their parents booked sunset viewings and dinners under the stars. I felt scruffy and slightly smelly and the internet had slowed to a crawl so I packed up the laptop and wandered back to the tent. A water pipe had burst and Oscar and Dylan were stripped to their underpants, racing sticks in the river of churning red mud. I couldn't remember ever seeing them so dirty or so happy. I plonked down on the ground and watched them play, wondering how they had adjusted so easily into their new life. In less than six weeks they had gone from having an entire cupboard full of games and toys to messing around happily in the mud with sticks.

Before we left home a lot of my anxiety was about how much stuff we needed to take. What clothes did we need to pack? Two pairs of shorts each, plus jeans and trackie daks and maybe pyjamas. A minimum of three t-shirts, two long-sleeved tops and two warm jumpers. Raincoats. Lots of underwear and socks in case it was hard to do washing. What kind of shoes should we take? Would runners, walking boots and thongs do? What about games? Toys? Books?

A few DVDs to watch on the laptop on cold or rainy days that we had to spend inside the tent? Should we have a couple of footballs and a soccer ball and a tube of tennis balls? If tennis balls, then racquets? Bicycles for everyone or just for the boys? Would they need helmets? How many pots would I need to cook our meals? Could we get by with only two forks each? Did we need cereal bowls and soup bowls and spare bowls 'just in case'? Would towels for showering and towels for swimming be enough? Four tea towels, or six?

Despite what I had thought of as a radical cull of our belongings, I knew now that we had brought far too much. At least one box in the trailer was full of stuff we didn't need. More importantly, I couldn't think of one thing we had left at home that we were missing. Certainly not the cupboard full of toys.

Later that afternoon we drove out to another viewing point and jostled for a good position to watch the sun set over Uluṟu.

'What's meant to happen?' asked Dylan. By now he had seen lots of excellent sunsets, but so far this was the first one that involved travelling 10 kilometres in a traffic jam to a car park.

'If yer lucky, the Rock'll go off', said a man standing next to him in the crush.

The Rock failed to go off that night, stubbornly fading from shades of red to grey to black with no spectacular moments of purple in between. The crowd around us declared the sunset a fizzer and stomped off disappointedly to their cars.

The walk around the rim of Kings Canyon in the Watarrka National Park, 320 kilometres from Uluṟu and an optional detour for many travellers to the Red Centre, was only 6 kilometres long but the park brochure included a warning about the extremely difficult climb to the top of the canyon. One of our guidebooks called it Heart Attack Hill.

The day before, we had woken the boys up when it was still dark and driven to the viewing platform halfway between Uluṟu and

Kata Tjuṯa to join another throng for the sunrise. We gave up trying to squeeze onto the platform for fear of knocking over one of the carefully placed tripods. All the cameras were aimed at the silhouette of Uluṟu that was emerging from the darkness as dawn broke. We sat behind the crowd, set up a small gas ring to make coffee and toast and, with our backs to Uluṟu, watched the red mounds of Kata Tjuṯa light up as the morning sun's rays bathed them in a warm glow. As the other tourists packed up their equipment and got back on the buses we heard a man ask, 'Is that the Olgas?' Like Uluṟu, this area has been officially returned to its Aboriginal name. And, just like Ayers Rock, many people still only know it by its European name.

Later that morning we dragged the boys along the Valley of the Winds walk at Kata Tjuṯa – an 8-kilometre trudge over loose rocks and up steep inclines. At one point the path veered away in a large loop away from the rock formations and out onto the hot, exposed landscape. The view back to the golden-red stone mounds was incredible but, with nowhere to shelter from the sun and the heat from the rocky ground radiating through the soles of our shoes, it was too hard to stay out there long enough to take it all in. It had reminded me far too much of the Flinders Ranges.

This time we decided to be sensible and just walk along the base of Kings Canyon. Dylan wasn't keen on doing another long walk, and James and I had to keep reminding ourselves that he was only six. It was a short stroll along the creek bed in the shade of the canyon walls. While we looked at the map on the sign where the tracks diverged, a couple with two little boys bounced down the track from the rim walk.

'How was it?' asked James.

'No problem', the man said. 'It's not that hard once you get up there. It only took us about two hours.'

James and I shared a look. 'I'll just go and grab some more water', I said.

In the end we spent four hours in the canyon. After the initial climb of 1000 steps, which the boys bounded up, the track circled the canyon's rim and gave us uninterrupted views to the horizon. We took a detour down a long, steep and rickety flight of wooden steps to the permanent waterholes aptly named the Garden of Eden. It was cool in the shadow of the rock walls around us and when I dipped my hand in the water to test it, it was colder than I had expected. We dangled our feet in the clear water and watched tiny fish dart in and out of the shade of giant palms and tree ferns. Insects flitted across the water, moving so quickly that I couldn't be sure if they were dragonflies or giant mosquitoes. The voices of the hikers on the rim far above floated down to us on the breeze. They sounded slightly flustered from where we were sitting. In this tiny unexpected oasis, the few people around us seemed to have fallen into a stupor. Swimmers drifted gently from one side of the pool to another, occasionally pushing themselves along with a lazy kick that didn't even break the surface of the water. A young couple sat surrounded by the contents of their packs, balancing books on their knees. One man was asleep, curled up on the rock with his head resting on a rolled-up towel.

I felt sorry for the people above, stuck up there in the heat of the day, unable or unwilling to take the time to climb down the steps and relax by the water. We ate our sandwiches and then decided that not having bathers wasn't a good enough reason not to swim and spent over an hour floating around the pool in our underwear. Refreshed and slightly damp, the walk back up the staircase was easy.

Our campsite was at a cattle station just outside the national park. We'd chosen it because it had a fire pit, but signs asked campers not to collect wood from the camping area, instead giving directions to a spot in the scrub just off the road. James and Oscar drove out to get the makings of a bonfire.

A few kilometres along the road they turned down a sandy track into the scrub. Twenty metres along, there was a small mound of sand that was less than a metre high. It was no great obstacle. The car powered over it and they drove on until they found a dead desert oak conveniently close to the track. They took turns to cut it up with the axe until it was in pieces that were small enough to load onto the roof of the car. Realising that he had forgotten to bring a spare rope, James balanced the wood in an intricate pattern beside the spare tent, the bag of wet weather clothes, the fishing rods and the golf clubs that were stored up there.

They got back in the car. James drove slowly and carefully so as not to upset the delicately balanced load. At the small hill, he inched the front of the heavy vehicle up and over the mound. The extra load pushed the back of the car down into the soft sand of the track. With no traction from behind, the front wheels lost their grip and sank into the sand on the other side of the lump. The belly of the car sat on top, like an elephant suspended in a sling. No amount of cajoling, reversing, changing gears or swearing could make the car move.

James had moved the compressor, snatch strap, tyre repair kit and jack into the car, but the shovel was still in the trailer. He found a shovel-shaped piece of firewood on the roof.

'Come on, Oscar. Let's dig.'

Twenty minutes later, he realised that the further they dug into the compressed sand the more likely it was that the car would squash them like bugs as it settled into the space they were creating underneath it.

They walked out to the road to flag down a passing car. After waiting for fifteen minutes, James decided to go back and try to build a platform of logs under the back wheels. He left Oscar under a tree on the side of the road. Ten minutes later, two young German men stopped for the little blond boy sitting alone in the middle of nowhere. When he explained why he was there, they drove down the track to help with the rescue. James hooked the two cars together with his snatch strap and they were free in thirty seconds. The Germans were rewarded with a six-pack of warm beer that James had in the car.

Back at camp, Dylan and I had only just started to wonder what was taking them so long.

James had vowed never to drive the same road twice if we had a choice. Instead of retracing our route back to the Stuart Highway to get to

Alice Springs, we decided to take the Mereenie Loop. An unsealed track, it ran north from Watarrka National Park, past Hermannsburg, and met up with the sealed road to Alice on the edge of the West MacDonnell Ranges. It passed through Aboriginal land, so we needed to get a permit from the Kings Canyon Lodge.

In the hotel lobby, the receptionist gave me a Mereenie Tour Pass booklet and a form to fill out and asked for $2.20. 'I've had to train myself to say "Two dollars and twenty cents"', she told me. 'I used to say "Two twenty". People were having heart attacks because they thought I meant two hundred and twenty dollars.'

The Mereenie Loop travelled through the country of Albert Namatjira. When I was a kid, I had seen prints of his watercolours hanging on the floral papered wall of 1970s lounge rooms. By the time I had finished university, I had absorbed enough cultural theory to understand that Namatjira's work was an example of Indigenous artists being persuaded to see their landscape through European eyes and paint it accordingly. In his work, the vibrant and stark landscapes of the Central Desert had reportedly been softened and rendered in pale shades of mauve and blue to appeal to white art critics and buyers. As we came over a rise in the road, the country below us sang in pastel hues of purple, yellow and green. The sky faded to white on the horizon and the light was hazy and diffused. The white trunks of huge ghost gums glowed as if they were lit from the inside. It looked exactly like an Albert Namatjira painting.

We camped at Palm Valley that night. Its crevasses and gorges were lush with palms and cycads, relics of central Australia's tropical past. Recent rain had created small pools in the hollows of the rocks and tadpoles darted in and out of the sun. We shared our fire with some Distance Education inspectors. They were on holiday, but their regular job involved travelling to remote cattle stations and communities and checking up on kids who were enrolled in School of the Air. They talked about families they had met who hired young women to work as governesses, often teaching a whole family of children at different year levels, from early primary onwards. Most only lasted a year, they said. The isolation got to them. The ones most likely to leave early were girls from cities down south, and then the mothers had to take over all the teaching as well as cooking for the station hands and working on the property.

For once we kept quiet about the length of our trip. I secretly hoped that they would assume we were just on a quick trip to the Red Centre. I didn't want to encourage any questions that would reveal our own dismal attempts at homeschooling. I was particularly ashamed as I thought about our most recent attempt at school in the open air shelters beside Uluṟu, which had ended with me declaring that if the boys wrote three postcards each I would count it as a full day's schoolwork. I wouldn't have lasted more than a few weeks as a governess when I was in my early twenties. Or even now.

We were ignoring all the sections of the workbooks that involved art, sport or major projects. Art, we reasoned, would be covered as the opportunity arose. We had already visited the small town of Hermannsburg, which was established as an Aboriginal mission in 1877 by German Lutherans. Hermannsburg has always been known for its artists. Albert Namatjira was the best known of Hermannsburg's painters and now the ceramics made by the women of Hermannsburg Potters are displayed in galleries around the world. We had walked through the historic buildings, looked at the paintings and pots, and lingered over old photographs showing Aboriginal children gathered outside whitewashed churches.

Reading was more contentious. When we left home, some of our friends had raised their eyebrows when they found out that we weren't planning to buy the boys any electronic games or DVD players to use in the car. 'They can read', I had said.

And they did. The back of the car was littered with filthy, torn books. They often picked one up off the floor, opened it to a random page and started reading from there. Although I hated seeing books treated so carelessly, Oscar and Dylan really did love them. They just didn't read the way most people did: from the beginning to the end, one book a time.

I didn't want to risk their joy of reading by turning it into work. I put a red line through the reading exercises in the schoolbook and wrote a note to the teachers to explain why we weren't doing them. They wrote back, saying that reading for comprehension was a skill that had to be learned and practised. I tried for a while, asking the boys questions like 'Who was your favourite person in that book?' and 'Did you like the ending?' Mostly they ignored me and I couldn't blame them. All my questions sounded fake, and for good reason. I hated talking about books. 'What's that you're reading?' was one of the worst things anyone could say to me when I was lost in a story. If the questioning continued – 'Good story, is it? What's it about, then?' – my heart filled with hatred. Reading was an intensely private experience for me. Writing book reports in high school had been excruciating. I could only ever do them if I was indifferent about the text.

There wasn't a lot the Distance Education teachers could do about it anyway. We were thousands of kilometres away.

By ignoring half of the workbook, school was only taking us about an hour and a half each day … on the days we did it. It took three weeks to get through each package, which meant that we spent, on average, an hour a day on school. When I thought of it that way, it worried me. I added up the hours they spent reading, the time we spent in national park centres looking at the displays and talking to rangers, and the maths skills they were getting as they checked out road signs to see how far we still had to drive each day. They were also picking up a lot about Australian nature, geography and history. Not to mention life experience. Other campers, particularly the older couples we met, kept telling us that the experience we were giving our sons was the best education they could get.

'They'll learn more in a year on the road than they would sitting in a classroom', was something we heard over and over again. I hoped they were right.

Chapter Eight

Dylan was bursting with excitement about the caravan park in Alice Springs. 'It has two jumping pillows. That's one for me and one for Oscar. And three pools and a BMX track. And,' he paused for suspense, 'you get free pancakes on Sundays!'

We hung out in Alice for a week and Nannette flew down from Darwin to spend the weekend with us. We set up the two-man tent for the first time and put the boys in it. Nannette slept in our tent, her first camping experience for decades. Growing up in a small village in Scotland, she had spent lots of her holidays camping. They had been cold, wet and miserable, made worse by clouds of biting midges, and she had vowed that when she was grown up she would never ever camp again. This was why I had never been camping as a child. She had spared me the same misery.

We visited the Reptile Centre, where James draped a huge snake around Dylan's neck as Oscar and I shuddered in horror. We'd wandered around the dry heat of the Desert Park and seen a huge wedge-tailed eagle swoop down in a demonstration of its hunting skills. We stood in Standley Chasm in the middle of the day and saw the sun make a very brief appearance overhead. Another evening we went to a didgeridoo show that made very enthusiastic use of a smoke machine, sombre voice-overs and aerial photography of the iconic Red Centre. James, with his theatre background, found it excruciatingly kitsch and couldn't bear to watch it but Oscar joined the performers on stage to bang a bongo drum in the finale. The next night Dylan discovered his inner performer too, getting up in front of a crowd of campers at the singalong to tell a long joke about three bank robbers who hid in sacks to evade the police. On our final evening in Alice, we lined up with the rest of the campers to look through a telescope at the craters of the moon and the rings of Saturn.

Packing up took a lot longer than usual, as the two-man tent proved to have inner dimensions roughly equivalent to the TARDIS. Out of it came books, pens, toy cars, balls, clothes, shoes and very tiny Lego pieces. A small mountain of stuff piled up that then had to be packed into the right boxes to give us a fighting chance of finding any of it again. James had insisted that the boys set it up and take it down themselves. When they started crying, we gave in and helped them.

All the other tourists were going north, chasing the warmth but, after dropping Nannette back at the airport, we went south. Our plan was to drive to Western Australia across the Nullarbor Desert.

Four hundred kilometres south of Alice Springs, we saw a Japanese cyclist pedalling along the highway. All I could see on his bicycle was a small pack, a blue tent and three water bottles. He smiled and waved as we passed him.

'We're not in a hurry', said James as he pulled over to the side of the road. The cyclist stopped and chatted in halting English, laughing the whole time, and showed us an old kangaroo bone that he had found on the side of the road. We offered him water, which he politely refused.

'We've got Tang', said Oscar.

The man's face lit up at the thought of a sugar hit so we filled one of his bottles with the warm orange liquid and shared it with him. Using mostly huge gestures and the names of countries, he explained he was cycling across all the continents from north to south. He had already ridden from Egypt to Cape Town and was going to South America next. Australia was the easiest, as the sealed Stuart Highway covered the exact direct route he wanted to travel, but he was finding the road trains terrifying. He mimed the swooshing of the big trucks for us, still laughing even as he mugged an exaggerated expression of fright. We understood that he had to get off the road when they roared past so that he wouldn't be sucked under the wheels by the wind they created. At night he camped 50 metres from the road, feeling much safer here than in Africa, where he had been worried about lions. When we waved goodbye and climbed back into the car, the boys said he was the happiest person they had ever met.

A bit further down the highway we drove past a group of Aboriginal men standing beside a broken-down car. They gave us a wave, but it was a token, dispirited one. Clearly lots of cars had already driven past and they weren't expecting us to stop.

James kept going and I looked across at him, surprised.

We had been warned several times not to stop for Aboriginal people on the road. 'Nine times out of ten', we were told, 'they've just run out of petrol.' I'd never understood why that was a reason not to stop. Running out of petrol was a serious thing on these roads. Several hundred kilometres could separate the nearest roadhouses. James shared my discomfort. From his days working on cattle stations, he knew better than most people how deceiving distances could be out here. What took an hour to drive in a car was an impossible walk in the dry heat of the desert.

Now he looked back at me and shook his head. 'I don't know why I did that', he said as he slowed down and pulled over. 'I feel really ashamed of myself.'

He turned the car in a wide arc and we drove back. We stopped behind the dusty, burgundy Commodore. One of the young men came over. Another man stood by the car and there was a young woman in the back seat. James got out and, after a bit of discussion over the raised hood of the car, he slid into the driver's seat and tried the ignition. Nothing happened.

The men were huddled over the engine. Oscar and Dylan had disappeared into their books so I got out, carrying what was left of our snacks. I gestured at the woman, offering the fruit and a drink, but she shook her head and looked away. I stood and watched as cars flew past us. They were going so fast I could only catch glimpses of the curious looks their passengers were giving us.

James came back. 'They reckon the battery's flat, and it is, but it's because they ran out of petrol then kept trying to start the car again. I could jump-start it, but we've only got diesel in our jerry can so they need to get petrol anyway. We'll have to tow them to the next town. Marla's only about 50 kilometres down the road.'

As James wielded our heavy tow rope, tying one end to the back of the camper trailer and then crawling under the front of the Commodore to find a spot to attach it to, the Japanese cyclist sailed past us and waved. The Aboriginal men seemed to be having a quiet argument. Neither of them was helping James with the rope.

Within a few minutes, our strange road train was on its way: the car, the camper trailer, a length of rope and a Commodore with three reluctant passengers. Dylan looked up briefly from his book to wave at the cyclist as we passed.

It was late in the afternoon when we pulled into the roadhouse at Marla. James tried to stop the other car at the petrol pump but frantic waving from the driver made it clear that they didn't want him to do that. He pulled up in the parking bay instead. One of the men went to the public phone box and the other two people stayed in the car. James untied the rope and had a quick conversation with them before coming back to us.

'I don't think they want to be here. They've got no money for fuel. He reckons they've driven from Docker River.'

I looked at the old Commodore. Docker River was in Western Australia, more than 700 kilometres away. 'Who's he ringing? Should we give them money to fill up?'

'It's not just the petrol, they're going to need a new battery too. I think he's trying to get someone to come out and pick them up. We probably should have just brought him in to make the phone call. I think they would have preferred to stay out there.'

I looked around at the concrete forecourt of the roadhouse. There was a road train and a few cars like ours in the car park. Through the windows I could see a couple of men in singlets and big hats sitting at the bar and a woman and three kids clustered around the ice-cream freezer. A red arrow pointed to a grey concrete motel block and an empty dirt campground, both of which looked as unwelcoming as any I'd seen. The Commodore looked very out of place. The two people in the back had slid so far down in their seats that they were nearly invisible. The man in the phone box was squatting, gesturing as he spoke.

We ended up spending the night in the campground. We couldn't get anywhere else before dark and, unlike the Japanese cyclist, we were too scared to camp alone beside the road. At that time, Nannette was very involved in the Darwin trial of Bradley Murdoch for the murder of Peter Falconio on the Stuart Highway in July 2001. Nannette's job involved working with the witnesses and victims of the crime, including Falconio's girlfriend, Joanne Lees, who had escaped from Murdoch after he tied her up with cable ties and forced her into his ute. We knew too much about that case for comfort and were seriously spooked.

We had a quick meal of pasta and bolognaise sauce and went to bed early that night, not keen to even go anywhere near the bar. When we packed up at dawn the Commodore and its occupants had disappeared. We hadn't heard the car leave in the night, so we didn't know if they had managed to buy fuel or if they had been towed by someone who came to help. Looking up and down the highway and seeing nothing but flat scrub in every direction, I couldn't even imagine where they had gone.

'Do you think we did the wrong thing?' I asked James.

'I don't know. I thought we were helping. I guess we didn't really ask what they wanted us to do.'

Coober Pedy, nearly 700 kilometres south of Alice Springs, was founded in 1915 after the fourteen-year-old son of a miner who had been searching the area unsuccessfully for gold came across pieces of opal lying on the ground. Eight days later the first opal claim was pegged. Since then its population has fluctuated as wildly as the price of opal. Now with 3500 residents from more than forty nationalities, tourist brochures often described the town as 'cosmopolitan'. In reality, it seemed to be populated almost entirely by obsessive, reclusive, middle-aged white men who would have had difficulty fitting in anywhere else.

It is not a hospitable place. Temperatures reach 45°C in summer and plunge to below freezing in winter. There are almost no plants to be seen anywhere, partly because of the lack of rainfall but also, I suspected, because most of the town has at some point been dug up by prospectors.

Many of the houses are underground or in caves dug from the side of hills. These dugouts are often far more comfortable than above-ground homes. The temperature in the dugouts is always about 25°C and shelves, alcoves and even new rooms can be dug at will. Some even have swimming pools and billiard rooms carved out of the hillside.

The novelty of the dugouts was enticing so we booked into the underground campsite Tim and Sue had told us about. It was like a rabbit warren, with long underground corridors lit by wall-mounted lamps and punctuated by small alcoves that had been carved out from the rock. We dragged down our mattresses and doonas and pillows and lay them on the white, chalky ground. There was only just enough room for our bedding and James couldn't stand up straight. As other people arrived, they politely looked straight ahead as they walked past the opening to our bedroom. Dust floated gently down onto our beds.

We spent most of that day in Coober Pedy noodling for opals in the tall, pyramid-shaped mullock heaps on the outskirts of town. Oscar and Dylan sieved through the piles of discarded dirt, looking for scraps of opal that the miners had missed. When they didn't find any treasure, they gave up, running up and down the heaps instead. They were soon covered from head to foot in fine yellow dust. We brushed them down and went back into town to go on a mine tour.

According to our guide, who was also the owner of our campsite, Coober Pedy's history was full of bitter feuds, lost fortunes, mysterious deaths and lives ruined in a fruitless search for opals. He told us outrageous stories that all had the theme of old-fashioned resourcefulness running through them. The tour ended with a detailed description of how to make explosives out of Vegemite and soap. I didn't have to look at the boys to know that they were sharing a conspiratorial look and wondering about the contents of our kitchen box.

That night we played cards in our alcove before going to sleep. Noise echoed through the corridors – we could hear every whisper, every snore and every rustle as the other campers turned over in their beds. When we woke up the next morning, we were covered in a thin film of white dust that had collected in our eyes and noses and ears. After weeks of being woken by wind or rain or the light of early sunrises, it seemed that an underground home really suited us. We were the only people left. When we emerged, blinking, into the daylight, we realised that not only had we slept through the sounds of everyone else packing up and leaving, but we had also missed the first rainfall for more than a month. I was glad we didn't have to pack up a wet tent, but I wasn't in any hurry to spend another night underground. Coober Pedy, I had decided, was the strangest place I had ever been.

As we drove south, dark clouds followed. It became a race between us and the weather. We were hoping to have our tent set up before the rain caught us but 60 kilometres from Port Augusta, with a road train lumbering up behind us, one of our tyres blew. The car lurched to one side and James cursed as he steered it off the road. As he changed the tyre, the first raindrops spattered down and sizzled on the bitumen.

It was dark and pouring by the time we eventually drove into town and found a caravan park. We made our way to the site we had been given to find a river of mud flowing through it. We didn't bother going back to the office to ask them to try again. James just set the tent up on a neighbouring site that had the advantage of not being almost underwater. The boys and I huddled in the car until he had finished. 'There's no point in everyone getting wet', he had said. When he was done, we drove straight back out of the park and hunted down a pizza restaurant.

It was still raining the next morning so, after a quick stop to have our tyre fixed, we drove straight past Whyalla and down the Eyre Peninsula. The coastline was supposed to be beautiful but we couldn't see anything except rain, mist and heavy cloud. The rain finally stopped late that afternoon, just as we entered Coffin Bay National Park.

After an hour of very slow driving on soft sand we arrived at the Black Springs campground. It was deserted and looked damp and miserable. Despite the looming black clouds above us, we decided to try the next campground a bit further on, past Seven Mile Beach. Twenty minutes later we met a vehicle coming the other way. The driver was surprised to see us towing a trailer. He said the track was soft and boggy and also impassable at high tide, which was in half an hour. We had to turn around. By the time we got back to Black Springs it was dark and raining. Again.

It rained all that night and most of the next day. James had to dig a trench to stop the water running directly into our tent. It was cold and I was miserable and my misery infected the boys. They went back to bed after lunch and refused to come out. James decided he was already wet and it couldn't get any worse, so he wandered to the beach with his fishing gear. Oscar and Dylan sat in the tent and created comic books starring characters called Super Dood and Piranha Man. I photocopied them later and posted them back to the Distance Education teachers and called them that week's schoolwork. James came back with whiting so we had fried potatoes and fresh fish for tea and the boys complained about the bones.

Again, it rained all night. We had to get up every hour to kneel on our bed and push the roof of the tent up with our hands to stop the water collecting and seeping through the canvas. The rain finally stopped the next morning, so we checked the tide chart and decided to have a look at Seven Mile Beach, a stretch of pristine white sand accessible only by boat or 4WD. I was nervous about driving so far along the beach alone, so I was relieved to see fresh vehicle tracks on the sand. Within minutes a car came hurtling past us and disappeared back down the track, the way we had come. We were on our own.

We parked at the base of the biggest sand dune I had ever seen, leaving the car doors wide open, and the four of us climbed up the hill together. The boys threw themselves down the slope, rolled down in a cloud of white sand then raced back up and did it all again. My mood lifted as I watched them have the most fun they had had for days. I walked along the narrow ridge of the dune, placing one foot carefully in front of another, trying not to slip down either side. The dunes stretched for miles along the beach, golden mountains smoothed out by the constant breeze. Their perfection was marred only by our footprints. I sat with my back to the ocean and looked out over the dunes, mesmerised by how far they marched inland.

Looking down at the beach twenty minutes later, I was horrified to see that the tide had turned and was coming in fast. Some of our tyre tracks had already been swallowed by the water. Shouting at the boys to hurry, we slid down the dune on our bottoms and jumped back into the car, spraying sand everywhere. I closed my eyes and gripped the dashboard. I couldn't watch as James nudged the front wheels into the water to give us enough space to turn the car around. I felt the wheels sink into the wet sand and realised we had been incredibly stupid. I imagined us sitting halfway up a sand dune watching the car disappear into the sea. We took off down the beach in a race against the tide. It was only a few minutes before we reached the track but it was long enough for me.

My black mood was back and so was the rain. It poured again all night.

The next day we took advantage of a fleeting dry spell. We packed up our soggy tent, filled our damp bags with wet and sandy clothes and got bogged in a patch of wet sand as we drove out of the park. Earlier that morning, when I had stumbled through the rain and mud to the tiny toilet hut, I had disturbed a very damp kangaroo and her joey who were sheltering there. As she had bounded reluctantly off into the bush, she turned back to me. We shared a look, one mother to another, and the meaning was so obvious that I laughed out loud: 'This is shit, isn't it?'

Before we left home, we had set ourselves a budget of $1000 a week. James's cousin had done a similar trip the year before with his wife and their three kids, and he had worked out that they spent $800 a week. James and I are the kind of people that can't walk out of the front door without spending $50, so we thought $1000 would be about right. We thought we might even be able to save up for a few special treats. We wanted to go on a helicopter flight in the Kimberley and a snorkelling trip on the Great Barrier Reef. I was secretly hoping that we could get out of the tent and stay in a hotel for a few nights as well.

Nine weeks into the journey we were already $2000 over budget.

Fuel was a big expense; one week we managed to spend $600 on diesel alone. We were also going through a lot of alcohol; when you're camping, every night feels like Friday. And we were eating very well. I had a lot of spare time and I spent most of it planning meals. The boys would have been perfectly happy with sausages and two-minute noodles every night, but that wasn't my idea of a good way to spend a year. We ate curries, risottos, steaks and lots of pasta. When we felt like a roast, we cooked butterflied legs of lamb on the campfire. We ate crayfish in Robe and oysters in Coffin Bay. They were great meals, but they weren't cheap. On top of that, we had already spent $450 on blown and punctured tyres.

'I don't see how we can spend any less', said James.

'We could give up alcohol.'

He looked horrified. 'You can't sit around a campfire without a beer. It just doesn't feel right. We're on holiday.'

I tried not to worry too much. Even if we did overspend, it was unlikely that we would ever look back on this trip and regret a moment of it. Anyway, in a few days there wouldn't be anywhere to spend money. We were about to cross the Nullarbor Plain. We were finally heading for Western Australia.

Chapter Nine

My proposal of a ban on alcohol fell over within hours of arriving in the tiny coastal town of Streaky Bay. At the local pub that night, the boys drank Fanta, James and I drank shiraz and we lashed out on a $10 roast dinner. For a few hours we were indoors, we were cosy and warm and there was football on the television. We were all glowing – we had showered for the first time in six days. Back at the tent the sheets were clean and so were all the clothes in our bags. The kitchen box and fridge were crammed with food. The boys had new novels to read, a stack of activity books and a box of new pencils, and we had hours and hours of Harry Potter books to listen to.

I was preparing for the Nullarbor as if it were a three-day siege.

When we were first planning our trip, people often asked if we were going to Western Australia. When we said yes, that was our plan, a look of concern usually appeared on their faces. 'You know you'll have to cross the Nullarbor?'

There were two types of people: those who had never done it and never planned to, and the ones who immediately told us their number, either as a badge of honour or a warning.

'We've been across six times now.'

'I've done it once, and I'll never do it again.'

Despite being repeatedly told that the Eyre Highway was the most boring road in the country, I was still surprised at how dull it was. I knew that just a few kilometres to our left the sea was pounding on cliffs. To our right, about 60 kilometres away, the Indian Pacific – the world's longest straight stretch of railway – passed through the ghost towns of Tarcoola, Cook and Loongana. But for hours after we left Ceduna all we could see was a perfectly straight road with orange dirt and very short, scrubby bush on either side. The view was almost familiar, iconically representative of the Australian outback, and I could easily imagine a family of kangaroos bounding along the

horizon, emus racing alongside our car or wedge-tailed eagles feasting
on roadkill. I had to make do with my imagination, though, as we
didn't see a single sign of life.

After 300 kilometres we had a welcome break at Head of Bight,
just like the southern right whales that come here to give birth to their
calves every winter. We drove the 12-kilometre access road and paid
the entry fee at the brand-new whale viewing centre.

'Whales! Whales!' cried the boys as they pounded along the
shining, freshly cut planks of hardwood.

'No whales', I said, reading the brochure. 'It's the wrong time of
year. They won't be here for another month.'

We walked to the lookout, letting the breeze blow the car smells
out of our hair and clothes. I hadn't realised we were so far above sea
level. Below us, waves pounded against the cliff like fists on a locked
door. Leaning against the railing, it was easy to imagine ourselves
standing on the edge of the continent.

Back in the car, a few kilometres further on, we noticed tracks
heading off the road towards the sea.

'Let's take another look', said James, pulling onto the track and
parking beside a sign that read 'DANGER. The high overhanging
cliffs on this coast are very dangerous. The actual edge of the cliff is not
readily seen. Approach with caution particularly in windy conditions.
Children should be kept under adult control at all times.' We climbed
out of the car and ventured warily towards the cliff. My head swam as
I looked down and I had to check that the boys weren't anywhere near
the edge. Another vehicle arrived and the people who got out started
setting up their tent just metres from the cliff. I thought they were
very brave. I wouldn't be able to stay here overnight, for fear that one
of the boys might choose that night to take up sleepwalking.

Late that afternoon, we arrived at the quarantine stop. I had
seen posters about it in Ceduna, but I had pictured it being like the
fruit bins that used to sit on the highway between Victoria and South
Australia. Those had worked on an honour system and usually just
prompted a rush of orange-eating and arguments about whether
or not avocados counted as fruit. This was more like a checkpoint

separating warring nations. Uniformed officials guided the cars into a single-lane queue and handed everyone a plastic bucket and a leaflet. I remembered the huge shop I had done the day before and felt very stupid for not taking the information more seriously. Ahead, we could see cars being searched, all the doors open as quarantine officers poked around inside. As we waited I read the leaflet, which listed all the prohibited items that might carry pests, weeds or diseases into Western Australia.

'It says we have to throw out all our fruit and vegetables, unless they are cut up. Nuts and honey too. Have we got honey in the trailer?'

'No', said James.

'Yes we do!' said Oscar.

'*No*, we don't. We *finished* it. This morning.' James couldn't have been clearer.

'Hi there', chirped the quarantine officer at my window. She was young and blonde and looked exceptionally healthy. 'Carrying any fruit or vegetables with you?'

'Heaps!' said Dylan joyfully.

I pulled out the esky from the back of the car and opened it up.

She smiled. 'Grapes!'

The contents of the esky went into the plastic bucket: grapes, two oranges, a lettuce, a head of broccoli, beans, two corn cobs and a sweet potato I had been planning to roast in our next campfire. I wondered if she would notice the absence of onions and potatoes. They were stored in the cupboard that was built into the tailgate of the trailer. I looked around for sniffer dogs.

'Anything in the fridge?'

Standing on the tailgate, I opened the fridge and took out a punnet of strawberries and another of cherry tomatoes. Her smile nearly cracked her face in half.

'And what about in the front? Any fruit?'

'We don't eat much of that', I said, for once wearing my family's aversion to fruit like a badge of honour. Dylan stuck his head out from behind the woman, whom he had been following with an air of awed admiration.

'Mum has more oranges beside her', he said. Traitor. She looked
at me expectantly.

'They're *cut up*', I said. I could tell she was disappointed.

Oscar looked into the bucket. 'What happens to it?' he asked.

'Oh, it all gets discarded', she told him, beaming at her haul.

As we drove off, Oscar sighed happily. 'This has been the best
day of the trip so far.'

James reached deep down under his seat and pulled out a plastic
container of dried fruit and nuts. 'She missed this.'

Twelve kilometres west of the border we stopped at Eucla. Eucla,
with a permanent population under 100, is nevertheless the main
stopping point for vehicles travelling on the Eyre Highway. At the
campsite, all the cars and caravans were lined up in neat rows. None
of the vans were unhitched from their vehicles – it was more like a
car park than a campground and everyone seemed poised for a quick
getaway the next morning. There were no campfires, no-one talking
to the neighbours, no kids racing around on dusty bicycles or kicking
a footy. This was just a place to refuel vehicles and grab some sleep.
The woman behind the till at the roadhouse, which also served as
the local store, motel and pub, looked surprised when I asked if they
sold fresh vegetables. She reluctantly fetched a piece of limp cauli-
flower and half a capsicum from the kitchen for me. We didn't even
bother unhitching the trailer from the car and were gone well before
eight o'clock Eucla time. Towns on the Eyre Highway between Eucla
and Caiguna operate on the unofficial Central Western Time Zone,
taking a halfway position on the ninety-minute difference between
South Australia and Western Australia. We had put the clock on the
dashboard back forty-five minutes when we passed the official road
sign about the unofficial time zone.

Back on the very straight road again, the monotony had some
advantages. I found that I could read without getting sick and,
although the logistics of folding the paper took a bit of working out,
I managed to get through *The Weekend Australian* from cover to cover
for the first time in my life. James was able to concentrate on our
Spanish language CD and drive at the same time. By the end of the

third track we had all mastered the very useful phrase, '*No es possible para usted así*' ['This is not possible for you this way']. Oscar used the Travel Scrabble set to create a crossword and Dylan amused himself by very carefully covering every square inch of his body with a complex pattern of sky-blue texta dots. At Cocklebiddy we put all the clocks back another forty-five minutes to join the rest of Western Australia and, instead of feeling as if we had gained time, it was as if we had just slid down the longest snake on the board.

We finally reached Norseman. Despite being a proper town with shops and a pub and a real caravan park, Norseman looked to be as much of a transit station as Eucla. The lady at the tourist information centre took one look at the boys' exhausted, miserable faces and gave them each a certificate.

'This is to commemorate that you have crossed the Australian continent on the Eyre Highway, following in the footsteps of Edward John Eyre.'

Reading the brief history of Eyre's crossing I realised that, despite the sketch on the certificate that depicted him as old and balding, he was just twenty-six years old when he led the eight-month expedition that opened up a land route between Australia's eastern and western shores. And only twenty-five when he trekked to the edge of Lake Eyre and wrote so eloquently of his bitter disappointment.

Much later I found out that at Eucla, only a few minutes' walk from where we had spent the night, there were ruins of the old tele-graph station, huge sand dunes and magnificent views of the ocean. The whole place was teeming with birdlife. I felt ashamed that we had raced along the Nullarbor so quickly. Next time, I thought. Next time we will stop and camp on the edge of the cliff and explore all the places that we dismissed as empty and dull.

The next day we went to Kalgoorlie and stood on the edge of the Super Pit. This monstrous hole in the ground was Alan Bond's idea.

In the 1980s, he decided this would be a more efficient way to dig gold out of the ground than all the individually run underground mines that used to operate in Kalgoorlie's Golden Mile. Four hundred metres deep, 3.5 kilometres long and 1.5 kilometres wide, the pit is almost too large to comprehend.

'Are those trucks real?' asked Dylan.

Tiny yellow vehicles trundled along the tracks carved into the walls of the pit. It wasn't a big stretch to imagine a huge, invisible toddler towering above us, pushing them along with his chubby hands. Two truck tyres lay on the ground outside the observation shelter, all black and fat and huge. We stared at them and tried to put both of these visuals together and get a sense of just how big the Super Pit was. We failed.

After the Super Pit, we thought about going to the Crusty Demons motorbike stunt show but the prices were so steep that we couldn't justify it. We satisfied the boys' curiosity by hanging around outside the venue and watching the rehearsal. Young men hurtled in the air, spinning in full somersaults and clinging to the handles of their motorbikes. It looked as if they were flying and carrying the bike along with them.

The story around town that day was that the Crusties had had a mishap on the way to Kalgoorlie. The road train holding all their gear apparently collided with a goat, causing the petrol tank to burst into flame and destroy several valuable motorbikes. Local gossip held that it was an insurance scam. Few people were prepared to argue with a group that reputedly had strong ties to the Hells Angels, but they expressed an interest in seeing the goat who could destroy a road train.

At Lucky Bay in Cape Le Grand National Park, the beach curved for miles around a calm turquoise bay, protected from the ocean by hills and sand dunes. The fine white sand squeaked under our feet as we walked. Dylan pushed his arms deep into the damp sand on the water's edge and when he pulled them out they looked like they were coated in cream.

One morning, after the boys did schoolwork and I cooked a big pot of lentil dhal for lunch, we decided to walk to the end of the beach. In 1802 this was the spot where Matthew Flinders, who was circumnavigating the Australian coastline in the *Investigator*, took shelter from a storm. Forty years later the bay again lived up to the name Flinders had given it. Seven months into their expedition across the Nullarbor, Edward John Eyre and his last remaining companion, an Indigenous man named Wylie, were almost dead from starvation and thirst when they spotted a French whaling ship in Lucky Bay. The captain offered to take them on board, but Eyre was determined to complete the final 300 kilometres to King George Sound on foot and accepted only supplies of food and water. What Wylie thought of this decision can only be imagined.

I was fascinated by these stories of early Australian settlement. The more we travelled, the more the huge distances and beautiful but harsh landscape impressed themselves on me. 'Just imagine it!' I would say, failing to interest the boys in the history around us.

The day turned out to be hotter than we had expected and halfway along we needed to swim. None of us had bathers and we didn't want to have to walk back in wet, sandy clothes, so we stripped off.

This was our first skinny dip, but they quickly turned into a habit. The boys became experts at whipping off their clothes whenever James shouted, 'Family nudie swim!' We would all race into the sea, splashing and shouting to combat the shock of the cold water. This first time, it was such a warm day and the beach felt so isolated that James decided to continue on our walk completely naked. At the end of our walk, just as we were inspecting a plaque commemorating Flinders's naming of the bay, an elderly couple appeared from nowhere and got a full frontal view of James. The boys and I nearly wet ourselves laughing as he hopped about, trying to get his pants back on. On the way back, we had another swim, but this time we stayed in the water when we saw the couple approaching. They pretended we weren't there and marched on up the beach, eyes front.

Back at the campsite, a neighbour told me that he had seen two kangaroos knock the pot of lentil dhal off our table and eat the contents. A crow had also discovered the eggs, which I thought I had hidden by putting a tea towel on top of them, and the empty shells were scattered through the scrub nearby. I knew that the loss of the eggs was totally my fault, but I was cross about the dhal. That would have been the basis for quite a few meals and it hadn't occurred to me that any of the local wildlife would have a taste for lentils. The roos had been efficient, though – there wasn't a scrap to be seen on the ground outside the tent and the pot had been licked clean.

Our plan was to go to Margaret River next, but the boys wanted to go to Wave Rock. James wasn't enthusiastic. He got out the maps and showed them how far it was. 'Look, we're here, near Esperance. And we're going here, to Margaret River, on the coast. Now, here's Wave Rock. It's about 400 kilometres inland. It's like going along two sides of a triangle instead of just one.'

Oscar looked up at him. 'But isn't that what this trip is all about?'

He was absolutely right, so we drove for five hours to see a rock. It turned out to be a very nice rock and it really did look like a wave. We weren't the only ones to drive a very long way to see it. Four young Japanese women had driven from Perth in a tiny hire car as well. They had thought they would be able to get there and back in a day. Their maps were deceptive: it was a 680-kilometre round trip. They spend the night huddled in their car, running the engine and the heater as the temperature dropped overnight.

Back on the coast, we discovered the small town of Denmark. It was a beautiful town, full of cafes, bookshops and antique dealers and surrounded by forests, wineries, cheese factories, honey producers and happy fat cows in green fields. I loved it. It was like a mixture of two of my favourite places: Fitzroy and Daylesford. We stocked up on second-hand books and refilled the fridge and kitchen box. But there was a reason for Denmark's lushness: it never stopped raining. At the first caravan park we went to, the entire camping ground was underwater. At the next, we were kept awake by a droning noise that James was so convinced was the sound of motorbikes on a racetrack that he spent an hour driving around trying to find it. Back at the tent, we tracked the source to a colony of tiny green frogs living in a stormwater drain just metres from our camp. We only lasted one night before we booked into a bed and breakfast near Pemberton, giving ourselves three precious days out of the tent.

When the rain finally stopped, we visited the giant karri trees in the forest around Pemberton. Seventy years ago, the tallest trees had pegs hammered into their trunks so they could be climbed and used as fire lookouts. Tourists can climb them now, so James went up first, then came back down for Oscar. I tried too, but I was so scared I had to come back down before I even got halfway up. Loose wire fencing was looped around the tree, forming a kind of protective cage, but there was nothing to stop anyone falling down. On the ground, Dylan – who knew his own limits better than I did – watched with me as James and Oscar made it to the top and stood on a platform that was over 60 metres above the ground and swaying in the breeze. I was stunned by their bravery and had to remind myself that Oscar was only eight.

Afterwards we sat and ate our muesli bars and watched other people stand at the bottom and lose their nerve. A woman wearing knee-length stiletto boots and tight jeans, whom we had heard speaking in Spanish to her friends, tentatively climbed up the first few pegs before stopping and looking down nervously. James couldn't resist: '*No es posible para usted así.*'

Margaret River lived up to its reputation as one of the best wine regions in the country, but the best bit for us was that the wineries had playgrounds for the kids. We alternated wine-tasting stops with visits to the chocolate factory and dairies, filling all the space in the car with bottles of wine and bags of treats.

At the Leeuwin–Naturaliste National Park, which runs in a thin, north-to-south strip along the coast from Cape Naturaliste to Cape Leeuwin and takes in surf beaches, limestone caves and the Boranup

Forest, a sign warned: 'This is an alcohol-free campground'. We thought it might have been a joke, but when the ranger drove up to collect our fees he assured us it was true. We pretended we were only asking out of curiosity, then sat around the campfire later and sipped our expensive red wine illegally from tin mugs.

Several hours after we had gone to bed a bus of teenage girls arrived on a school camp. They spent ages setting up their tents to a soundtrack of high-pitched squealing and giggling. Later that night James made two terrible discoveries. The first was that overindulging in chocolate, beer, cheese, venison and wine can lead to a debilitating case of stomach cramps and diarrhoea. The second was that one of the schoolgirls had apparently been so freaked out by the pit toilet that she had decided the safest approach was to stand on the seat and squat from there. Unfortunately, she mustn't have had a torch. If she had, she might have noticed that the lid was down before she shat all over it.

In the town of Bunbury, which billed itself as 'cosmopolitan' but seemed more like one giant suburb, we headed straight for the familiar comfort of the BIG4 caravan park. As we drove through the quiet streets, the boys wondered if it might have two jumping pillows and perhaps even a games room. Maybe – they hardly dared dream it – there would even be a television. When we arrived, there was one jumping pillow but no children playing on it.

'They're probably all off doing stuff', I said, trying to cheer them up.

I wasn't holding out much hope. There were no other dusty camper trailers. Not even one motorhome with a couple of tiny bicycles clinging to the back. Instead, cul-de-sacs lined with permanent demountable homes and their trim garden beds circled patches of neatly mown grass that appeared to be the camping sites. We found our site and as we reversed the trailer onto it, a man came out of his front door and glared at us. We were setting up on his front lawn and he wasn't happy about it.

The boys went exploring and came back to report that there were no kids, the jumping pillow wasn't inflated, they couldn't find a games room and all the little houses had concrete gnomes out the front.

I opened one of my tourist books and had a closer look. We had come to Bunbury to see the wild dolphins at the Dolphin Discovery Centre. We were trying to avoid having to go to Monkey Mia, the tiny town further north that was famous for its dolphins. But in the list of 'Things to do in Bunbury', the dolphin centre wasn't the highlight. The must-see attraction was Gnomesville, 'the magical home to over 3000 gnomes who have migrated there from all over Australia and around the world'.

James took the boys to explore the town while I took advantage of all the empty washing machines and dryers to clean everything we owned. A gardener came past and stopped for a chat. 'Have youse been to Gnomesville?' he asked.

'No, not yet', I confessed. 'We might go tomorrow?' I have always been a terrible liar.

He glared at me. 'Don't tell me yer one of those people that don't like gnomes', he hissed before slumping off in disgust.

The Dolphin Discovery Centre was as grey and sad as the weather. Its laminated posters and display panels about life cycles managed to make dolphins as dreary as a school project. When a dolphin did finally come into the official 'interaction zone', I hurried into the water in my undies to get close to it. It stayed just long enough to snatch a fish from the guide before disappearing back to sea. The boys were so cold that they wouldn't wade in any further than their ankles and James had refused to get in the water at all.

As we left town, the sun broke through the clouds, warming us through the windscreen and glinting on the water. We rolled the windows down to catch the warm breeze and our spirits lifted. Behind us we imagined Bunbury still squatting miserably under a grey sky.

In Perth we stopped to pick up Nannette, who was joining us again for a few days, squished her into the back seat with the kids and drove 250 kilometres north to Perth's favourite fishing and camping spot,

Sandy Cape. This time we didn't bother setting up the separate tent, we just put down an extra mattress for her between the two boys. Privacy had become a less pressing issue for us and five in a tent didn't seem much different to four. The campground had no fresh water, no showers and the foulest pit toilets we had ever smelled, but the rest of the place was beautiful. James slung a rope over a tree branch and made the boys a swing. That night, for our first time in the west, we saw the sun set, like a ball of orange fire being extinguished as it slipped into the sea.

Over the next three days we explored the dunes and filled Nannette in on what we'd been up to in the six weeks since we'd left Alice Springs. James tried to fish from the beach, but had to give up when a pod of dolphins insisted on lolling around in the shallows beside him. The boys rolled down the sandhills and buried each other in the warm sand. The days slipped past easily without much getting done and I realised how much the pace of our lives had slowed down. At home, every day seemed to be punctuated by activity: cooking, tidying, cleaning, activities to amuse the kids, more food preparation, shopping, more cleaning and tidying, bored kids needing to be entertained, work deadlines, school homework, 'must-watch' television ... on and on, relentlessly, every day. Now we got by with the bare minimum of cooking and cleaning, and a sand dune, a rope swing and a couple of books were all the entertainment we needed.

One day we drove to the Pinnacles in the nearby Nambung National Park. We wandered around the huge expanse of yellow sand exploring the weird, skinny rocks that seemed to be growing up out of the ground. They were entirely random – tall ones, short ones, skinny ones and fat ones. Sometimes there were lots of them all clumped together and then there would be a bare patch with just one solitary sentinel. I tried to get my head around the thousands of years of erosion that had resulted in these strange rock formations, but it was too hard. To me it looked like an alien landscape or even a set from a bad science-fiction sitcom from the 1970s. I half-expected them to move when I looked away. We spent hours playing a daylight version of spotlight that involved hiding behind the rocks and sneaking up on one another.

Nannette helped us by taking over the boys' schoolwork. Before changing careers and studying law, she had been a primary school teacher for more than 20 years. She had much more skill and patience than us and they got a full day's work done every morning with very little whingeing. One day I overheard her ask Dylan to come up with a sentence using the word 'for'. He thought about it and then said, 'Oh, for goodness sake, put that down!' I heard my own voice in his and was thankful that he had censored my more usual phrasing.

Nannette told me the boys seemed to have grown up a lot in just a few months. When I watched them doing the dishes that night – still bickering but getting the job done pretty efficiently – I decided she was right. Most days they were on the move all the time, running around with huge bursts of energy, then collapsing in a heap for a few minutes before heading off out again. When they were little, I used to joke that boys were like puppies: you had to walk them twice a day or they would destroy the house. I was trying to be funny, but the truth was that their energy had always exhausted me. Sometimes I had envied my friends with daughters, who seemed to be happy to spend entire afternoons sitting still and doing craft.

Now I realised that they had needed more than regular exercise all those years. They had needed freedom. Out here – where they could run, wrestle, shout, jump, swing, roll down hills, throw sticks and stones, dig holes, sing silly songs at the top of their voices, lie in the grass and climb trees – I had never seen my sons happier.

The open spaces seemed to calm them down as well. I wondered if their constant motion and noisiness in the city had been a response to the boundaries and restrictions that I kept placing on them. Some of them had been necessary: it was my job to make sure they didn't run out onto busy roads or fall off our balcony. If I was being honest, though, part of it was also that I was scared for them. When they were wrestling, I imagined dislocated shoulders and broken arms. When they played at sword fighting, all I could think of was eye injuries. I had spent years trying to shut them down but now I was learning to trust them and let them explore their world the way they wanted to.

When it was time for Nannette to leave, I drove her back to Perth – but not without taking a wrong turn onto the highway and getting just a little bit lost. We stayed overnight with her friends but as we ate dinner in a lovely Thai restaurant, making adult conversation and drinking expensive wine from a proper glass, I felt strangely restless and out of sorts and realised I missed my family. I woke up at dawn the next morning and was back on the road two hours later. When I got to the campground just after noon Dylan said, 'Why are you back so early?'

James grinned at me from his camp chair where he sat with his left foot up, nursing a beer. They had spent the previous morning at an abandoned tip, throwing old bottles into the heap. After that they had played at being gladiators on the dunes and James had broken a toe as he tumbled down, head over heels, clutching both boys and rubbing their heads into the sand.

Steep Point is the furthest west you can go on Australia's mainland. Beyond it, in Shark Bay, lies Dirk Hartog Island – just off the coast, close enough to see and only fifteen minutes by barge from Steep Point. The water is shallow and calm and flat on the bay side of the point, protected from the ocean by the island. On the other side, the towering cliffs that give Steep Point its name plunge into the Indian Ocean. Apart from people determined to stand on the edge of the country, like us, Steep Point mainly attracts devoted fishermen for whom the beach is just a convenient place to launch boats. Most of the campsites were empty.

We set up the tent just a few metres from the water's edge and the boys were immediately welcomed by a big silver fish which almost beached itself next to them. They chased it in and out of the clear shallow water for an hour and it kept coming back for more. They were beside themselves with excitement at having a pet fish.

An hour after arriving we had our rods in the water at the front of our tent and within minutes the boys had caught two flathead, a bream and a whiting. We cooked them on a fire on the beach and went to sleep listening to the water lap gently on the sand just outside the tent.

When the ranger came by in the morning to collect our camping fees we told her about our fishy friend. She said it was a poisonous toadfish with razor-sharp teeth, a fiercely territorial nature and an evil temperament. The year before, one had chased a man out of the water and bitten his toe off. She also mentioned there was a tiger shark in the bay at the moment and advised us to 'just have a look around before going swimming'. But there were also dugongs and humpback whales and turtles around the point, and stingrays and more fish than we had ever seen right on our beach. Later that morning, a school of dolphins swam past us and one hurled itself high out of the water in what seemed like an act of pure joy.

At the top of the cliffs, we found a wooden sign that said 'Steep Point: Westernmost point of Australia'. We took a photo and then drove along the ridge, getting out of the car to walk along the edge of the cliffs and look down at the pounding waves.

'So where are the bloody whales then?' James said.

A spurt of white foam at the bottom of the cliff caught my eye. 'Right there.'

The first whales of our trip were wallowing around where the dark rock face disappeared into the ocean. We followed them on foot as they cruised up the coast. When they had gone, we stood on the edge of the cliff and watched giant turtles gliding gracefully in the water below us. I saw a flash of white near the horizon and I looked up just in time to see a humpback whale throw itself out of the water and hang in the air for a moment before slamming back down onto the surface.

Further along the track, a group of men were fishing from a rocky ledge. Holes drilled into the rock held their rods and the lines dropped down the side of the cliff into the deep water. When the rod bent and jerked, they sent a grappling hook down the line to grasp the fish and haul it up. They only fished at dawn and dusk, spending the rest of the blindingly hot daylight hours and much of the night drinking. Along the cliff's edge, plaques marked spots where people had died. Some had suffered heart attacks. Others, barely in their twenties, had fallen and drowned on the rocks below.

There were no women in any of the fishing camps. They looked to be the most basic of set-ups: humming generators powered fridges that I would have bet held little more than beer and sausages, and most of the men must have been sleeping in their cars, because the only other shelter I could see were a couple of half-heartedly hung shadecloths. When I asked if any of them had brought their wives, one man told us that he and a friend had brought their families along for the first time the year before, but not to this spot.

'You camped down on the beach?' he asked. We nodded. 'Yeah, that's where we were. I woke up one night and I could hear waves. Waves! Down there it's dead flat all the time. I got up but it was pitch black and I couldn't see a thing. I walked down to the water and this wave hit me. By the time I got back to the tent, the water was halfway up the beach. My mate, he grabbed his baby out of its cot just before the whole thing went underwater. We lost everything. Some bloody tsunami set off this monster wave that made it all the way here. If it wasn't for that' – he gestured towards Dirk Hartog Island – 'we'd all be dead. Anyway, the missus doesn't want to come back here anymore.' He finally noticed my horrified face. 'Nah, you'll be right. Once in a lifetime thing, they reckon.'

On the way out of Steep Point, we were flagged down by a man standing at the side of the road beside his car. One of his tyres was completely shredded. The road was so rough that he had driven on it for a few kilometres before realising he had a puncture. He needed James's help because it was a bit tricky for him to get down and crawl under the car to position the jack properly. He only had one leg. His wife couldn't help – she was very overweight and was firmly wedged in the passenger seat, pressed up against the dashboard, with a little white dog on her lap. Together, he and James jacked up the vehicle – and the wife and her dog – and changed the tyre.

Our next stop was at a tiny roadhouse on the turn-off to Monkey Mia – a 220-kilometre round trip off the main road.

'Everyone's going to ask if we went', I said.

James groaned. 'It's just so *far*.'

'Yeah, like Wave Rock', said Oscar.

We found a caravan park in Denham and at eight o'clock the next morning we were at Monkey Mia. The dolphins turned up right on cue, just as they had since the 1960s when the local fishermen began feeding them. They snorted around in the shallows, hassling for fish and sucking up to the handlers during the fifteen-minute talk before grabbing their food and taking off. Despite their worldwide fame, they didn't really do much for me. There didn't seem to be much dignity about the whole thing.

Oscar was so underwhelmed that we had to drag him away from the playground to make him stand in line with all the other children and admire the dolphins.

'But we've seen heaps of dolphins and this is the first playground for ages. It's got *swings*.'

Chapter Ten

We arrived in Exmouth in June, right at the end of the whale shark season. Whale sharks migrate up the west coast and pass through Ningaloo Reef between April and July every year, presumably to feed in the nutrient-rich waters associated with the coral spawning that happens in early March. Weirdly, very little is known about where they go after that. An entire ecotourism industry has sprung up around them, based mainly out of Coral Bay and Exmouth. Fast boats, spotter planes and crews of dreadlocked young people head out early every morning with boatloads of tourists in search of sharks. The Canadian man who was renting our house had told me that swimming with whale sharks on Ningaloo Reef was the best thing he had ever done in his life.

The only problem was that I wasn't very good in the sea. I could swim laps in the safety of a 50-metre pool, but when I looked underwater in the ocean I panicked about what was lurking in the dark depths and in the murky water behind me. I would spin around in circles, desperately trying to keep tabs on everything around me, and end up out of breath and sick with anxiety. So far on this trip, I had only snorkelled if James was beside me. I had pretended to be comfortable about it because I didn't want to scare the boys. They had never seen *Jaws*. There was no need for them to inherit my fear.

James wasn't with me that day. We had both wanted to go but the thought of trying to entertain the kids on a small dive boat for a whole day was too horrible. We would have had to take turns at getting in the water and, with some of the boats only reporting a single sighting in a day, it could have been a very expensive and frustrating day out.

Only one boat at a time was allowed to approach a whale shark. When the call came in from the spotter planes that there was one in the area, our driver raced to get us to it first. Ten of us lined up on the platform in wetsuits and snorkel gear, ready to leap in when our boat stopped in front of the shark.

'Go, go, go!' shouted the guide. 'It's a big one. It's coming towards us now. Make sure you can see where it is and get out of its way.'

I flopped into the water and stuck my head under to have a look. In my excitement, I had forgotten to put my mask on. I panicked and tried to scream but I had also forgotten to put my snorkel in my mouth. After coughing up some seawater and adjusting my gear, I put my face back under and saw a massive whale shark coming towards me. It was only a few metres away and I had to kick furiously to get out of its path. It was cruising quite slowly, completely oblivious to the people splashing beside it. I could see every single one of its markings. It looked like a living dot painting in turquoise and white ochre. Hundreds of little fish were escorting it on its journey through the ocean. Just once, its distinctive shape registered in a primitive part of my brain – *oh my god, that's a shark* – but for the most part it was a peaceful and awesome experience.

'Did you see the shark?' one of the other swimmers asked me when we were all back on the boat. I wondered if he thought I was stupid. It had been the size of a bus. 'No, I mean the *shark* shark. The bronze whaler that was circling us further down.'

At that moment I thought that my first swim with a whale shark would be my last, but then I remembered James was staying at the caravan park with the kids so that I could have this experience. I'd done my research. No-one had ever been taken by a shark in this part of the world. I steeled myself to jump back into the sea nine times that day and swam beside six more whale sharks. I didn't stop being frightened, but I decided that it was better to be scared than miss out.

The last time I jumped, only five other people went in. The shark was moving fast and I couldn't keep up with it or the rest of the swimmers. When I surfaced, the boat had drifted away and I was completely alone in the water. I raised my arm and waved, as we had been instructed, to signal that I wanted the boat to pick me up. I tried to stay calm as it approached, but my legs were scissoring frantically below me, just like that famous image from *Jaws*, and I started to panic. By the time I climbed on board, I was shaking and sweating and I felt sick. But I had no regrets. I went to sleep that night dreaming of shouts of 'Go, go, go!' and massive beasts that moved gracefully through the water.

At Ningaloo Station we camped behind a sand dune, 20 metres from the water. Although we saw a large group of vans in a fishing camp as we drove in, there were only two other camps on the long stretch of beach near us. The sea was perfectly still, protected from waves by the reef just offshore. After a very quick set-up, behind a sand dune to protect us from the sea breeze, we stripped off for a swim. James and the boys jumped in first and just as I was getting ready to follow them I saw three large dark shapes in the water heading towards them. For a horrible moment I panicked, frozen to the spot and unable to call out, but when a dark brown snout broke the surface of the water I realised with relief that they were turtles. James swam towards them to get a closer look but they were surprisingly fast and raced away as soon as he got close. Later, resting at the top of a sand dune, we watched a metre-long reef shark cruising slowly through the shallow water.

For the next week, time drifted past slowly and we got sandier, smellier and more serene. We spent a whole day drift-snorkelling over the reef that was just a few metres from the shore. The current pulled us along over the top of coral formations that were home to thousands of brightly coloured fish. Dylan was still a little nervous in deep water so I stayed close to him, and realised that calming his fears about sharks and other sea creatures helped reduce my own *Jaws*-related anxiety. Oscar didn't seem to know what fear was and James sometimes had to swim out to bring him back closer to the beach. Often we would look up and realise we had drifted so far along the coastline that it was a very long walk back to the spot where we had dumped our towels and drinks.

One afternoon James and the boys made bows and arrows out of reeds, fishing line and sticks. Oscar – barefoot and wearing nothing but a pair of torn shorts, a quiver of arrows attached to a belt and a bow slung over his shoulder – announced he was off to hunt the wild goats we had seen grazing on the dunes earlier that day.

'Sure', said James, not even looking up. 'Bring back dinner.'

An hour later, it occurred to us that this might have been a bit rash. We stood on the top of the closest dune and scanned the horizon. Eventually we saw him about a kilometre away, stalking a couple of uninterested goats. He waved at us and kept going.

'He'll come back when he's hungry', said James.

Food was becoming a problem. As the fridge emptied it had to work harder to stay cool. We were completely out of fresh fruit and vegetables and had gone through most of the meat. We were eating fish that James was catching, and working our way through our canned and dried food stores.

Fresh water was also an issue. We had arrived at Ningaloo with 80 litres in the tank underneath the trailer and another 10 litres in bottles and casks. Even though we were using seawater to wash dishes and relying on daily swims to keep ourselves clean, we couldn't get by on less than 20 litres a day. Curious about what the people in the fishing camp did for water, we drove round to ask.

We stopped at the camp of the first person who smiled and waved, and introduced ourselves. Tony was in his sixties, tanned and skinny like most of the fishermen we had seen in Western Australia, and wearing the standard uniform of old, baggy shorts and thongs. He laughed when we asked our question.

'There's heaps of fresh water around here. I've got my own bore. I dug it myself. You go and get some containers and I'll take you up there.'

We drove back to our camp and collected our jerry cans and water bottles and then followed Tony's car. He drove back along the main track for a few kilometres before turning off along a rough path behind the dunes. He stopped in a long flat valley, surrounded by sandhills on all sides, climbed down from his car and pushed aside a heavy rock to reveal a hole about 20 centimetres wide. A white plastic bucket with the bottom cut out of it stopped the walls from falling in and in the bottom, about half a metre down, was a pool of water.

'Is it fresh?' asked James.

'Most beautiful water you'll ever taste', said Tony as he scooped some out with an old soup ladle.

James bent down and tasted it. 'It's sweet', he said, surprised.

Tony grinned. 'Yep. And there's lots of it.'

He went to the back of his car and came back with a small shower pump, which he connected to the cigarette lighter socket of his dashboard and turned on. He put one end of the hose in the water and the other in one of our jerry cans. Water poured out in a slow, steady stream.

'Takes a while', he said, leaning on the bonnet of his car.

Half an hour later we had 60 litres of water and permission to come back if we needed more. Tony put the rock carefully back on top of his bore. Looking around, we noticed lots of unusually large rocks in this small sandy valley. They were all bores that had been dug with the most basic of implements. Tony had used his soup ladle.

A few days later the weather turned nasty. A storm came in late one afternoon and the night was full of wind and rain. Our supplies were almost exhausted and James was worried that if it got too wet the road out might be too boggy to get through. The next morning we packed up and made a run for it. The track was slippy in places, but soon we were back on the bitumen, heading for Karratha.

I'd been warned that sites for tourists were hard to find. Western Australia's mining boom had attracted workers from all over the country. So much labour was needed that the wages on offer were amazingly high, but the towns weren't equipped to house all the people who came to cash in. Many of the short-term workers had to stay in caravan parks.

I dragged out the soggy, sandy guidebooks from beneath my seat and, as soon as we had mobile coverage, began ringing around. There were no powered sites anywhere from Dampier to Roeburne, in Point Sampson or in Karratha. Eventually we managed to find an unpowered site outside the caretaker's residence at the caravan park in the Karratha Industrial Estate.

We set up on a patch of grass, which we shared with four taciturn middle-aged mine workers who slept in their cars every night. They cooked their evening meal on a small brick barbecue then balanced their plates on their knees, watching game shows on a tiny television. The television was mounted on the shelf of an alcove, above a bar fridge where they stored their food. It cost them $400 a week each, they told us. They didn't seem to mind too much. If they didn't blow too much cash on beer, they predicted that they could earn six times more in a year than was possible in their hometowns. They were gone by five every morning. They left quietly, not bothering with breakfast, just waking up and driving off in their cars without even getting out.

We spent the next morning restocking the fridge, spending a shocking amount in a supermarket that had to be the most expensive in the country. The savings we had made by not spending any money for over a week were wiped out with one trolley-load of groceries. More money went on getting a tyre fixed, but in Karratha, where every tradesman was swamped with work, James couldn't find anyone to do such a mundane job as fixing our compressor and he had to try to do it himself.

One of the places I wanted to see was Hearson Cove. Like Broome's Roebuck Bay, the exposed mudflats on the night of a full moon created the illusion of a staircase of moonlight. We'd missed that by just a few days, but I had read that it was a good swimming beach so we packed a lunch and went for a drive.

Hearson Cove was very close to one of the Burrup Peninsula's ancient rock engraving sites. For thousands of years, people recorded stories and legends by carving pictures on the dark-red boulders that formed gorges and caves all along the coast. The significance of these sites was just being recognised. The day before we arrived, the rock art had been placed on the World Heritage list. We stopped there for a while to wander through the rocks, and soon lost count of the engravings we had found. Every rock face told a story.

When we got to the beach it was obvious there had been a party, probably on the night of the full moon. Empty beer bottles and twisted cans lay half-buried in the sand and we could see the remains of bonfires. Cigarette butts were strewn down the beach and plastic chip packets were caught on twigs in the scrub. Beside one fire pit I saw a pile of discarded condoms. A few dirty nappies lay nearby, their contents pecked at by scavenging seagulls. Everything was covered in sand and there were no bins anywhere. I made a half-hearted attempt to pick up the cans but they were heavy with wet sand and I had nowhere to put them.

I turned my back on the beach and found myself gazing at the mess of pipelines, chimneys and towers of the liquid natural gas refinery, just a few kilometres away. The view placed the filth behind me in perspective. What would be the point in looking after one small beach when, everywhere you looked, people seemed to be doing their best to destroy everything that had been held sacred.

The Pilbara hides its beauty well. It would be easy to drive the main highway and see nothing but scrub and red earth for hours and wonder if there was any water or life to be found. But my guidebook promised that Millstream Chichester National Park, just 150 kilometres from Karratha, had a large shady campground by a river. For ages it was hard to believe we were going in the right direction. The road was dusty and all we could see around and in front of us was scrappy scrub and bare hills. Yet quite suddenly, after driving through a gap in the hills, we found the campground. As promised, it was on the bank of a wide brown river, shaded by huge river gums. At dusk, the sky filled with the frantic white fluttering of thousands of corellas returning to roost. Their raucous squawking was deafening and we had to communicate with hand signals for nearly an hour as they called to each other, shrieking and fighting and bickering. A steady stream of ragged, dusty, stained feathers fluttered down from the trees, interspersed regularly with drops of guano that fell as steadily as rain. Most of the poo ended up in the river, forming a greasy film and accounting for the sweet smell of decay that rose from the water.

At least it was a designated 'No Generators' site. We had spent too many nights trying to sleep through the rumbling of generators. As well as the noise, which shattered the peace as effectively as a lawnmower cranking up on a lazy Sunday afternoon, the diesel fumes were often overpowering. Generators were also the sign of a campground where people disappeared into their vans to cook dinner inside and watch television. There was a terrible loneliness in being the only ones still outside in the dark, listening to the muffled sounds of game shows and current affairs programs leaking out from the curtained windows around us. We preferred the places where everyone stood around a communal fire, jostling for position to drop a rusty old metal plate on the coals to cook sausages and swapping stories about their travels.

On our way out of Millstream, on our way to Karijini National Park, we passed the access road to Wittenoom. A large blue sign with a skull and crossbones on it warned about exposure to the blue asbestos that had been mined there fifty years ago: 'Inhaled asbestos dust may cause cancer.' James was curious and made a case for going to have a look at the abandoned town. We took a vote on it. He lost three to one.

At Karijini, Western Australia's second largest national park, we were excited to find that we would be amongst the first people to camp at the new eco-resort. It was owned by the local Indigenous people and managed by a private ecotourism company and the main building was so new that it was still being painted. I loved the idea that, deep in the heart of mining country, a space had been created by the people who had lived in this land for thousands of years to share it with visitors.

The suburb where we lived in Melbourne was once home to the largest Indigenous community in Victoria. Many of the families had been displaced from their homes when they were razed to build high-rise housing commission estates, but there were still health and legal services, childcare and community centres. Despite all this, I did not personally know one Indigenous person. The kids' primary school was full of children from all over the world – more than twenty nationalities were represented in a school with fewer than 150 pupils – but, to my knowledge, there were no Indigenous students. I understood how a long history of division could result in a society where one group of people never interacted with another, but for some reason I thought that outside the cities and towns things would be different. So far that hadn't been the case. We seemed to be carrying an impenetrable bubble of Anglo-Australia with us as we travelled.

At the reception area, a very white woman sized us up, her nose wrinkling as she inspected our scruffy, dusty clothes. When we asked if we could book a campsite for two nights, she sniffed. 'You'll be lucky. We're fully booked out from Monday.'

'I think it's only Thursday', I said, although I wasn't absolutely sure.

She reluctantly admitted she did have a spare site and indeed, when we drove into the campground, there were at least ten to choose from. We picked one beside a tree with a sturdy branch that was begging to be turned into a rope swing.

As I organised a meal of sausages and salad and James put up the swing, the sun dropped behind the red hills to the west, leaving behind a completely clear sky and the first twinkling of thousands of stars. The day had been so warm that on our way into Karijini we had swum at Hamersley Gorge, where the dark red rocks betrayed the presence of iron ore more obviously than anywhere else we had been in the Pilbara. We had lazed around on the warm rocks and eaten lunch in our bathers with our legs dangling in the cool green water, but when the sun set that night the temperature dropped twenty degrees in a matter of minutes. Within half an hour we went from shorts and t-shirts to a full load of all the warm clothing we owned. James dug out beanies, scarves and fleecy jumpers from the bags in the back of the car while I shivered beside the brand-new communal electric barbecue. We were cooking and eating our meal alone again, but this time it was because everyone else had sensibly eaten when it was still warm and were now safely hiding in their tents or vans. The park had a 'no campfire' rule, so it wasn't possible to do any kind of socialising in this bitter cold.

The same thing happened in reverse in the morning. I climbed out of bed at first light to get ready for a day of hiking in the gorges. I put on both my jumpers and a beanie and my fingers were stiff and frozen as I tried to pump water out of the tank to fill the kettle. The sun slid over the horizon and ten minutes later I had stripped off to my T-shirt and promised James and the boys that it was much warmer outside than it was inside the tent.

Extremes in temperature dogged us for the next three days as we walked through gorges made from dark red rock. It was this rock that made the Pilbara irresistible to mining companies. Iron ore deposits were discovered in the early 1950s and the region now produces nearly all of Australia's iron ore exports. More than 100 million tonnes of iron ore are removed every year, transported on heavy-duty railway lines that carry the longest trains in the world – 200 cars stretching for up to 3.75 kilometres – to Port Hedland or Dampier and loaded onto ships mostly bound for China.

In many of the high-walled crevices, the water got little, if any, direct sunlight. In some places we had to clamber along thin rock ledges just above the water. James negotiated one gorge by placing all four limbs on either side of the narrow gap, inching along above the stream. The boys and I had to splash through it, ankle-deep in the freezing water. The sharp rocks in the river bed meant we had to keep our runners on and our shoes soaked up the cold water until we couldn't feel our toes. At Kermit's Pool in Hancock Gorge, James and I stripped to our bathers and plunged into water that was so cold that for a moment I couldn't breathe.

On the second day we found all the other campers. Fortescue Falls was a luxuriously wide staircase carved from layers of red rock that formed the base of a generous waterfall. Clear fresh water cascaded down into a green pool surrounded by lush ferns and giant white river gums. The whole place looked exactly like a set from a 1950s Hollywood movie. Beautiful European backpackers sunned themselves on the rocks, all with small bikinis, long tanned legs and golden hair. Their dreadlocked boyfriends leapt exuberantly from the top of the gorge into the pool. The place was packed. Everyone was staying at the other campground in the park. It was so full that the rangers had set up an overflow site in a nearby clearing.

On our last night we rugged up and went to a star-gazing talk. We tipped our heads back and tried to find familiar constellations like the Southern Cross and Orion's Belt in the mass of stars above us. The Milky Way gleamed like a white brushstroke across the crowded sky. The astronomer told us that the local Indigenous people didn't look up to the night sky, fearful of catching sight of a falling star. They believed that these were spirits falling to earth and that watching them might invite their unwanted attention. He showed us the shape of a massive emu in the black spaces within the Milky Way and said it was a protective spirit that looked out for all of us. We were transfixed, and looked for the emu every night after that.

Unable to cope any longer with the extremes of temperature, we left the next morning. On the way out we spotted an Aboriginal man – the first we had seen in the park – cleaning the barbecue.

Chapter Eleven

At the visitor centre in Broome I stood in a queue and listened to the woman at the desk say the same thing over and over again. 'Have you got a booking anywhere? No? Then your best bet is the overflow campground at the showgrounds on the other side of town. They'll let you stay for a couple of nights while you find somewhere else or move on.'

In my hand I had the brochure for Chile Creek that I had picked up months earlier at the Aboriginal community of Iga Warta. While I was waiting my turn, I also found a booklet listing several Aboriginal communities that ran tourism businesses on the Dampier Peninsula, north of Broome.

When I got to the front of the queue I held them both out. 'Can you tell me if we would be able to go to any of these communities and do some camping? We haven't booked anything.'

'The only camping up there is at Middle Lagoon and Cape Leveque. Cape Leveque is booked out, you won't get in there. You might get into Middle Lagoon.'

'What about Chile Creek?'

'You can't camp there.'

'But it says in their brochure you can', I said.

The woman sighed. She turned to a man beside her. 'Any camping up at Chile Creek?'

'They're not one of ours', he told her.

She turned back to me. 'We don't do bookings for them. Sorry, I can't help you with that.'

I looked at our map. The people at the camping shop in Melbourne had marked Middle Lagoon with an orange cross. Chile Creek was further up the peninsula, almost up at the top, near booked-out Cape Leveque. Middle Lagoon it was, then. I didn't want to risk driving an extra 100 kilometres on a dirt road to Chile Creek if we couldn't camp when we got there. I was also nervous about driving into an Indigenous community, no matter how friendly the brochure sounded, without some kind of reassurance that it would be okay.

Outside, the footpath was packed. We navigated the crowds awkwardly, bumping into people constantly. We all seemed to have lost our ability to negotiate busy streets, somehow taking up more room than we used to and being unable to anticipate other people's movements. We sat shivering in an air-conditioned cafe for twenty minutes waiting for coffees and wondered why we used to enjoy doing this so much. After spending a small fortune in the supermarket we left Broome to drive up the corrugated, sandy and slippy road to Middle Lagoon. The road acted as a filter, keeping out people with cars and caravans that couldn't cope with off-road conditions. When we arrived, the campground was busy but not crowded. Tents and dusty off-road vans nestled under gum trees that circled a central bathroom and laundry area. Lots of washing flapped on the lines, mostly bathers, kids clothes and towels, and bikes were strewn on the grass. It was one of the most welcoming campgrounds we'd seen in ages. A German woman in the office gave us a campsite on the top of a sand dune, which looked down onto a small cove with a tumble of rockfalls at either end.

The Kimberley has the second-largest tides in the world. Over the course of a day, the water level rose up to 9 metres until it lapped at the base of the dune, then pulled back until we could wade for ages and still only be knee-deep. At low tide, rocky outcrops were exposed in the bay. As the sea returned, they became islands before disappearing underwater.

In Melbourne it was the July school holidays, so I declared it was for us as well. We had a holiday from our holiday. No packing up, no long drives, no school. We let it all go. The boys were on the beach at sunrise with a gang of other kids and had to be dragged back in at dusk. One day, they all decided to be pirates. As the tide came in, they paddled out to the closest rock, claiming it as their own. When the water rose, they climbed aboard their boogie boards and navigated to the next, higher one. We watched from the beach with the other parents, taking turns to keep an eye on them. The older boys shuttled the younger ones across the water on boogie boards and then came back for supplies of drinks, sandwiches and biscuits. When the tide flowed all the way in, they retreated to the rocky outcrop at the northern end of the beach. Here they were above the high tide mark, but would be cut off from the beach for hours.

When they disappeared from view for a while one of the dads swam over to check on them. He found them all huddled in a rock pool that filled and foamed with seawater with every wave, like a natural spa. Annoyed, they waved him away, telling him this was a 'kids only' spot today. As the sun set and the water retreated, they trudged back to shore, as exhausted and happy as I had ever seen them.

We did drive further up the Dampier Peninsula but we had lost track of the days and didn't realise that it was Saturday. The communities of Ardyaloon and Lombadina were closed to visitors on weekends. I had hoped to go to Chile Creek as well – after all, I had carried their brochure halfway around the country – but the access road was off the Lombadina road and we didn't feel comfortable about driving down it when the community was closed. We stopped in at the supermarket at Ardyaloon to buy lunch and asked the young white woman at the till if there was anywhere we could go. She gave us a map and marked the road to the trochus shell hatchery, and said tourists could go there on weekends. At the end of the road, near the ramp where boats were launched, we watched a tourist fishing charter leave. A young Indigenous man stood at the back of the boat as it took off and an older man sat at the helm. I envied their four passengers, not for the fishing experience, but for the conversations I imagined they would have with these men about their lives and their culture.

A large black man in his fifties leaned on a dusty red Volvo sedan that didn't have one window intact. He wore a huge black cowboy hat that was painted in red, white and yellow, with a feather stuck in the top. His long white hair hung in two thick plaits.

He beckoned to James. 'Hey, brother, where you from?'

'Melbourne', James confessed. I had never felt so white in my life.

'Ah, my sister, she lives in Melbourne! Nice country down there.'

I looked around me. The sea was a colour I had never seen before. It was brighter than the dark blue I was used to – more like a deep turquoise – and it seemed to glow as if it was lit from below. It was very warm, almost too hot, but there was a cool breeze. Hundreds of tiny islands jutted from the water, rocky and red. The sea boiled and foamed around them as the tide rushed in. He thought Melbourne was nice country? He had to be kidding.

'A man down there, he sells my paintings. I fly down for shows, meet people. All the time. I go overseas too. I'm a world-famous artist!' He eyed us. 'Where you stopped?'

'We're camping at Middle Lagoon.'

'What you doing down there? You come camp on my country. I got a block just over there.' He waved vaguely in the direction of the sea. 'You camp with me. I'll show you my country, tell you stories, teach the kids to catch crabs. I have white people all the time. Specially if they're pretty women! I talk to all the visitors. I'm sick of talking to this mob', and he gestured towards the town. 'I'll make you laugh.'

Here it was. An invitation to do what I had been wanting to do since we left home. This was a chance to have an actual, authentic, real-life experience with Indigenous culture. Except that, when I had imagined this meeting, it had always been a scenario that I somehow controlled. I didn't know what to do in this situation.

James mumbled something about having already paid for a few more nights at Middle Lagoon.

'That's okay. You think about it. I'll give you my number, you call me. Bruce Wiggan. Everyone knows me.' He wrote a mobile number on a scrap of paper and, as he handed it to James, he came in close and said something so quietly I couldn't catch it.

'What did he say?' I asked as we drove back through the quiet town.

'He said he knew we were coming. He said he'd dreamed us. Like he'd called us here.'

I raised my eyebrows. 'That's a weird thing to say. Was he just teasing, do you think?' James just shrugged.

A few days later I went to the phone box opposite the Middle Lagoon office and dialled Bruce Wiggan's number, promising myself that if he answered I'd ask for directions to his camp. He didn't pick up and I was ashamed to feel a vague sense of reprieve.

Nannette flew in from Darwin – we had planned to have a week with her in Broome, but instead we drove to town, collected our mail, stocked up on supplies, and brought her back to Middle Lagoon. She didn't seem to mind being dragged away from civilisation again. At least this time the toilets flushed and there was a shower block.

That night we sat outside the tent and watched the sun set. Unseasonal clouds streamed across the horizon like the slipstream left in the wake of an invisible celestial craft. Their scalloped edges turned golden, burnt orange, vibrant bright red and, finally, a deep, soft lavender. The light bathed us in the warm colours of fire. Just beyond the point, two humpback whales spouted and slapped their tails on the water.

James taught Nannette to snorkel at Middle Lagoon. He adjusted her snorkel, showed her how to waddle backwards into the water so that she wouldn't trip over her flippers and told her there was nothing in the water that would hurt her. Ten minutes later, having been distracted by an octopus hiding in a crevice in a rock, he looked up and couldn't see her. He finally caught a glimpse of a snorkel in the distance. She had been following a brightly coloured fish and was nearly half a mile out to sea. He caught up with her and brought her back closer to land and revised his earlier words with the caution that *close to the beach* there was nothing dangerous. Further out, there were bull sharks and crocodiles.

Our next-door neighbour on the ridge was a man in his late fifties, travelling alone in a cute triangular pop-up van. The only real problem with being on his own, he told us, was that it was always his turn to wash his dishes. Oscar and Dylan said they would do them, for a price. I suggested to James that we invite him over to our fire for a beer while they worked.

'I don't think he drinks beer', James said.

I fossicked around in the back of the trailer. 'We've still got some of that stuff from Margaret River. It's probably got a bit hot, and it's bounced around a bit …'

'No. We can't give him that', James said, slightly panicked. 'He's a winemaker. He's won awards. Winemaker of the year, or something like that.'

He did come over after dinner, bringing a bucket of dirty dishes and his own bottle of very nice red. I set the boys up with warm, soapy water and our cleanest tea towel and joined the adults around the fire. As our neighbour explained to Nannette why pinot was the only wine worth drinking, the giggling behind us got louder and louder.

'What's going on?' I asked Oscar.

'These glasses!' he said. 'They've got no handle bits!' He meant stems. The boys were washing very expensive Riedel glasses in a plastic bucket. Our neighbour grinned at me and raised the chipped melamine mug we had given him for his wine.

After dropping Nannette in Broome with promises that we'd be in Darwin within a few weeks, we headed down one of the country's classic 4WD routes. The Gibb River Road, originally a stock route, runs 700 kilometres from Derby to Kununurra through some of the Kimberley's most beautiful and rugged country. Its notoriety had waned in recent years – mining exploration had led to major improvements to the road – but it still divided round-Australia travellers into those who did the Gibb and those who didn't.

At Windjana Gorge we saw hundreds of freshwater crocodiles slide out of the murky dry-season waterhole to sunbake on the sandy riverbank. They were greenish brown, scaly and leathery, with long snouts that tapered at the end and identified them as freshwater crocodiles. Freshwater crocodiles, unlike their saltwater cousins, pose little threat to people. Although saltwater crocodiles can live in fresh water just as well as they can in the ocean, there was no way that they could navigate the waterfalls and escarpments to get this far inland. Nor could they survive the dry season, when many of the creeks and waterholes dried up. It was hard to believe so many of the freshwater crocodiles could survive in such a small body of water. At night we gathered a gang of kids from the communal campfire and took them into the gorge with torches. James had been spotlighting before and showed us how to look directly down the beam of their torch and see the crocodiles' eyes reflect it back, shining like red Christmas lights. High-pitched squeals were soon echoing around the gorge.

Just past the Windjana Gorge turn-off, a sandwich board on the side of the road announced that a Snack Stop was open. A dirt track ran beside the Lennard River and a caravan was set up at the highest point of the bank. The man in the caravan was in his mid-sixties, small and compact with a grey beard that ended in a sharp point at his chin and drew my eye directly to the hole in his trachea.

He opened a sliding window to hand out my tea, placing the cup on a shelf attached to the outside of the van. On the shelf sat a sugar jar, a mug full of teaspoons and a tub of sweet biscuits that he picked up and rattled vigorously as if to say 'help yourself'.

When everyone had been served, he came out of the van and walked over to a small telescope mounted on a tripod on the edge of the high river bank. He shifted his cigarette into his left hand and placed a stained finger firmly on the open hole in the centre of his throat.

'Here, come and have a look at this', he rasped. 'There's a young male croc on the bank over there.'

I bent to look through the telescope. There he was, perfectly framed in the centre of my gaze, lying on the sandy bank on the other side of the river.

'How do you know it's a male?'

He grinned at me. I'd just walked into his trap and he was delighted. He put his hand back up to his throat. 'Because it's got its bloody mouth shut!' he cackled.

We lingered on the Gibb for days. At Lennard Gorge we followed an unmarked track through high grass to the edge of a crevice that hid a narrow gorge with waterfalls at one end. Piles of rocks placed there by other travellers marked a safe path down the side of the steep cliff. At the bottom we threw ourselves, hot and sweaty, into the cool water. The boys shrieked with pleasure and a grey water monitor slid from its warm rock ledge into the water without leaving a ripple.

At Bell Gorge we clambered over the rock walls of the gorge and climbed down to the pool where a waterfall crashed into the water. We spent the day moving from one side of the gorge to the other, first chasing the warmth of the sun after swimming in the freezing water, then hiding in the shade. We went through all our food and drink, but the water was fresh and cool and sweet so we drank it as we splashed under the pounding waterfall.

At the tiny community of Imintji, we ate ice-creams on the wooden verandah of the roadhouse. The shopkeepers were Queenslanders who clearly loved the place. Jenny, a compact blonde woman who bustled around in constant motion, said that in the evenings she baked cakes and muffins and pies in the oven of their house to sell in the shop. 'Because it's hard to bake when you're camping, isn't it? And people like a treat.'

Her husband, Stan, a white-haired man built on a larger scale than most people, rolled his eyes and smiled. 'Doesn't make any money', he said, but I could tell he didn't mean it.

At Galvans Gorge, a sandy track led to a tiny oasis where water tumbled down into a dark green pool surrounded by ferns and palm trees. A rope swing attached to an overhanging limb of a huge gum tree cried out for some serious Tarzan action and we obliged.

From the rock wall above the swimmers a large Wandjina, the traditional spirit of this area, looked down on us sombrely. It was the first one I had seen and I found it mesmerising. Painted in red ochre on the rock face it had a halo around its head and huge dark round eyes, fringed with long lashes, peering out of a pale face. There was a long, skinny nose but no mouth. I had read about it in the guidebooks. Senior law men used to restore the Wandjina at the end of the dry season to keep the spirit fresh and strong and to ensure the return of the rains. Many of the paintings are thought to be at least 4000 years old, but in traditional terms they are not 'art' as they were never originally painted by people. They simply *are* the spirits. They left their images behind when they returned to the spirit world.

We lingered so long in the water that by the time we reached the roadhouse – and the three or four houses that seemed to be all that made up Mount Barnett – it was early afternoon. It was too late to attempt the one-hour walk to Manning Gorge that made Mount Barnett a popular stop on the Gibb River Road, so we paid our camping fee, got permission to set up anywhere in the campground and prepared to spend the night. We got a whiff of the toilet block and put up the tent beside a huge, gnarled boab tree that was close to the river. Looking around the deserted campground, I noticed another camper trailer that was exactly the same model as ours. But it looked different somehow – it was squarer, more solid. I peered through its open flywire windows. Something funny was going on in there with the tent poles. I called James over. He stood and looked for a while, then nodded.

'I've been doing it wrong.'

He went back to our tent, adjusted some poles and suddenly our saggy tent, which had a tendency to collapse at one corner, was as solid and square as it had been the first time we put it up five months ago.

To get to Manning Gorge the next day we had to swim the Manning River. We pushed a day's supply of snacks, towels, shoes and our camera across in two crumbling white polystyrene boxes supplied by the campground for exactly this purpose. It was an hour's hike to the gorge and it was worth every step. The circular pool was wide and generous and had large flat rocks around the edges to lie on. The boys found a sloping rock covered with an inch of rushing water and used it to slide down into the pool, then clambered back up and did it again and again. Tiny freshwater leeches collected on their bare backs every time. When the boys noticed them, they just casually flicked the tiny black creatures off each other. I was surprised by how relaxed they were. I wondered where my kids – one of whom had been known to run screaming from a blowfly – had gone. They were still five months away from turning seven and nine but sometimes, like when they were helping around camp or hiking beside us on long walks, they seemed a lot older than that. At other moments, they played together just like they did when they were two and four, and life was all about having fun and getting as dirty as possible.

We decided to ignore the advice we had been given that the road to Mitchell Falls was too rough for our camper trailer. After a decadent lunch of burgers and chips at the hotel at Drysdale River, we set up a very basic, one-night camp on the bank of the King Edward River. The river was wide, but fairly shallow – we had crossed it just before reaching the designated camping area and the water hadn't even come up over our wheels. Nothing on this road seemed to be as difficult as people had told us to expect. The next morning we were up at six o'clock, ready for a full day of waterfall exploration. It took more than two hours to drive 70 gruelling kilometres of rocky, corrugated road. The car shook and rattled so loudly that we couldn't even talk to each other. At some point the cover on our front indicator began to come loose and James had to throw it in the back to fix later. When we arrived at the Mitchell Falls campground we realised we hadn't got up early enough. A busload of elderly people had almost completely booked out that day's helicopter flights. We paid for the last available flight down from the falls and walked up. At the top of the falls the water was filled with the elderly people who had flown in. They were doing breaststroke and complaining about the quality of their packed lunch.

The helicopter had no rear doors and only two lap belts in the back. We put Oscar in the front beside the pilot and wedged Dylan between us in the back and held on to him as tightly as we could without hurting him. The helicopter tipped a little as it took off and I could feel the weight of my body wanting to slide out the open doorway. I was grateful for the incredible noise because it meant I could swear loudly until I was able to calm myself down and breathe normally again. The view of the gorges from above was incredible. Although this was the middle of the dry season, water was still cascading down from the escarpment and creating massive waterfalls. Despite flying this route many times a day, the pilot had an enthusiasm for the landscape that was infectious. At one point he pointed to the horizon to make sure we could see the faint blue line of the coast in the far distance and then traced the path of a wide river all the way from the ocean to the gorge below us, finally pointing down into the gorge where the dark shape of a large saltwater crocodile lurked at the base of a thundering waterfall. We buzzed with excitement about our flight the whole way back to the campsite.

Back on the Gibb, the first 50 kilometres of road was smooth and flat until, with no warning, there was a faint hissing, then a bang and the back end of the car began to wobble. We had a flat tyre. It wasn't just punctured. A rock had slashed the side wall, leaving a gash nearly 10 centimetres long. We pulled over onto the side of the road and ate lunch under the shade of a tiny tree while James changed the tyre. Forty minutes later we were again on our way.

Five kilometres further along the road James felt another wobble at the back of the car. This time a tyre on the trailer had blown. He replaced it with our one remaining spare wheel.

Ten minutes later it happened again. All we could do this time was take a wheel off the trailer and put it on the car, then leave the trailer on the side of the road and hope we made it to Home Valley Station, 55 kilometres away. Just as we were ready to leave, two workers from a mine near Drysdale River stopped and offered us their spare tyre. After another round of tyre changing, and with the trailer back on, we got to Home Valley just before it closed. We parked the trailer, drove the car to the workshop and returned the borrowed wheel. By the time we realised we had left the trailer outside the furnished cabins instead of in the designated campground, our three-wheeled car was locked in the deserted workshop. We ended a long, exhausting day by pushing the one-tonne trailer through soft sand to the right spot.

'Easier with a car!' laughed two men as they walked past us on their way to the bar.

The Home Valley mechanics were at work early the next day and we were back on the road with a full set of new tyres just after breakfast. Nine kilometres down the road we reached the Pentecost River. I'd been worrying about this for the whole trip. The river was 200 metres wide and well known for being full of saltwater crocodiles. There was no bridge or barge: the only way to get across was to drive and it looked a lot wider and murkier in real life than it had in the pictures and videos I'd seen.

A small car was sitting on our side of the river and it turned out to belong to the men who had laughed at us the night before. They were worried about the crossing. If the water was too deep it might get into their engine and stall their car in the middle of the river. After extracting an apology from them, we tied their car to the back of the trailer and drove slowly into the river. Muddy water lapped at our wheels and seeped in under the doors, but it never reached our bonnet.

When we were safely across, we got out of the car to high-five each other and take photos of the next vehicle crossing behind us. There was a whole lot of debris floating in the water, bobbing about in the waves we had made. The men we had towed had left their rear hatch door open and now their stove, their food and all of their cooking equipment was floating down the river. One of them put on his thongs and took a few steps towards the river, clearly planning to wade in and rescue their things. At the same time, we all saw the red sign warning that large estuarine crocodiles lived in the area. Entering the water without a car or boat, it advised, was a very, very bad idea. He stopped well back from the edge and watched their gear disappear around the bend.

Chapter Twelve

At El Questro Station – a cattle station that had been turned into a huge tourist resort and was known either as 'the jewel in the crown of the Kimberley' or 'Kimberley Disneyland', depending on whom you talked to – the boys tumbled out of the car to wrestle on a patch of perfect green lawn. In the office, the woman behind the desk smiled. 'Lots of kids do that. You must have come off the Gibb.'

El Questro had a range of accommodation options. Its central hub had a motel and a large campground with shower blocks and laundries. We wanted one of the bush sites further along the river. We had been told that these were the best spots to get and were highly sought after, so when the woman confirmed that there was one available we couldn't believe our luck. We drove past the campground with its warm showers and flushing toilets, past the families and kids playing footy on the grass and past the communal fire pits, to our private site far away from human contact and amenities.

Ten minutes later we went back to reception and asked for a site in the campground instead.

El Questro divided opinions amongst travellers. We had been warned that it was a tourist trap: expensive, kitsch and unauthentic. The natural hot springs were only open to regular people before midday. In the afternoon, the rich had it all to themselves. A helicopter flight over the ranges to secret fishing spots with a private guide was so expensive they didn't even bother advertising it in the campground, and the variety show after the Saturday night all-you-can-eat barbecue buffet was hilariously awful in its camp Aussieness.

We loved it.

We spent a whole day cruising Chamberlain Gorge in a small battery-powered boat. We explored the rocks, swam in spots where the sun had warmed the water, and hung fishing rods off the back. Every hour we waved at the tourist boat as it cruised past us with its

full load. Walking El Questro Gorge the next day, we realised how fit
and adventurous Oscar and Dylan had become. The first half of the
walk was a difficult trek through a rocky river bed, then we had to
swim across a deep, cold waterhole and climb over several huge boulders that blocked the entrance to the second, narrower section of the
walk. Lots of adults took one look and decided not to go any further
but our kids didn't hesitate.

We restocked at the nearest town, Kununurra, just 110 kilometres
away, but not without checking that we wouldn't have to hand over
all our fresh fruit and veg at the border. Less than 40 kilometres out
of town we watched a line of cars travelling in the opposite direction
submit to a quarantine inspection, kicked the footy and drove into
the Northern Territory. Instead of driving straight to Katherine,
James wanted to visit Montejinni Station, the cattle station where
he had worked as a jackaroo more than twenty years ago. It was a
250-kilometre detour along the Buchanan Highway. He said it would
be an easy drive; the road was sealed and it wouldn't take more than a
few hours. Either his memory had failed him completely or someone
had come along in the past couple of decades and covered the bitumen
with sand and rocks and corrugations. It was a beautiful drive, though,
and James spent most of it telling us long stories about riding for days
on horseback to muster herds of wild cattle, slaughtering beasts to
feed the men, eating corned beef three times a day and being so cold
at night that he had to wear every single item of clothing he owned.

We pulled in to the roadhouse at Top Springs at dusk. Just
14 kilometres north of Montejinni, it used to be James's local pub.
I had expected a small town, but it was just the Top Springs Hotel
at the junction of the Buchanan and Buntine highways, the dusty
campground behind the pub, and little more. After setting up, we
wandered back into the pub and James asked the barman if he had the
phone number for Montejinni. He did, but warned us that everyone
there had probably gone to Katherine for the annual camp draft that
weekend. James rang, but there was no answer so he left a halting
message on the answering machine, trying to explain who he was and
saying we would like to visit.

In the morning we decided to take the chance and drive down to Montejinni anyway. When we arrived at the homestead, the cook, Pauline, came out to meet us. She had heard James's message and knew exactly who we were. She showed us around, asking James which buildings were new since his time and filling him in on the fate of the people he remembered. Not much had changed in twenty-two years apart from a couple of new sheds and some trees that had grown taller. Equally familiar to James was the news that one of the ringers had been arrested for fighting the night before and was now locked up in Katherine.

Pauline took us into the huge kitchen and within minutes she had loaded up the long table with a feast of pikelets, cake, apple crumble, custard, cheese and a platter of corned beef and pickle sandwiches. I was stunned at the amount of food she had produced and she explained that her main job was to keep the men well fed. She cooked everything in bulk and always made sure that the fridge was full so that they could help themselves at any time. We ate until we could barely move, although James politely declined the corned beef. Pauline seemed surprised at how little we had managed to put away and insisted on packing us a bag of food to take with us.

By the time we reached Darwin a few days later, we were more than ready for a couple of weeks out of the tent. Nannette had booked us two weeks in an apartment and we couldn't wait. We would have a toilet of our own, a bedroom for the boys and a separate one for us, a television and two swimming pools to choose from.

At the end of the fortnight I had arranged to fly back to Melbourne for a few weeks to work and earn some much-needed cash.

Although the accommodation was a gift, we still managed to blow our weekly budget in Darwin. We had to replace all our tyres and the car needed a thorough service. We decided to wash it first, in case the mechanics took one look and decided it wasn't worth putting in much effort to fix up such a bashed-up, filthy vehicle. The back door hadn't closed properly for weeks, so there was a fine film of greasy red dust over everything inside. As red mud piled up in our bay of the carwash we realised that a solid seam of compressed dust in the door seals was causing the problem. The more we blasted it with the high-pressure hose, the more red dust washed out from hidden cracks and crevices. Scratches and dints revealed themselves as we scrubbed and wiped and soaped and hosed the car, but after an hour it was almost white again.

We spent that fortnight as happy tourists. We ate hot, oily prawn satays at the Mindil Beach market, the golden juice tracing a garlicky river down our arms. At Mick's Whips stall, James proved that his jackaroo stories were true by cracking a stockwhip so loudly that it stopped people in their tracks. At Parap on Saturday mornings we queued for freshly pounded pawpaw salad and plastic tubs of curry laksa ladled from huge silver vats. We fed stale bread to the fat milkfish at Doctors Gully and spent a day wandering around the Wildlife Park. We had timed our visit to coincide with the Darwin Festival and left the boys with Nannette a couple of times so we could see some shows. The next Sunday, the *NT News* social pages featured a half-page picture of us, looking cleaner and more relaxed than we had seen ourselves for months, sitting in the open-air Festival Club sharing a bottle of wine and a plastic bowl of chicken curry. We watched lots of television and found ourselves constantly going to the fridge and the cupboards for easily accessible cold drinks and snacks.

On my last afternoon in Darwin, I sat on the edge of the swimming pool with Nannette. I watched my family messing around in the water and thought about how much I would miss them during my three weeks away. The pool had a shade cloth suspended above it like a sail and the boys decided they wanted to touch it. Dylan went first, crouching on James's shoulders and gripping his hair tightly. James sank underwater and then sprang up, propelling Dylan up and forwards. Dylan stretched his arms high but just missed the dark blue canvas. Oscar went next, confident that his extra height would get him there. As James pushed away from the tiled floor of the pool,

Oscar leapt straight up, brushed his fingertips on the sail and crashed back down.

We all heard the crunch as he landed directly on top of James's head.

James staggered, tilting over and coming close to losing his balance and falling into the water. He got himself to the edge of the pool just as I reached him and I helped him up the steps. He collapsed, lying flat on his back on the brick patio. 'I think I might have broken my neck', he said faintly, his face twisting in pain.

Nannette ran to the apartment to call an ambulance but he called her back. 'I'll just lie here for a while. I'll be all right in a minute.'

Five minutes later, he was obviously not well. He had a searing headache but, more worryingly, he was vague and disorientated. He didn't want to go to hospital but, when we insisted, he agreed on the condition that we didn't call an ambulance. I helped him into dry clothes and the four of us supported him and got him into the car.

At the hospital, I let James out at the front door and went to park the car. When I walked into casualty he was nowhere to be seen. The triage nurse had fast-tracked him into the ward, but not after telling him off for not calling an ambulance immediately. By the time I found him, after getting a small lecture myself for driving him to hospital, he was flat on his back in a neck brace, shivering violently under a thin cotton blanket.

Over the next five hours, they did X-rays and scans of his neck. At ten o'clock, just four hours before my flight was due to leave, I rang Melbourne and told my boss I might not be coming. Finally the doctors were convinced that no damage had been done to his spinal cord and let us leave. They gave James a box of painkillers and told him to take it easy for a few days. Back at the apartment he collapsed on the bed, only stopping to say, 'Call back and tell them you're still coming.'

I argued with him, but he was insistent. We needed the money to top up our dwindling supplies of cash. And, he said, the three of them were looking forward to a few weeks of boys-only time. 'No washing, no showers, no vegies, no sweeping out the tent. We're going to have fun. We already have plans', he added ominously.

I knew he was making most of that up to make me feel better, but Nannette agreed that I needed to go and promised to help with the boys for the next few days. I finished packing my bags, called Melbourne again to say that I was on my way to the airport and left worrying about how he would manage to pack up the apartment and get back on the road the next day, let alone cope without me for the next three weeks.

When I called the next morning from the St Kilda flat where I was staying with friends, James said that he hadn't slept a wink all night. Both boys had climbed into bed with him and he had spent the night squashed between their hot, wriggly little bodies. His neck was still so stiff and sore that he couldn't turn his head.

That day, as I sat down at my old desk at my old workplace, wearing my old winter clothes that felt heavy and unfamiliar next to my skin, James slowly packed our new life back into the trailer and drove slowly and carefully down to Litchfield National Park. While I was freezing in Melbourne, they were cruising around the Top End. When I talked to them, they seemed happy and relaxed and I wondered if they were having a welcome break from my nagging, but James said that it was just that they were taking a break from actually *travelling*.

I was busy at work, but in the moments when I stopped and looked around me at the people I had worked with for years, or sat at a dinner table with our oldest friends, I felt as lonely as I could remember. For the last six months, when I couldn't see the kids I could always hear them. The four of us slept in one tent and prepared all our meals, ate and cleaned up together. When we bush-camped, we all washed in the same bucket. We argued a lot, but it was hard to hold grudges or sulk when three other people were laughing at you, so disagreements blew over quickly. Without them, I felt as if half of me was missing. It was hard to concentrate and even harder to sleep.

There was something else troubling me as well. I had some news to break to our friends. The Canadians who were renting our house had been in touch a few weeks earlier. They had been asked to stay on in Melbourne for another six months and they wanted to keep living in our house. As I told this story to Astrid, who had been forwarding our mail, fielding calls from friends and relatives when they hadn't heard from us for a while and passing on messages from Distance Education wondering where our workbooks were, she looked at me accusingly. 'You're not coming back, are you?'

We weren't. It had only taken us a couple of minutes after reading the email from our tenants to decide. We couldn't think of one good reason to go home yet. We weren't ready to return to our old lives. I tried to explain how this decision, which seemed so huge, had actually been one of the easiest we had ever made. Our friends were curious to know exactly what it was like – the freedom, the open spaces, living with such little *stuff* – but I couldn't find the right words to describe it. All I had was a small ball of loneliness in the pit of my stomach. I wanted to go back.

Three weeks later, even after an evening flight to Darwin and an early morning bus trip to Katherine, I was so happy to be back in the heat and dust with my boys that I couldn't stop talking. As we drove down the Stuart Highway to Mataranka, where they had been camped for several days, I wanted to know everything that they had done while I was away and I had messages to give them from their Melbourne friends. But all three of them had begun the marathon task of reading the entire Harry Potter series and the boys were so deep in their books that they could only raise their heads and nod a polite response before diving back into the pages. When we got to the campground, James abandoned me for Harry too, so I wandered around aimlessly, trying to wind down and rediscover the slow pace of camping life.

After a day of lolling in the tree-lined thermal pools for which Mataranka is famous and then sitting in the local pub's open-air bar watching Collingwood make it into the preliminary finals, we packed up for a trip across the Gulf Country. A shopping spree in Katherine meant that we were carrying quite a lot of alcohol and we were worried about getting through the Gulf Country to Queensland. The most direct route was the Roper Bar Road, but it travelled through Aboriginal land and the Federal Government's Intervention had come into force in the Northern Territory the day before. It was now an offence to travel through certain areas carrying alcohol.

I called the Katherine police station to check. They still weren't sure how the laws affected the Roper Bar Road but advised us not to carry any alcohol. The *NT News*, however, had a front page story that said that as long as you were travelling straight through the banned areas it was permissible to carry 'thousands of dollars' worth of alcohol. We left with all our cargo.

After hours of driving we pulled into the Butterfly Springs campground at the southern end of the Limmen National Park. Covering 10,000 square kilometres, Limmen is the second-largest national park in the country. According to our guidebook, the only safe swimming spot in the whole park was Butterfly Springs, a tiny rock pool with a lacklustre waterfall at one end. Hot and dusty, we hurled ourselves into the water before realising that it was stagnant and a bit smelly. We decided that the tiny trickle of water leaking down from the rocks qualified it as flowing so we stayed in.

We set up camp under some flowering gums and made friends with two other groups who pulled in after us. Despite the temperature still hovering at 25°C well after the sunset, we lit a campfire and sat around it late into the night. The air was heavy with the smell of bushfires in the area and the sweet, cloying scent of pollen from the trees around us.

In the morning we woke to a droning noise that was so loud that the air practically vibrated with energy. Native bees were busy harvesting the blossom from the gums. We were fighting a losing battle against the soporific effects of the sound of the bees and the sickly sweet smell from the trees so there was little point trying to do any schoolwork. Instead we explored the Southern Lost City. Eerie sandstone pinnacles towered above us and we wandered around silently, staying close to each other. Smoke haze from the nearby bushfires made visibility difficult and the view from the lookout was obscured by smoke.

The following day we had planned to go to the fishing camp at King Ash Bay, which was 150 kilometres to Borroloola and then another 50 kilometres out to the coast of the Gulf. Half an hour into the drive we passed a sign to Lorella Springs Station. It said there was camping, beer, showers, natural hot springs, great fishing and waterfalls. We turned off and drove 40 kilometres to have a look. The managers were a bit surprised to have people arrive so early, but they were very friendly. We spent hours in the warm thermal pool, paddled an old wooden rowboat up the stream to where the hot water bubbles out of the earth, slid down a natural rock waterslide and checked out a twenty-year-old sea eagles' nest with a huge mound of discarded turtle shells and small animal bones beneath it. Cooling off in a waterhole, we nervously kept an eye out for crocodiles, as we had been advised.

According to the woman who lived at Lorella Springs, we should have done the same thing back at Butterfly Springs. It was home to a pair of freshwater crocs. 'They're not man-eaters or anything but, you know, they could break a bone if they had a go.'

Our route was now being dictated by James's need to watch Collingwood progress through the AFL finals series. Their next match was against Geelong on Friday night. We had been told that King Ash Bay, 130 kilometres away, was 'very nice and it has a pub with a TV'. When we arrived on Thursday, it was a dry, hot dustbowl on the banks of the Macarthur River. Saltwater crocodiles made the water completely off-limits for swimming and there were no trees or shade to alleviate the heat. A little white dog skulked under a caravan, looking as miserable as I felt. Two women – fishing widows, I presumed – hurried past with plastic baskets of washing, heading for the grey concrete toilet block. There were no families here at all. I couldn't imagine what we would do here for forty-eight hours.

I hated it so much that I refused to get out of the car. James insisted on driving around to look at campsites, but I was so angry that I wouldn't speak to or even look at him. Eventually I accused him of being so obsessed with football and fishing that he was ruining our trip. He said I was too uptight, that I couldn't cope with a bit of adventure and that my silent disapproval of everything he did was chipping away at everyone's enjoyment. Half an hour later we were still arguing so nastily that the boys pleaded with us to stop. We drove out of King Ash Bay, went straight through Borroloola without stopping and turned back on the main dirt road and headed for the Queensland border. Furious at being forced to leave a place he had thought was pretty much perfect, James said that we would bloody well camp in the bush that night and we did, but not until we had driven nearly another 200 kilometres.

We spent Thursday night on a hill above the Robinson River. At sunset, the smoke haze turned the sky purple and the sun hung like a huge crimson ball on the horizon. Sunrise brought exactly the same colour palette. The sun rose in the pale grey sky, shining a terrifying bright red through the smoke. It looked as raw and angry as I had felt the day before.

We stuck with our tradition and kicked the footy into Queensland, 160 kilometres along the road from our camp. Signs on the road had advertised hot food and cold drinks at the Hell's Gate roadhouse, just 50 kilometres from the border, and we promised the boys that we would stop for morning tea. When we arrived it was closed. I jumped out of the car, clutching the phone number for the nearest campground at Adels Grove. It was still nearly 170 kilometres away, but I was hoping to make amends with James by ringing ahead to check that they had a television and would be showing the football that night. But there was no phone – the phone box was as empty as the roadhouse.

It took us more than three hours to reach Adels Grove. Before checking if there were any campsites available, James marched up to reception and asked if they had a television. Yes, they did. Would they be showing the football?

'Nah, mate. We did that last weekend, but there was too much whoopin' and hollerin' so we're not doin' it again.' The man behind the bar had no sympathy for James. 'You're in the outback now, mate.'

We all piled back into the car in silence. I felt terrible. I knew how much this meant to James. The nearest pub was at Gregory Downs, 90 kilometres of unsealed road away. Despite the long and disappointing day they had already spent in the car, there was no whingeing from the boys. They knew this was deadly serious.

'Three hours to go', said James, grimly. It was already after two o'clock. Thank goodness it was a night match.

When we got to Gregory Downs, the boys and I hovered anxiously as James spoke to the woman behind the long, towel-lined, wooden bar of the pub. 'Yeah, no worries. The telly'll be on. Just camp down on the river, everyone else does.'

He grinned at her. It was the first smile we'd seen from him in more than twenty-four hours. 'Fantastic. We just drove nearly 700 kilometres to watch this game.'

We chose a shady spot on the river and had swimming races until it was time to go back for dinner and the football. At first, James and Oscar were the only people paying attention to the game. Everyone else was playing darts or singing along to the jukebox. By the final quarter, however, with the score at 62–67, the whole pub was whoopin' and hollerin'.

In the end, Collingwood lost by five points. James was philosophical about it but Oscar had truly believed that they would kick a goal in the final seconds and win their way into the Grand Final. When the siren went, it was too much for him and he burst into hot, painful tears. James was so proud that he went out to the public phone box and rang friends in Melbourne to spread the news that his oldest son was now a true Pies supporter, heartache and all.

We trailed back to the river under the bright moonlight, slept until late morning and woke to the sound of the river rippling past our tent. When we stopped into the pub on the way out to thank them for a great night, they asked if we would like to stay on and work for a while. I glanced at the neat little one-room school across the road and gazed around the vast arid landscape that I was beginning to see the beauty in, and tried to imagine what it would be like to belong here. It felt good in that moment, but we declined the offer. We were going to Cape York.

Chapter Thirteen

From Karumba, there were three ways to get to the top of Cape York. We could take the sealed road that curved south, forming a gentle smile on our map, and finished 1100 kilometres later in Mareeba, north of Cairns. From there, we could head up Cape York on the main Peninsula Development Road, which ran up the centre of the peninsula like a spine. This was the easiest and fastest route.

Alternatively, we could go north on the unsealed Burke Development Road, which stretched up promisingly for more than 200 kilometres before turning south to meet up with the sealed road 100 kilometres west of Mareeba. Both of these seemed like the long way round, and we would also be backtracking on our return journey down the Cape.

But our map also showed a shortcut. At the northernmost point of the Burke Development Road, a dotted line ran from Dunbar Station to a point about halfway up the main Peninsula Road. It would knock about 600 kilometres off the trip.

We went into Karumba for advice. The officer on duty at the police station was the largest man I have, and will ever, see in my life. From his great height, he pointed out that between the road and the track lay the Mitchell River. Dunbar Station charged $500 to tow bogged vehicles out of it. The carpenter who was fixing some cupboards in the police station piped up to say that 98 per cent of people got through the river without being towed and that we'd be fine. The butcher down the road said her dad was working on a road plant up there and he had heard there was quicksand in the Mitchell River. The local RACQ man thought the river crossing would probably be okay if we let our tyres down.

No-one really seemed to know much about the track on the other side of the river. The policeman did ask why we wanted to go that way. We told him it was to save time. He laughed down at us, but in a nice way.

James decided we may as well go and have a look, so we packed up the trailer and drove 250 kilometres to Dunbar Station. A man working in the yard said that the year before they had towed 150 cars out at $50 a time. This year, after they put up a sign saying the fee was $500, they had only towed six vehicles. 'We go over in the utes all the time, but there's no way I'd tow a trailer. It'd get bogged in the sand and turn into an anchor.'

We were so close to the crossing that we thought we may as well drive down to see it for ourselves. There were people camped on the other side of the river, so James waded across for a chat, keeping an eye out for crocodiles.

'A guy did it with a trailer yesterday, but it took him eight goes', one of the men said. 'We'll give you a tow if you get stuck. $500.'

At two o'clock, after nearly an hour of standing at the bank of the wide, shallow river, James decided we should give it a go and started deflating all of our six tyres.

I had always known this was going to happen. Every one of the 250 kilometres we had driven up to Dunbar Station was another kilometre out of our way if we had to turn around and head south, and James couldn't resist a shortcut. I had $500 in my pocket that I'd withdrawn from an ATM before we left Karumba, just in case.

Sweating slightly, his mouth tense, James put the car into low range and gunned the motor. Lurching on the soft sand, the car entered the running water, found some traction on the riverbed and ploughed on and up the steep bank on the other side, following the tracks made by previous vehicles. Oscar and Dylan shrieked with excitement. The campers stood up, gave us a round of applause and waved their stubbies in the air. 'Best crossing we've seen yet!'

As James got the compressor out to pump out our tyres, one of the women asked where we were going to camp that night. I looked at my map. 'I think we'll make it to the Peninsula Road.' I was hoping that we could have dinner at Musgrave Roadhouse, a popular stop on the Peninsula Road that had accommodation, a pub and – it was rumoured – a pool table. She looked at me a bit strangely and went back to her friends without another word. I wondered if I'd misread the map. I checked it again. It was less than 200 kilometres and we still had about five hours of daylight.

One kilometre from the river crossing, the road turned into a goat track. We had to creep along very slowly in first gear, wheels bouncing in and out of ruts and gullies in the hard yellow clay. We were averaging about 10 kilometres per hour. James sat forward and up high in his seat, looking over the bonnet for dangerous washouts in the track, fallen trees, axle-breaking holes, sandy patches and buried rocks. The track had them all. At five o'clock we realised we weren't going to get anywhere near Musgrave that day. We found a clearing on the side of the track and set up camp for the night. A car drove past as we messed about with the tent and the big Aboriginal man driving seemed surprised to see us, but gave a friendly wave.

The next morning the track got even worse. I checked my map. Where we had expected there to be a road turning off to outstations, there wasn't one. Where there were signs, they pointed to places I couldn't see on any of our maps or road atlases. I had seen a detailed map of Cape York a few months earlier but I hadn't bought it at the time, not wanting to have even more bits of paper at my feet. I thought we'd be able to pick one up when we got closer, but there hadn't been any in Karumba. If we didn't find some kind of landmark or sign soon, we'd have to consider the possibility that we had taken a wrong turn somewhere.

After two hours of very slow going I was estimating how much fuel we would need to get back to Dunbar Station. We could probably go another 30 kilometres before we wouldn't have enough diesel to get back safely. I told James, but he just nodded tersely and I knew he'd already worked that out. Navigating the trailer around a fallen tree, we saw a ute up ahead. Two young men were refilling their fuel tanks from jerry cans.

'Are we still on the Musgrave Road?' James asked.

'Yeah, mate, don't ya have a GPS? How shit is this road! Fifty kays to go!'

We didn't have a GPS. We didn't have any mobile coverage either. We had done some research on the expense of buying or hiring a satellite phone and decided against it, but we did have a UHF radio that we had bought and had installed in Perth. With a range of only 5–20 kilometres, depending on the terrain, the UHF was limited in its effectiveness in very remote areas, but the EPIRB was still tucked into the pocket in the door beside me. It gave me some comfort to know that we could send a distress signal that would summon help but the more we travelled, the more we realised that everywhere we went, so did lots of other people. Seeing the man driving past in his ute last night had reminded me that people did live out here. We were on a track that, unlike the road out to Halligan Bay on Lake Eyre, was used by locals getting to and from other communities or towns. We were starting to think that it would actually be quite difficult to get somewhere so remote that help wouldn't drive past within a few hours.

Three hours later we drove past the sprawling sheds and out-houses and fences of the New Dixie cattle station, just a few kilometres from the Peninsula Road. When I closed the final gate behind us and looked back the way we had come, I saw a sign that said 'Road to Dunbar Station impassable. Drive at own risk.'

We turned onto the smooth, well-graded Peninsula Road, giddy and slightly hysterical at what we had just done. At Musgrave Roadhouse, the halfway point between Cairns and the tip of Cape York, we queued in the kiosk to buy pies, sausage rolls, soft drinks and chocolate. We sat in green plastic chairs on the grass and wolfed our snacks as if we hadn't expected to ever see food again. All around us, people were complaining about the terrible state of the Peninsula Development Road and the toll it was taking on their vehicles. We couldn't help ourselves. 'We took a shortcut.' But we had to admit that, although it had knocked 600 kilometres off the trip, we had only saved ourselves two hours of travelling time.

At Archer River, another Cape York stopping point with a roadhouse, pub, accommodation and campground, we treated ourselves to what we decided were probably the best burgers in the country. We chatted to some people who were travelling in a convoy with four other vehicles, and they invited us to tag along with them. An older couple in their group had done the drive up to the tip of Cape York several times before. We had assumed that they were all friends but it turned out that, at some point in the last few days, the older couple had collected four carloads of first-time travellers and offered to lead them.

'They really know the ropes and if anything happens you'll have people around to help you out.'

We weren't tempted. To us, the older couple seemed determined to latch onto these nervous travellers by instilling in them an irrational fear about what lay ahead. The man had already irritated James by expounding loudly on every subject from tyre pressure to fuel consumption.

Although we weren't experts on any of these subjects, we thought we knew enough to be sure that the man's predictions of disaster had little connection with reality. The Gibb River Road, spoken of in hushed voices by some of the travellers we had met, was positively busy and the Peninsula Development Road seemed that way too. The main difference was that, while the Gibb River Road attracted a lot of European and American tourists, the Cape York track was almost completely populated by Australians. I could never work out why, but perhaps it was because any trip up the Cape was, by necessity, one that required you to retrace your exact route on the way home. It wasn't 'on the way' to anywhere: it was more of a pilgrimage.

Cape York, the pointing finger at the north east of Australia, is split in two by the Peninsula Ridge. The ridge is the northernmost end of the Great Dividing Range, the third-longest land-based mountain range in the world. It runs down Australia's east coast from Cape York, through Queensland, New South Wales and Victoria. It forms the Blue Mountains, the Australian Alps, the Snowy Mountains, Mount Kosciuszko, the High Plains, and the Grampians. On Cape York, water on the western slopes of the Peninsula Ridge drains into the

Gulf of Carpentaria. On the eastern side, the rivers flow into the Coral Sea, flooding the Great Barrier Reef with fresh water and nutrients.

The history of European settlement in Cape York echoes that of Central Australia. Alice Springs was originally settled as a telegraph station in 1871 while, in Cape York, construction on an overland telegraph began in 1862 and was mostly completed in 1887. One particularly tricky stretch relied on horses to carry telegrams until the final section of galvanised cast iron poles carrying a single wire was finished. You can still see remnants of the posts and wires deep in the scrub of the Old Telegraph Track.

The largest town on the peninsula, Weipa, began as a Presbyterian mission in 1898. Back then, thousands of hectares were set aside as an Aboriginal reserve. Huge deposits of bauxite – the ore that produces aluminium – were discovered in the area in 1955. Over the next decade most of the land was converted to a mining lease and a railway and port were built to transport the ore directly to Japan.

We were visiting Weipa because James had flown there a few years earlier to install the lighting in the new Western Cape Cultural Centre. The Weipa–Napranum Reconciliation Committee had built the centre to tell visitors about the Indigenous culture, environment and history of the region. The idea was to promote reconciliation and encourage visitors to respect the culture and lands of the local Indigenous people. The project took years, but it eventually opened with a showcase of displays contributed by the local communities of Aurukun, Mapoon and Napranum. James had been proud to be involved in something so important.

When we arrived, the centre was deserted. At first we thought we might be too early or that maybe it wasn't open every day. As we walked around, peering in the windows to catch a glimpse of the displays, it was clear that it had been abandoned. When we asked at the visitor centre, we were told that after several years of sporadic staffing and disagreements amongst the management committee, the centre had closed two months earlier.

Deflated, we continued on to the local campground. It was set right on the water and was generously planted with shady gum trees. It also had the twin attractions of a swimming pool and hot showers. The only disturbing thing was the list of rules they gave us. Along with sensible advice about not cleaning fish by the edge of the water because of the local crocs, was the rule that pig dogs had to be locked in their cages at all times. Some of the caged dogs had large radio receivers on their collars to track them as they chased feral pigs through the bush.

That afternoon, two cars plastered with AFL logos pulled up beside us. The men who climbed out, unfolding their long legs in relief, were holding a clinic at one of the local communities the next day. They said we were welcome to come, so we took the boys for a day of footy with a group of Indigenous kids. It was the first time I had seen Indigenous kids play football and I was amazed at their skill, their ability to keep running despite the extreme heat and the fact that none of them were wearing shoes. The only other white boy was the son of two schoolteachers, Nathan and Letitia, from Bamaga at the very top of the Cape. They invited us to visit them when we got up there.

For a lot of people, the main reason for being in Cape York was to drive along the 360-kilometre Old Telegraph Track between Bramwell Junction and the Jardine River. It was a narrow, corrugated and rocky track with lots of river crossings. The approaches were sometimes very steep and all the crossings required careful navigation around submerged rocks and deep holes.

We drove along the Old Telegraph Track for a while. We had decided to have a go at the notorious Gunshot Crossing, but on the way there we got stuck behind a tour bus that was axle-deep in the sand. The driver told James that all of his passengers were 'about seventy, not out' and not much help at digging the heavy wheels out of the sand. We unhitched our trailer and pushed it off the road, then tied a rope to the bus and towed it two kilometres to a firmer section of the track. An hour or so later, back on the main road, we again found ourselves behind the bus. It was stuck in the mud at the final creek crossing. We couldn't drive around it, so we returned to the Old Telegraph Track and drove along a very rocky track into the campground from the other direction. That experience was enough for us and we stuck to the main road after that.

Eliot Falls, 280 kilometres north of Archer River and in the middle of the Jardine River National Park, was one of the most beautiful swimming spots we had seen. A wide, slow river trickled over a waterfall into the pool below. A smaller creek rushed in from the side. Where it flowed into the pool there was a tiny rock hole that filled with bubbling water. We took turns to sit in its fizzy coolness. We spent a whole day swimming and floating and doing bombs from the top of the waterfall.

At Jardine River we paid a fee that bought us a return trip on the ferry. It was also a permit to bush camp on Aboriginal land between there and the tip of Cape York. While we were waiting for the ferry to be winched across from the other side of the river we drove around to the old crossing for a look. We had heard people complain about paying to cross the Jardine, talking instead about the original crossing further upstream. We got out of the car and looked at the point where the track dived into the water. The river was at least 50 metres wide and was flowing fast. We guessed it could be as much as five metres deep but, aware that crocodiles were common in the area, we didn't wade in to check. Years ago this had been the only place to cross the river. Back then, timber planks were placed on the sandiest sections and the entries and exits were clearly defined. The other bank now looked overgrown, dark and steep: a perfect crocodile lair.

The people who resented paying the ferry fee were usually the same people who argued they shouldn't have to pay to enter Aboriginal land. To me, $100 to ferry our car and trailer across a river and back and allow us to camp on someone else's country seemed like a bargain. We returned to the main crossing, drove the car onto the large steel barge and were winched across in less than five minutes.

The next morning we wasted no time getting to the top of Cape York. Homemade wooden signs with painted arrows saying 'This

Way to The Tip' were nailed to trees along the track. At the end of the road, we followed a path into a small section of dense rainforest, through the trees and out to a large expanse of flat red rocks. We clambered along the rocks until we were standing on a small summit. Less than 200 kilometres to the north, across the Torres Strait, lay Papua New Guinea. I had read that on a clear day the mountains of Papua New Guinea were visible from where we stood. I couldn't see them, and doubted that was even possible, but I felt a satisfaction and a thrill of achievement. It was unlike the feeling I had at Steep Point, looking west towards nothing but ocean for thousands of kilometres. Standing here, I felt as if one giant step could take me somewhere new and exotic and exciting.

Thrilled with how adventurous we were, we walked down to the final 50-metre section of the Australian mainland to find forty elderly people milling around, taking photographs of each other. The official sign was mounted on a steel post that was concreted firmly into the rock bed. It looked about as significant as a parking sign. In small, aqua writing, it declared that we were standing at the northernmost point of the Australian continent.

Over the next hour, just about everyone we had camped near in the past fortnight turned up and we all took turns taking each other's pictures by the sign. James had decided to fish, but at the same moment that he finally hooked something, the black akubra hat he bought in Alice Springs nearly six months earlier flew into the water. I saw him consider whether or not to throw himself in after it and then stop himself as he remembered that crocodiles and tiger sharks patrolled the channel.

That night we stopped in at the general store in New Mapoon, one of the five communities that make up the Northern Peninsula Area at the top of Cape York. New Mapoon is home to about 300 people. We ordered a pizza and the man who ran the store sat on the wooden verandah with us and chatted as we ate. He said that he leased the store from the local council and that it was a goldmine. The only problem was finding reliable staff. It was a familiar story and we had heard it at most of the roadhouses in remote communities so far.

At the moment, his main employees were three young Indonesian men whom he had sponsored under an immigration scheme. They lived in a caravan behind the store. They cooked a great curry, he said, although hot chips and pizza were still his bestsellers.

When he said that he was thinking of selling the business, James glanced at me. The man must have noticed, because he told us that if we were interested, he could email us the information. 'Mind you, what you see in the books isn't the half of it. That's why I'm getting out. When I bought it, I thought we'd stay ten years and make enough to retire on. That was only four years ago, and I reckon we're set up now. Besides, the wife hates it here.'

My skin crawled a little. New Mapoon was created in the 1960s when the people from Mapoon, near Weipa, were forcibly relocated to allow bauxite mining leases to be granted on their land. If he was making a fortune, it was out of the pockets of people who had been displaced from their traditional land and dumped onto someone else's country. He had a captive market amongst the families who weren't able to get anywhere else to shop.

'And', the man went on, 'the lotto people have been in touch. They want me to stock scratchies. They've done their research and they reckon this could be one of their biggest selling outlets in the state. Now, fair enough, you might not think that's a good idea. It'd be up to you. But if it doesn't happen here, you can bet your life they'll just buy them somewhere else and then where'll you be?'

I sat on the verandah and wondered what it would be like to live here permanently, not as a quick fix for a meagre superannuation fund, but to build a different kind of life. It was hard to imagine, but I knew that if we were to do it, scratchies wouldn't be involved.

We did have to earn money somehow, though. Our decision to rent our house out for another year had changed the nature of our trip, but we hadn't yet worked out how to manage that. Our savings had nearly run out and, while the rent the Canadians were paying was covering our mortgage, we were soon going to have to work to fund our travelling. We had no plans about what we would do for money when we returned to Melbourne, more than a year from now, but I tried not to think that far ahead. Also, the school year would be ending in a few months. Our homeschooling experiment had worked out fairly well so far, but I didn't think we could extend it for much longer. 'They'll learn more from travelling than they will in a classroom' must surely have some kind of limit. I was worried that we'd almost reached the point where the reverse would be true.

The next afternoon we fished off the sun-bleached wooden wharf at Seisia, the smallest of the Northern Peninsula Area communities. We jigged for live bait, the tiny fish that clustered in shimmering schools under the pier. When we caught one, we put them on a larger hook to cast out to sea for larger fish. Dylan refused to fish and instead perched on a wide wooden post on the edge of the wharf, deep in the world of Harry Potter. When the afternoon ferry arrived from Thursday Island, Oscar and Dylan were fascinated by a fair-skinned, sandy-haired boy who was about fifteen years old. He had switched from chatting to them while the ferry docked to speaking an exuberant and completely incomprehensible language as he helped the Thursday Island women haul their colourful striped bags along the wharf to waiting cars. We caught a few English phrases in the musical stream of words and realised he was speaking the local dialect, Torres Strait Creole.

The next day we drove to Bamaga, the administrative centre of the region, to visit Nathan and Letitia, the teachers we had met at Weipa. We asked them about the language we had heard. As the kids bounced on their trampoline, they told us that most of the local people spoke several languages, Creole among them. English was a third or fourth language and often wasn't spoken at home. Despite this, English was the only language used at the school. They also confirmed many of the stories we had heard about very low levels of school attendance in remote Indigenous communities. The main goal of their school was to teach basic literacy and numeracy. They admitted to often being frustrated but they were philosophical about it. Up here, strongly held cultural practices and traditions took precedence over Western education.

Looking over at their five-year-old son, Letitia said that they would probably only stay a few more years. As much as they loved the place and their jobs they wanted a better education for him than he could get here. Most of the white kids were sent down south to boarding school as soon as they were old enough. The idea of sending my boys away to school was unthinkable and I knew that the man in New Mapoon would have to keep looking for buyers for his business.

Driving back down the Cape, we visited Lockhart River, famous worldwide for its contemporary Aboriginal artwork. We spent a couple of hours at the workshop, looking at the paintings and prints and chatting to the artists who worked there. We chose a few pieces that we couldn't resist, justifying the purchases to ourselves with the fact that prices at the workshop were much less than we would pay in a gallery at home. They charged our credit card with a low-tech swipe of a carbon paper receipt and arranged to post the canvases to Astrid's address in Melbourne for us.

We had bought one huge canvas and two linocuts by the same young artist and James commented that it would be a small windfall for him. The man wrapping the artwork shook his head. 'No, it doesn't work like that. The best thing he could do would be to move away from here and go down to Cairns. That money'll be gone in a few days. Once his family get to know about it, he'll have to hand most of it over. The most successful artists from here, they all live in town. It's the only way they can hold on to the money they make.'

We drove out, disturbed at how little we understood the issues that were part of everyday life in remote communities.

Chapter Fourteen

On our way down the Cape York Peninsula, I decided I should have a go at driving. James claimed to get horribly carsick in the passenger seat but he surrendered the keys with good grace. I should have been practising more. I drove too fast into a patch of sand and the car skidded sideways, all one tonne of it completely out of my control. Too scared to put my foot on the brake in case it made the car slide more, I wrestled with the steering wheel. In my panic I didn't notice that the car was heading straight for the high bank at the side of the track. James leaned across and grabbed the wheel, pulling it round sharply and shouting at me to brake.

We came to a stop with the car at an angle halfway up a mound of sand and the trailer jack-knifed across the track. I tried to hand the keys back to James but, after calmly talking me through how to straighten us up again, he insisted I keep driving until we reached the sealed road. Very carefully and much more slowly, I drove us to Cooktown.

In Cooktown, the northernmost town in Australia, located on the mouth of the Endeavour River and just over 300 kilometres north of Cairns, we spent a long time reading the display panels that described what happened there in 1770. Captain Cook and his crew had spent seven weeks living alongside the local Indigenous people. Cook's men transgressed local custom by killing sea turtles and refusing to share the meat and the Indigenous men expressed their frustration by burning down the sailors' camp. Later, the two groups came together at a place now known as Reconciliation Rocks. Cook handed out clothing and blankets, but a few days later the gifts were found in a heap, discarded as valueless.

This story, with its layers of cultural misunderstandings, struck a chord with James and me. We felt as if we understood just as little about Indigenous culture as those white men more than two hundred years ago. We read the panels and talked with the boys about what had happened, and how it had all gone wrong. James said he was always wary of doing the wrong thing, like Cook's men had. That was why he was so reluctant for us to go into Indigenous communities, even those that welcomed visitors. My argument was that if we didn't make an effort, even if it made us feel uncomfortable, we would go home to Melbourne understanding just as little about Australia's Indigenous people as we had when we left. The boys took the opportunity to remind us that, unlike James and me, they had never climbed Uluru, proving that they had more respect for Indigenous culture than we did. They were still only six and eight years old, so by the time we left the museum, their favourite part was a verse from one of the displays: 'Captain Cook chased a chook all around Australia. He lost his pants in the middle of France and found them in Tasmania.' But we had just had a serious conversation about racial tension in Australia and our feelings about it, and I couldn't imagine that ever happening in Melbourne.

At Cape Tribulation, the part of the Daintree National Park that has been set aside to house and entertain backpackers and other tourists, Oscar entertained a busload of Japanese tourists by cracking a stockwhip and posing for photos. James and I laughed when we saw him holding court in the car park of the pub. With his filthy clothes, bare feet and long tangled hair, our son from the inner city must have looked to them like a genuine Aussie kid from the outback. As I watched him, I noticed an air of relaxed playfulness that I couldn't remember him having in the city.

I had seen changes in both boys. They were developing a quiet confidence and could have serious conversations with adults without any self-consciousness. Many of the older campers we had met had told us how much they had enjoyed talking to the kids. Some of them were probably just missing their grandchildren, but I had overheard some of those conversations and realised that Oscar and Dylan sounded a lot more grown-up than they used to. The way I spoke to them had changed too. I used to have a different voice that I used for the kids: slightly higher pitched, a bit slower and much more considered than the one I used with adults. If I lapsed into that voice now, its patronising tone made me cringe.

Something else I had noticed was that I was no longer trying to protect the boys from my moods. We lived too close together for there to be any point trying to hide when someone was frustrated or angry or grumpy or sad. I had a tendency to sulk and then explode. Once, when they had been mucking around in the back of the car and ignoring me when I asked them to stop, I shocked all of us by unclipping my seatbelt and throwing myself into the back seat, slapping and shouting at them. We were all seeing each other in our most horrible moments, and we were all coping with it. It was dawning on me that this was what people meant when they said travelling with their kids made them a closer family. I thought that on this trip I would be getting to know Oscar and Dylan better. It hadn't occurred to me that I might have been a bit of a mystery to them at times too.

South of Cape Tribulation the rainforest gave way to cane fields that stretched as far as we could see. We were on our way to Port Douglas, the resort town 66 kilometres north of Cairns that would be our first experience of city living since Darwin eight weeks earlier. Astrid and Anthony were already there with their three children, having their annual tropical holiday to recover from the tail end of Melbourne's miserable winter weather. We navigated the smooth asphalted roads that seemed too narrow for our big car and parked outside their apartment. Oscar spotted them hurrying towards us from the beach, lugging bags, damp towels and sandy buckets and spades. Astrid dropped her load to hug us all and I suddenly realised how much I had missed them. We spent the next few days catching up, although we had trouble dragging the boys from the apartment to do anything but eat. They were mesmerised by the television and the luxury of being indoors as the tropical rain fell in sheets outside.

James's sister, Liz, was also in Port Douglas. She owned a restaurant in the main street with her partner, John, but they lived in Mission Beach, 140 kilometres south of Cairns. A month earlier, when they heard we had decided not to go home at the end of our first year of travelling, they had invited us to stay with them in their brand-new house. I was very reluctant. It seemed like a huge imposition and I wasn't sure how they would cope with our noisy, half-feral boys. I had tried to explain this to James and Liz's stepmother. She heard me out and then told me she had reached a point in her life where she had decided to accept all invitations as they were offered: with grace and generosity. It was good advice and I took it.

When Astrid and Anthony left, we packed up and drove straight to Mission Beach. John met us outside the house with a huge smile, reassuring me that he really didn't mind us landing on him. He opened the front door with a flourish and we looked past the swimming pool to the palm trees that lined the beach and framed a view of Dunk Island. We walked through in awe. Two bedrooms and a bathroom at the front were ours. There was a sleek commercial-quality kitchen with a plumbed-in coffee machine, a lounge room with huge leather couches and a deck by the pool that held a Balinese-style pagoda and a day bed.

Dylan and Oscar ignored the television and pool in favour of something far more exciting: 'Soft beds, such soft beds!'

After eight months on the road, we were completely over camping.

Although there were only six weeks of term left, we enrolled the boys at the local primary school. They were as eager to go as we were to hand them over to professionals. At the end of the first day, Dylan had six new friends and assured me that he'd make more the next day. Oscar had a different approach. He had spotted a boy in his class who, just like him, had hair that was well below his shoulders and bleached by sun and salt water. It didn't take long for the other boy to notice Oscar and they became best friends. Sometimes when I was calling them home from the beach, I couldn't tell which of the two lean, tanned boys was mine.

The boys loved the routine of school. The only downside was that they came home with nits. It wasn't my first encounter with head lice, but the tropical ones were a lot more persistent than the ones I was used to. Every night, I soaked their hair in chemicals and painstakingly combed out all the creatures and their eggs. In theory that should have broken the cycle, but whenever I checked I found more of the tiny, elongated eggs clinging to a hair shaft.

One afternoon I asked one of the other mothers how she coped with it. She looked a little guilty and then let me in on a secret. The local vet had advised her to use an animal flea treatment on her kids. 'You just put it on their heads every three months. I do it in the holidays. They used to have nits all the time, and I haven't seen one since I started.' I seriously considered it for a couple of days before deciding to persist with my less drastic method for a while longer.

John was the manager of a local resort, the Horizon, and he organised jobs for James and me there. Built on a hill above South Mission Beach, looking out to Dunk Island, the Horizon looked as if it were gradually being engulfed by the rainforest. After a quick lesson on the coffee machine, I was rostered on the breakfast shift and James worked behind the bar in the evenings. Although we were back to tag-team parenting, the handovers were a lot less frantic than they had been in Melbourne.

'Where are the kids?'

'Dunno. On the beach, I think.'

'All right. See you later.'

I had to be at work early and I came to love driving through the rainforest at dawn. Sometimes I surprised a family of cassowaries who were loitering in the middle of the road or nosing around a wheelie bin. Nature was always nearby at the Horizon. Guests were warned that the large resident male cassowary that patrolled the paths between the cabins should be treated with wary respect.

The open-air restaurant was visited regularly by a lace monitor called George. When I heard screaming from the dining area, I knew George was doing his rounds. Sometimes we broke an egg into a bowl and put it down for him. It was important to do this quickly. George could smell an egg a mile away and would sprint towards it frantically, his long, curved claws scraping along the floorboards.

Snakes were also common visitors. One morning the receptionist had to be taken home after a tree snake fell from a door frame and draped itself around her neck.

'You work at the Horizon', a tiny classmate of Dylan's said to me, after I had been at work for just two days. Oscar's teacher had already introduced herself to James across the Horizon's bar. We had been warned that gossip whizzed through the three small villages of North Mission, Wongaling and South Mission. A small minibus trundled from North to South Mission a few times a day, and I suspected that it had some kind of magical ability to transfer knowledge as it drove along. You could almost see people waving at the bus, absorbing the news that someone had just been sacked for turning up to work drunk, then going next door to tell their neighbours all about it.

The only other public transport was one taxi, which was also a minibus. If you had drunk too much in one of North Mission's bars, you had to call the taxi and hang around on the street waiting for it to arrive. Eventually it would turn up and collect you and anyone else who had been wondering how they were going to get home. You worked out who was going where, although the driver already knew where you all lived, and handed over some money when you got out. It was a nice system, a bit like someone's dad coming to pick you and all your friends up from a school disco.

It would have been a very bad idea to drive home at the end of a big night out. The local police did a lot of hiding behind trees with radars and often set up roadblocks on the one road that connected the three towns. One night James was breathalysed in the front garden after coming home from work. A police car that had been hiding further up the road screeched to a halt across the driveway as he drove in and the policemen jumped out and grabbed him as he got out of the car. The breath test showed traces of alcohol and James admitted to having had one beer when he knocked off. The police officer finally conceded that he probably wasn't over the limit – or at least he wouldn't be by the time they took him to Tully, 40 kilometres away, for a blood test.

Until recently, Tully had the honour of being the town with the highest rainfall in the country and it still had a Big Gumboot right in the centre of town. Mission Beach regularly had more than seventy days of rain in a row and, when the wet season arrived, it was bombarded by electrical storms and tropical downpours. As lightning lit up the sky and the rain was so loud we couldn't hear each other talking, we were very glad we were not in the tent. And when the humidity hit 100 per cent, the temperature climbed into the high thirties and the sea was off limits because of stingers and crocodiles, we were very grateful for Liz and John's pool.

By Christmas, we still hadn't decided what to do next. Every day we had a new plan, but nothing seemed quite right. Sometimes we considered putting down roots in Mission Beach, perhaps even buying a house and starting a business. But then we would start daydreaming about heading back on the road and we couldn't imagine making a commitment that serious. For now, though, as rain continued to fall for thousands of kilometres in every direction, it seemed wisest to stay right where we were.

The Horizon closed for renovations in January and James stayed on as a labourer. It was hot and humid and every night he came home exhausted, drenched in sweat, covered in insect bites and streaked with mud. He distracted himself by talking about how great it would be if we had a boat. After weeks of nagging I gave in and agreed to spend $2000 on it, providing he came up with a system for getting it on and off the car without needing me to help.

James spent an evening designing an attachment for our roof rack so that we could carry it on top of the car. He took it to a welding company in Tully for a quote. The man looked at the drawing he had done in texta on a paper napkin, raised his eyebrows slightly, and said it would cost $980.

The next weekend, James drilled and screwed and bolted together aluminium struts and boat rollers and attached them all to the roof rack. On the way back to the hardware store for more screws, he spotted a little boat with a 'For Sale' sign on it. 'Do you reckon I could get that on top of my car?' Of course, the salesman said. It had been on a roof rack before. In fact, he had originally bought that very boat for himself. He had just been to Cooktown and he and his kids had cruised up the Endeavour River in it.

He couldn't have come up with a better line if he had been spying on us for six months. Although, given the way information travelled through Mission Beach, perhaps he had.

'How much do you want for it?'

'$1200 just for the boat. But I could do you a package deal with a motor for $3000.'

That afternoon, James told me the bad news. 'I know it's more than we wanted to spend. I've already wasted a bit of money, but maybe we should forget the whole thing.' His chin quivered a little. 'It's just, you know, I really thought it would be fantastic to have a boat. For the boys, they'd love it. Wouldn't you, Dylan?'

'A boat! A boat! We're getting a boat!' Dylan shouted obligingly.

The next day, we went to pick it up. As James and the salesman struggled to load it onto the car, it became obvious that this boat had never been upside down in its life. At one point, a wooden box on the floor of the boat clattered open, revealing a rusty battery.

'Probably have to nail that shut', the salesman muttered.

When he picked up the motor, James almost fell over. It weighed 50 kilograms. Next came the anchor, four life jackets, two oars, instructions on how to change over the registration of the boat, advice about how to get a boat licence because it would be illegal to drive this boat without one, details about how to mix the two-stroke fuel and run the motor in properly and a reminder to have the whole lot serviced regularly.

I looked into the back of the car. When we were on the road, it was packed neatly to the roof with boxes of food, school books, our fridge and two eskies for fresh vegetables and cold drinks. Now it was full of boat stuff. I tried to catch James's eye but he was handing over the rest of the cash and wouldn't look at me. We drove out of the yard silently.

At home, the boys and I watched as James wrestled the boat from the roof of the car. When he finally got it to the point where gravity was on his side, he managed to get out of the way just before it landed on his feet. Looking at the car, it was obvious that James's homemade boat rack had bent quite a lot during the very slow 4-kilometre trip from the boat shop. He hauled the outboard motor out of the back and dragged it into the house. Although he lowered it to the floor as carefully as he could, there was an obvious dent where it landed on the wooden boards.

Dinner that night was a tense, quiet affair. At eight o'clock the next morning James rang the shop and asked if he could return everything. They didn't seem surprised. That evening, we dismantled the twisted and bent structure from the roof rack and agreed to remain a family that fished from the beach.

Early in January, we decided we wanted to go back and spend more time in the Kimberley. I contacted every campground on the Gibb River Road to ask if we could work for them during the dry season. I knew it was a long shot, especially as I had to explain that we had two children and would have to spend time homeschooling them.

In February we got a reply from a cattle station near the Gibb River Road, offering us jobs running their campground. The boys wouldn't be a problem. The woman said that she had a teenage daughter and it would be nice to have more kids around. James would do general maintenance and my job was to clean the tourists' cabins in the morning and help the cook. She had also hired a governess, so when the campground was busy our boys could join in her daughter's lessons. We could start at the end of April.

It sounded perfect. We would still be living in our camper trailer and homeschooling the boys, but this time we'd be settled in one place and they could have regular lessons every day. They would have plenty of time to play and explore outdoors. The station was the kind of campground that attracted families, so there would always be other children for them – and people for James and me to talk to. We had one day off a week, so we could explore the gorges and waterfalls around the station and maybe take a couple of longer trips further along the Gibb River Road. The dry season ended in October, giving us a few months to drive back to Melbourne. There was even internet access at the homestead, so I thought I might be able to do a bit of work for my old clients in Melbourne in the evenings to earn some extra money for our return trip.

Everything was falling into place, except that James had been coming home more exhausted than usual and had been complaining of a nagging headache for weeks. At first we put it down to dehydration. Within minutes of arriving at the construction site each day, rivers of sweat were pouring down his back. He was constantly sore and achy but, given the hard physical work he was doing, that wasn't unexpected. One night he woke up shaking violently and complained that he was cold. I turned off the ceiling fan and found him a blanket. He fell asleep but soon woke again in a pool of sweat. His skin was hot and tight and when he got up for a drink his hands were so stiff he couldn't hold the glass. The doctor eventually diagnosed Ross River Fever, a mosquito-borne virus, and said that there wasn't much he could do. James could expect the symptoms to recur for up to twelve months.

Our last weekend in Mission Beach, in mid-March, coincided with the local government elections. A friend of Liz's was running for council so we went to a barbecue at the lifesaving club on Saturday evening to await the results. The kids got bored with all the talk of numbers and parties and votes and were running around outside in the dark, barefoot as always. We were watching them when Dylan gave a loud gasp.

'Snake! Ouch, it's bitten me!'

James picked him up and raced inside. There were two puncture wounds and drops of blood on Dylan's ankle. James grabbed a large tablecloth and wrapped it around Dylan's leg. Someone called an ambulance and the first-aid kit was found. We bandaged Dylan's leg properly, holding him firmly to immobilise the limb. A woman knelt down beside me and helped keep Dylan calm.

'The important thing is to make sure he's breathing as slowly as possible', she said.

For twenty minutes we sat beside him on the concrete floor. Lying on the ground, his leg bandaged to the thigh, he looked tiny and pale. His eyes were fixed on us the whole time, wide with fear. I knew that he trusted us completely, believing that if he did everything we told him he would be fine. I was terrified that we were going to lose him.

'He's so small, you know, if it was going to be bad it would probably happen pretty quickly', the woman beside me said quietly.

When the ambulance finally arrived from Tully, the paramedic checked his vital signs, re-bandaged his leg, loaded him onto a stretcher and drove us back to Tully Hospital. Two hours and several blood and urine tests later it was clear that whatever had bitten him wasn't venomous.

The next day, on his way to collect us from the hospital, James stopped at the lifesaving club and had a look around in the daylight. Behind the building, right where Dylan had been bitten, he found an old black rubber mat. It was rotting and falling apart and one of the rubber strips had two nasty pieces of wire sticking out from one end.

Chapter Fifteen

Leaving Mission Beach to drive back to the Kimberley, the trailer bouncing along behind us, we felt light and free. Everyone assumed their old positions: James at the wheel, the boys curled up in the back with a pile of books and me squashed in beside bags of maps and food and bottles of water. We were adventurers again.

But first, we were taking a major diversion. We had four weeks to get to our new jobs, and we had to make good on a promise we had made the kids when we left Melbourne. We were going to Wet'n'Wild on the Gold Coast.

On the way down the coast – on the first sunny day for weeks – we treated ourselves to a trip to the Great Barrier Reef. Oscar was born to snorkel. Like his grandmother, he had no fear and by the end of the day he had decided to study marine biology at James Cook University in Townsville and be a professional diver. He flitted around the reef for hours in his bright yellow stinger suit, only surfacing to eat. Dylan decided his career was going to be in photography, contenting himself by doing several trips in the tiny semi-submersible submarine that chugged around underwater at regular intervals, happy to view the coral and the fish through thick, clouded windows.

Heading south on the Bruce Highway was terrifying. By then we had driven on some of the roughest and most remote roads in the country, but I had never been as scared as I was when we were being tailgated by huge trucks pulling two semi-trailers. We made it to Brisbane, a bit shaken, and the next night James and the boys went to watch Collingwood lose by two points in the final minutes of the game.

At Wet'n'Wild, we were first in line when they opened the gates. It was a sunny, warm weekday in the middle of the school term so there were no crowds. We rode every ride at least twice, climbing the tall metal staircases back to the top of every ride without ever having to wait for our next turn. Oscar and Dylan only stood still long enough to eat and to let me slap sunscreen on their arms and legs and watch it slide straight off. We limped out, damp and exhausted, when they closed the gates and slept for twelve hours. Both boys declared that it had been the best day of the whole trip so far. Although I was appalled that a theme park could outrank all the other things we had done, I sort of agreed with them.

Before we left the Gold Coast we spent a couple of days with Tim, Sue, Troy and Kirralee, the family we had first met in the pub at William Creek on the Oodnadatta Track. They were just back from their trip, and we sat up late one night, drinking and swapping stories about the places we had been. Sue had been busy printing and framing photos and we laughed when we realised that we had some identical shots taken in exactly the same places. We worked out that our paths had continued to cross since Dalhousie Springs. Tim and I had been on different whale shark boats on the same day at Exmouth and we must have driven right past their campsite in Cape Range National Park on our way to Ningaloo Station. They had lingered in Western Australia too. Tim was a fanatical surfer and they had fallen in love with Gnaraloo, halfway between Carnarvon and Exmouth, and were hoping to go back there soon. They were still one of the few families we had met while we were travelling, and we still couldn't work out why that was. We felt like very lucky members of a very exclusive club.

After several long days in the car, we made it to the heart of the outback. At the classic Queensland town of Longreach, located on the Tropic of Capricorn and home to Qantas and the annual RM Williams Longreach Muster, we visited the surprisingly modern and large Stockman's Hall of Fame. James wandered around feeling nostalgia for his days as a jackaroo and ringer, the boys were captivated by the whips and knives and guns, and I shuddered at the photos of the conditions that the women had to endure in the early days of outback settlement. That night we found a free camp beside the Thomson River. We spent most of the night around a campfire with two men who were celebrating a sixty-eighth birthday. They had a guitar, a squeezebox and a plastic bucket of rum and orange juice that they invited us to share. We sang classic campfire songs with them, starting with 'Waltzing Matilda' and moving on to 'Kookaburra sits in the old gum tree' and 'Tie me kangaroo down, sport'. It was only when the birthday boy fell off his chair and into the fire, then declared himself as 'drunk as a cunt' that we decided we should take ourselves and the boys to bed. Their wives arrived back from bingo and gave them hell, and we laughed ourselves to sleep.

The next day we drove to Winton, which is not only the birth-place of 'Waltzing Matilda' but also has the world's only fossilised footprints of a dinosaur stampede. At the caravan park we showered in the sulphur-scented water, which was a less-advertised feature of Winton. The man at the caravan park said that you weren't considered a local until you no longer noticed the smell. 'Mind you, I've been here fifty years and it still stinks.'

I liked the Waltzing Matilda museum. It had a light and sound show with an animated swaggie telling his story and talking about why Banjo Patterson's song meant so much to Australians. There were rooms full of old bottles, early settlers' furniture, recordings of different versions of 'Waltzing Matilda' and hundreds of old photos. We had optimistically bought the full Winton Tourist Pass, so we also went across the road to see the life-size diorama of the dinosaur stampede. The building didn't seem big enough to hold a dinosaur, but wandering past a collection of crocheted doilies and old bottles, I found some small fibreglass dinosaur models lurking in the corner behind a faded picket fence at the back of the dusty shop. We stared at it, confused.

The next morning we drove to Lark Quarry, the site of the actual stampede. Bill the Dinosaur Man explained that the stampeding dinosaurs were about the size of chickens, but assured us that they had been running away from a much bigger dinosaur. We couldn't

understand why the chicken-size prints were running towards the
bigger ones so Bill told us to think of ourselves walking into a chicken
shed and then imagine the chickens running past us to avoid being
cornered. It was starting to sound much more like a scurry than a
stampede. But the footprints were definitely there and, as Bill told
the story and pointed at the fossils with a plastic T-Rex on the end
of a long stick, we got the picture and were a little awed. After the
tour, Oscar told Bill that he wasn't very interested in dinosaurs but
he would like to know more about the stuff that had killed them, like
comets and meteors. Bill seemed okay with that.

Our next stop was 360 kilometres west of Winton in the only
caravan park in Boulia, home of the mysterious Min Min lights that
have been reportedly seen in the area since before European settlement.
Back in the swing of camping, we were all set up in just seventeen
minutes. An hour later, two families drove in and spent an hour dust-
ing the outside of their campers before they even started unpacking.
As the adults put up tents, set up long stainless steel kitchen benches
and unloaded boxes of cooking equipment, their hungry children ran
around screaming and shouting and playing in the toilet block. At
nine o'clock a German man in blue pyjamas emerged from his caravan
and told them off. The kids were eventually fed and put to bed. At ten
o'clock, their parents finally started preparing their own meal.

It was that evening – because, of course, we wandered over to
meet them – that I realised I was turning into the kind of annoying,
know-it-all traveller that I had always hated. They told us that they
had decided not to take the Plenty Highway to Alice Springs because
they been told it was so corrugated and rough that it was virtually
impassable.

I couldn't help myself. 'Oh, that's complete bullshit. If it was as
bad as that, it would have to be the worst road in Australia.'

Before I knew it, I had told them all about the many places we
had been in the last thirteen months and no doubt gave the impression
that I believed I knew everything there was to know about road
conditions across the entire country. The next day James told me he
had seen them exchange looks as I talked. He knew those looks. They

were the same ones we swapped when people offered us unsolicited advice.

I was right, though. The Plenty Highway wasn't that rough. It was, however, so mind-numbingly featureless and boring that a game of I-Spy in the car only lasted four minutes.

'I spy with my little eye something beginning with C.'

'Umm … that cow over there.'

'How did you get that?'

'It was either that or "car" and I just did that one.'

Dylan and Oscar conspired for a while in the back and came up with a variation.

'Okay, so Level 1 is something real that you can see. Like the road. And Level 2 is something that's real, but you can't see it right now. So, maybe, like … a tree', Oscar explained.

'I want to go first!' said Dylan. 'I'm going to do Level 3.'

'What's Level 3?'

'Something that you can't see and isn't real. Ummm … I spy with my little eye something that begins with D', said Dylan.

'Dragon!' said the rest of us.

'That's not fair! How did you get that?'

We were so bored that when I found a shortcut to Alice Springs through the rugged but beautiful East MacDonnell Ranges we decided to take it. We spent the night at an almost deserted campground near Harts Range, 215 kilometres north-east of Alice Springs, that had the fantastic name of 'Spotted Tiger'. The only other people there were eight men, aged from their early twenties to late fifties, all heavily bearded and decidedly grimy. They were camped in the far corner with their dogs. We waved at them as we drove by but they just stared at us and didn't wave back. Half an hour after we set up they started up their chainsaws. James and I didn't sleep well that night. In the morning they drove out early, all wearing orange safety vests, and we worked out that they were a road crew.

In Alice Springs we visited the School of the Air, where we had a long conversation with one of the teachers about homeschooling. We swapped notes and realised that the workbooks we were using were very similar to theirs. We talked about how difficult we had sometimes found it to do the lessons with our kids, and she told us some parents employed young women with teaching experience. That explained the governess we would be meeting in just a few weeks. We watched a class of students from all over the Northern Territory have a lesson via a video link-up. They were all white, and I asked how many Indigenous students they had. The guide explained that most of their pupils lived on remote cattle stations. Indigenous children, she said, tended to live in communities that had access to a school.

On our way out of the Northern Territory a couple of days later, we stopped at the art centre at Yuendumu, 300 kilometres west of Alice Springs. While Oscar and Dylan checked out colourfully decorated music sticks and shallow bowls made from bark that the salesgirl told us were called coolamons, James fell in love with a triptych of the Seven Sisters constellation painted in achingly beautiful shades of purple and lavender.

The woman who ran the centre laughed at him. 'You can't have that. It's spoken for.'

The work had been commissioned by a gallery in Switzerland so even if we could afford it – which we couldn't – it wasn't for sale. She promised to ring James if the Swiss gallery changed their mind. We left, dreaming of winning the lottery.

Once we got outside the art centre, Yuendumu was a shock. It was the first time we had been in a Central Australian Indigenous community. Rubbish blew past as we drove to the general store for fuel and snacks for what was left of the afternoon's drive. Faded tin houses squatted in patches of bare dirt and plastic bags and nappies collected against the wire fences that divided each bare yard from the next. Rusting car bodies sat on bare hubs and leaked foam upholstery onto the ground. Scrawny dogs loped past in packs and paid us absolutely no attention. Neither did the people gathered in small groups on the porches of the houses, some of them warming their hands over fires burning in 40-gallon drums.

Ten minutes earlier, we had been fantasising about paying thousands of dollars to hang a painting on the wall of our inner-city house. It was a shock to be confronted with the appalling living conditions of Indigenous people in this wealthy country.

That night, 400 kilometres further up the Tanami Road, we camped out the back of the Rabbit Flat Roadhouse, run by a recluse who was notorious for chasing away visitors who dared to arrive on his days off. We sat around the campfire while the pastel colours of twilight slowly faded into the dark velvet of a desert night and talked about being homesick. I'd known something was brewing earlier in the day when both the boys had used the last of their pocket money to buy gifts for classmates they hadn't seen for more than a year.

I was homesick too. We'd been gone for more than thirteen months, travelled nearly 50,000 kilometres and camped in over a hundred places. We'd driven across deserts and through rainforests, snorkelled in coral reefs on both sides of the country, climbed mountains, camped on deserted beaches and met people from all over the world. It was a wonderful experience, but home suddenly seemed very far away.

That night the boys and I talked about the people we missed, and about how different it was to being in Melbourne. We talked about what our lives used to be like – James and I working and the four of us not really spending any time together. Sometimes all we seemed to do was argue about getting ready for school in the morning and about brushing teeth and going to bed in the evening. We rarely ate our meals together. On weekends, we would cross paths sometimes in the mad whirl of cleaning, shopping, washing and the kids' sporting activities. Oscar thought about that, and then said accusingly, 'When we were at home, we never *saw* you!' As if he'd only just realised.

James had been quiet during most of the conversation, but then he admitted that he wasn't looking forward to returning to Melbourne. He knew when we got home at the end of this year he would have to go back to a regular job and he wouldn't ever see this much of us again. That's when he would be homesick. He'd be missing his best friends – us. We were all silent after that, staring into the dying flames, wondering just what 'going home' would be like, and how much we would miss this life.

As I helped Dylan into his sleeping bag later he said, 'I felt different tonight. I felt happy. I could feel all this warmth and love coming out from you and Dad all the way over to us.' And in case I didn't get it, he added, 'Like flies to a sandwich.'

After a quick visit to the Wolfe Creek meteorite crater, made famous by the 2005 horror film based loosely on the murder of Peter Falconio, and an overnight stop in Halls Creek, the first town at the Western Australian end of the Tanami Road, we decided to make amends for missing the Bungle Bungles the previous year. At the turn-off from the Great Northern Highway to Purnululu National Park, 100 kilometres north of Halls Creek, several caravans and camper trailers were parked by the side of the road, and for good reason. The narrow, 53-kilometre track was notoriously rocky and corrugated and it took several hours of very slow driving to navigate the dry creek crossings, steep climbs and tight corners.

When we reached the surprisingly new and modern visitor centre at the end of the track, we were allocated a campsite a few kilometres south of the rounded rock formations that we had come to see. It was early in the season and the park had just opened, so there were only a few other camps set up and none near us. We put up the tent in the shade of a huge gum tree and settled in for an early night.

The next morning we began exploring some of the walking trails. We wandered along narrow sandy tracks that led into cool, dark chasms where the sunlight only managed to get in for an hour or so each day. We tested the peculiar acoustics at Cathedral Gorge, where sound travels around the huge curved walls so that a whisper at one end of the gorge can be clearly heard at the other. The track detoured around the base of the domes and we craned our necks trying to make out the orange and grey bands in the sandstone above us. The striped effect is due to different amounts of moisture in the sandstone. The drier layers display their oxidised iron content with their orange colour. The grey bands are the layers that hold more water; bacteria grow on these surfaces and turn them grey.

On the second day, we did schoolwork in the shade of a wooden shelter in the car park at the start of the Echidna Chasm walk. Helicopters buzzed above us and a sign warned walkers not to wave at them unless you were in need of emergency assistance. After an hour or so of sweating, literally, over maths sheets, we packed up the books and walked through the narrow gaps between the domes. We soon decided that there was no doubt that the best views were from the air. Reasoning that we were about to spend six months in a place where there would absolutely nothing to spend any money on, we drove to the airstrip that afternoon and booked a ridiculously expensive half-hour helicopter flight.

Our second helicopter ride was less terrifying than the one from Mitchell Falls the previous year. This time the chopper had doors and all four of us had seatbelts. From the ground, the famous beehive mounds had appeared to be clustered closely together, but from above we could see that there were hundreds of them that stood alone, separated by eons of erosion. In the middle of the range, where we had been walking, the sandstone folded and rippled, forming gorges that hid cool dark waterholes.

By Anzac Day we were in Fitzroy Crossing. James and the boys spent the afternoon in the camp kitchen watching Collingwood play against Essendon so I had some rare time alone in the tent. As I settled down to read, a familiar accent drifted across the campground.

'Whit dae ye mean ye didnae bring a hammer?'

'Oh, it disnae matter. Ah'll just use a big rock. Look, there's wun right here. That'll do the job no problem.'

'What's goin' on with this wee tent? There's ropes and zips everywhere. I cannae work it out.'

I peeked at them from above my book. They were definitely Scottish, I knew that already, but they looked as if they could actually belong to my family. I wandered over with our hammer. 'Would you like to borrow this?'

'Thanks, love', said the tiny, dark-haired woman. 'This bampot here forgot to bring oors.'

'Do you need a hand?'

'Dae ye know how tae put up one aw these?' she asked, waving her hand at a pile of blue silk and white rope.

As we worked, Linda and Andy explained that this was their first camping trip. I feigned surprise. They had only been in Australia for a few months, having just moved from Glasgow to Broome. This weekend was their first opportunity to explore their new home. They had driven 400 kilometres that day – a distance that was extraordinary to them – to have a look at Fitzroy Crossing.

We got the tent up and Linda peered anxiously inside. 'Ah'm terrified aw creepy-crawlies', she confessed. 'Dae ye think anything can get in there?' I assured her it would be fine, but suggested she close all the insect screens that Andy had unzipped and thrown open 'tae get some fresh air in'.

By the time James and the boys got back, we had been invited for a drink after dinner.

'Dae you two like ice-cream?' Linda asked the boys when we arrived, following the Scottish tradition of plying children with sweets at every opportunity. They assured her that they did.

I looked around, confused. I had helped them unpack their small car and hadn't noticed an esky. 'How did you bring ice-cream?' I asked.

'Och, that's an auld trick', said Andy. 'Dae ye not know it?' He lifted out a mass of soggy paper from a cardboard box. 'Ye wrap it up in newspaper. It's a brilliant insulator.'

The boys watched, fascinated, as he peeled away the paper to reveal a container of chocolate ice-cream. When he opened the lid, the contents were completely liquid. Which, to be honest, wasn't a complete surprise. The temperature hadn't gone below 30°C.

Andy frowned as he looked into the tub. 'Ah suppose it is a bit hotter here.'

As we drank ice-cream from our mugs, we told Linda and Andy where we were going and they invited us to visit them any time we were in Broome. We covered a lot of ground that night. It turned out that Andy was a quintessential Scottish man: an engineer who also happened to be a Reiki master. I told Nannette later I suspected that, in fine Scottish tradition, he had taught himself from a library book.

Oscar and Dylan were besotted with Linda. She was the first grown-up they had met for ages who was genuinely interested in everything they had to say. Andy threw in a few jokes to try to win them over to his side but it was too late. They were already calling Linda 'Aunty'.

As I was kissing Dylan goodnight he said hopefully, 'Mum, Linda could be related to us, couldn't she?' I agreed that it was possible. 'Yes, because she's a grown-up but she's even shorter than Granny Nannette.'

When we drove into the cattle station that was going to be our home for the next six months, a thin woman in an apron walked onto the front porch of the homestead and flapped her hands at us crossly.

'Didn't you see the signs? The campground's that way.'

We walked up the stairs, introduced ourselves to Diane and her husband, Glen, and explained that we were here to work. She frowned.

'I don't know what you're talking about. My husband and I have been caretaking here over the wet. We run the campground. They didn't say anything to us about it.'

'We weren't meant to be here until tomorrow, but we were definitely expected', I said. 'Could you call the owner?'

'I suppose so', said Diane. 'I hope you're not expecting to be fed. We've barely any supplies.'

'No, we're fine', James said firmly when he saw that I could hardly speak. The deal had been a minimal wage in return for our meals and free accommodation in the campground. We had brought some food with us, but not much. The nearest store was back at Imintji, three hours' drive away. That night I was too distressed to make conversation with the other families in the campground. When the boys went to sleep I lay in bed and cried.

'I can't work it out', I said to James. 'I spoke to the owner a few weeks ago. She knew we were coming. I can't believe I've dragged us all this way across the country for nothing. What are we going to do?'

The next few days were tense and uncomfortable for everyone. The owner was contacted and said that she had meant to get in touch and tell us that things had changed. Her daughter was unwell and the whole family were in Perth and unlikely to be at the property over the dry season. She thought the job would be too hard for us to manage on our own, especially as we had children to look after too.

'You're welcome to stay for a week. Until you find another job', she offered.

James and the boys helped Glen slash the vegetation on the access tracks to the nearby gorges and swimming holes that drew in visitors. I called all the local properties to see if they had any work. Although it was still early in the tourist season, all of the local campgrounds and tourist operations already had their staff in place. Most were sympathetic and said if we hung around for a month or two something might come up.

Our luck changed when I rang the Imintji roadhouse and spoke to Jenny, the lady whose homemade cake we had bought the year before. She said that the Derby Bus Service was looking for a school bus driver to do the daily run from Imintji to Mount Barnett and her husband, Stan, added they might need help in the store when the season picked up. I rang the bus company and the manager said to come into Derby the next day for a chat.

A few hours later, James and Glen drove back up to the house with Oscar and Dylan riding behind them in the old ute. I couldn't wait to tell them the news.

'Looks like we'll be on our way soon.'

'I know', said Diane, who had come out when she heard the ute approaching. 'They'll be gone tomorrow', she told her husband.

It was my first experience of the Gibb River Road's lightning-fast information exchange. It made Mission Beach look like it was on dial-up.

The bus company signed us up straight away. James's job would be to drive the Imintji kids 80 kilometres north-east along the Gibb River Road to Wananami Remote Community School at Mount Barnett. We had camped at Mount Barnett the year before, pushing our day's supplies across the Barnett River in polystyrene boxes and then walking to the waterfall at Manning Gorge. We had no idea then that, just across the road, was the Indigenous community of Kupungarri. Next we were interviewed by Jim, the CEO of the Aboriginal corporation that owned the Imintji roadhouse. Jim was a small, stout white man with a shiny bald head and a thick, carefully trimmed white beard.

'He looks like one of the Seven Dwarves', Oscar said with delight when we first met him. I bundled both boys outside to play before they could stuff this up.

We handed over our resumes and Jim added them to a teetering pile without even looking at them. We both officially had jobs at Imintji.

A few days later, we followed the bus on the morning run to school. The drive took an hour. The road dipped as it went through Saddlers Creek on the boundary of Imintji before turning slightly and stretching out across a huge expanse of sparse scrub. Although we had driven along this road before, everything seemed different now. Three slim boab trees leaned towards each other, their limbs entwined in an embrace. Haze from distant fires obscured the view when we reached the top of the Phillips Range. James followed the bus as the driver swerved from side to side, finding the smoothest section of the road, and I knew he was memorising every move.

The principal of the Wananami school, Gary, was a thin, pale man in his forties with jet-black hair and serious, intelligent eyes. He had spent almost his entire career teaching in remote Western Australian communities and met his wife in Halls Creek. Together they had worked in lots of schools, spending a few years in each and getting extraordinary results before moving on again. I got the impression they ran a very tight ship.

The school was divided into three classes: Kinder–Grade 3, Grades 4–6 and Secondary. I looked at Oscar and Dylan standing nervously in the playground while all the other kids played a vigorous session of kick-to-kick in bare feet. 'They'll be right', said Gary. 'They're all pretty good kids here. And footy's a great leveller.'

Driving back to Imintji, past the track to the cattle station where we had planned to spend the dry season, I was very thankful for the turn our lives had taken.

Chapter Sixteen

The Imintji store was a converted steel container on the Gibb River Road. Imintji itself was made up of 15 corrugated iron buildings that sat in the hard red dirt, fading in the sun. Five were homes to the three or four families who had chosen to live out bush rather than in Derby or Broome. Five young men shared another house. They were doing a TAFE program, learning skills while they did building and maintenance work around the community.

Most of the other buildings were empty and had become homes for dogs. Some of the houses – and the dogs – had been abandoned by people who had succumbed to the pull of town. Others were empty because broken plumbing and dangerous wiring had rendered them uninhabitable, even by local standards. The newly painted store and Stan and Jenny's house were outside the main community. They sat inside a neat square of bright green grass that was edged with flower-beds and fenced in tightly, like a child's farm set. Our caravan huddled under a tree in the corner of the garden, as if it was trying to hide. Behind the shop was a kilometre of dusty scrub, spinifex and grey boulders and, beyond that, an escarpment reared up to the sky and stretched out along the back of the community like the wall of a massive dam.

A tour company that leased land from the Imintji community had set up a wilderness camp in the gully beside Saddlers Creek. It was aimed at more well-heeled tourists than us; the kind that boarded buses and toured the Gibb River Road, sleeping in safari tents and being fully catered for along the way. The tourist season had just begun and a helicopter company was offering joy rides over the nearby gorges and waterfalls. Business was still slow. During the day, the helicopter mostly sat on a cleared patch outside the shop. At night the pilot, Jim, parked it in a fenced area inside the community. The flight logs were carefully monitored, but Jim often took a passenger when he flew the 100 metres from the parking spot to the store and back again each day. On the first afternoon at Imintji, James and the boys climbed on board for a bird's-eye view of our new home.

On our first official day of work and school, James and two very nervous boys left in the bus and I spent a full day in the shop with Stan and Jenny. I learned how to use the till; where to find the non-perishable stock that was stored in the dark shipping container behind the store; the importance of rotating the cartons of soft drink and potato chips to make sure they didn't spend too long in the heat before being brought inside the air-conditioned store; where the cleaning products were kept; and how to count, balance and record the day's takings.

Most importantly, Stan showed me the system for tracking how much diesel was pumped into the fuel tanks of the vehicles that pulled up out the front. The single pump was old and slow and a locked padlock secured the nozzle to the latch that released the fuel. When a vehicle pulled up, I grabbed my hat, the key and a greasy rag and went outside to greet them. Sometimes, especially if the driver was an older man, they were reluctant to let me handle the fuel pump; Stan would give them an encouraging smile and a wave from the shop's window. When the tank was full, I tore a page from the diesel-stained notebook from my pocket and wrote down the amount for them to give to Stan. If the store was busy and I was fuelling up several vehicles in a row, I'd make a separate note of the numbers and hand it to Stan through the window so he could make sure it was all paid for.

When the school bus pulled up outside at the end of the day, Oscar and Dylan jumped out with huge smiles and a new friend. Willie had a quad bike, and the three of them rode it around all afternoon, eating muffins that Jenny gave them. Dylan told me that he had a language class at school and had already learned a few words of the local Aboriginal language, Ngarinyin. Willie's mother, Cherylene, came into the store and asked if the kids could come over the next day to play on the trampoline and try a traditionally cooked bush turkey.

We really had fallen on our feet. For a week or so, anyway.

Ten days later, I was alone in the store for the first time. Stan and Jenny were off on a flight with Jim. He was timing a new flight and had asked them to come along and point out the waterfalls and gorges that would be the selling points for the tourists. Jodie, who worked at the tourist camp, had also gone with them.

It had taken Jenny a lot of work to get Stan to agree to the flight. She had been very excited: this was a chance for them to leave the store for a couple of hours.

Stan was terrified of flying and Jodie had been jittery and on edge that morning too. James had driven back to Imintji to pump diesel for me, arriving just in time to join in the teasing as Stan and Jodie waited to climb aboard. Stan was clutching his camera to his chest and I guessed he would take photographs the whole time to settle his nerves.

The store had been quiet all morning and I'd been managing on my own but, when a bus full of tourists pulled up outside, I was relieved to hear the familiar thumping beat of the chopper returning. The bus blocked my view of the landing spot and all I could see was the bus door swing open and the first passenger venture into the bright sunshine. I rang the buzzer to let James know that I needed help with the fuel.

Within a minute, the shop was full of people asking questions and ordering milkshakes and coffees. A queue had formed down the middle of the store and everyone seemed to be holding an ice-cream in one hand and a $50 note in the other. Just as I started to wonder why the helicopter hadn't landed, James ran past outside.

'It's crashed!'

I abandoned the sale I was ringing up and, for the first time in my life, dialled 000. What service? Ambulance, I guessed. What was my location?

'It's three hours' drive from Derby. The community's called Imintji. It's on the Gibb River Road, about 250 kilometres … (west? east?) west of Derby. A helicopter's just crashed outside.'

Hours later I realised I had placed us in the Indian Ocean, somewhere on the way to Christmas Island.

The operator was calm. 'How many people are in the helicopter?'

'Four, including the pilot.'

'Do you know what injuries they have?'

'No.' I heard the start of a wail in my voice.

A truck roared out of the community. Four men were riding on the tray, clinging to the cabin roof as the vehicle charged over the road and into the scrub. Relief weakened my knees.

'There are men going to help now.' I pushed past a few people on my way out of the shop. 'Where are they?' I shouted to the people standing beside the bus. The driver looked up.

'Over there', he said, pointing to the scrub on the other side of the road. 'Who's on the chopper?'

'Stan and Jenny.'

He winced.

'Are you there?' James's voice came from the two-way radio inside the store. I ran back inside.

'What's happening?'

'Everyone's alive. We're bringing them back on the truck. Jim's pretty bad, though.'

'Okay, I heard that', said the emergency operator. 'We're in contact with the Flying Doctors and we're trying to get you some help. Give me your number and I'll call you back.'

My hands were shaking as I called the tourist camp. 'There's been an accident. The helicopter's just crashed. Everyone's alive and we're bringing them back to the shop. You need to come up now.' Next I rang the helicopter company. 'I'm calling from the Imintji store. Your helicopter has crashed outside with Jim and three passengers on board.' And then the Aboriginal corporation in Derby. 'I'm calling from Imintji. The helicopter's just crashed out the front. Stan and Jenny were on it.'

The truck crawled up the road, with several men running alongside it. James was at the wheel, his face tense and serious. Stan sat in the passenger seat beside him. Stan's eyes were closed and he was leaning at an odd angle. As the truck turned into the driveway, I saw Jim lying on his back on the tray. Jenny and Jodie were hunched beside him. There was blood on the women's faces and their eyes were wide and glazed.

When the truck stopped, people began to move in towards Jim. A young man, who had been running with the truck, shouted, 'Don't move him. Leave him there.'

James looked exhausted and stern. 'We had to pull Jim out of the cabin. His legs were trapped. We grabbed him by the shoulders and pulled him out through the window.' He paused. 'I think his back is broken. He kept saying, "Don't move me, please don't move me." All I could smell was aviation fuel. I can't believe the whole thing didn't explode.'

He held out his trembling hands and looked at them curiously, as if they belonged to someone else. 'The others were already out when we got there. They were sitting in the dirt. I think Stan's done something to his neck. He's in lots of pain.'

A young woman came up to us. 'Water', she said. 'We need water. And blankets, I think.'

The inertia had broken. Cars had arrived and everyone was on the move. Jodie's boyfriend half-carried, half-walked her behind the store to the garden, where there was some shelter from the relentless sun. It was nearly midday.

Kevin, Imintji's TAFE instructor, leaned out the window of his ute. So far I'd only met him once. 'Have you called Llane?'

I shook my head, confused.

'You know. The nurse from Mount Barnett.'

'No. What's her number?'

Kevin shook his head. 'I'll go home and do it.' The ute did a screaming U-turn and raced back into the community.

I got bottles of water from the fridge and took them outside. People were gathered around Jim, holding up their clothing to shield him from the sun. His eyes were shut and he was pale and clammy.

Someone got a market umbrella from the garden and positioned it to give Jim shade.

Stan was lying on the grass behind the store. He seemed calm and told me he thought he was okay, except that his neck hurt. Jodie was curled up beside him. The people from the tourist camp were looking after them. Jodie was pale and unable to talk, flinching every time she moved. I found blankets to put underneath them to keep out the damp from the grass, and got pillows to raise Jodie's legs.

Jenny had made it to her house, but now she was lying flat on her back on the concrete floor. One of the young women from the bus was with her.

'Please, will you go and tell Stan I love him?'

Back out the front, a young man got out of his car and came towards me. 'We're shut', I said. 'You have to go to Mount Barnett.'

'I'm Matt', he said. 'I'm supposed to meet Stan and Jenny. I'm from the ABC.' A vague memory returned. The ABC was covering the annual Gibb River Road bicycle ride from Derby to Kununurra. Matt was here to interview Stan and Jenny about the store. 'There's an ambulance travelling with the cyclists. I'll go back and get them for you.'

The phone rang constantly. Emergency Services said they couldn't send an ambulance from Derby, but the Flying Doctors would be coming as soon as they could. Then the owner of Broome Helicopters called to tell us he was trying to release one of their large choppers from a fire-bombing job and get it to us.

'But the Flying Doctors are coming.'

'No', he said. 'I don't know what you've been told, but I've been talking to the guys here in Broome and they aren't coming. They don't have a plane in the Kimberley today.'

Journalists started ringing. I explained that we only had one phone and that I needed to keep the line free, but they wouldn't stop. I gave the phone to James and sat with Jim.

He opened his eyes and croaked, 'My passengers? How are they?'

'They're fine, Jim. You're the only one we're worried about. Your boss says to tell you he doesn't give a shit about the chopper, and he's going to get you out of here as soon as he can.'

His eyes fluttered and closed. For a long and terrible moment I thought he was going to die on the back of the truck, holding my hand.

Llane, the nurse, arrived in what seemed a very short time. Kevin told me later that she was notorious for driving like a mad woman on these roads. The first thing she did was give Jim a dose of morphine and we all felt huge relief until he said it wasn't doing anything for his pain. I remember thinking that if he was hurting, it must mean his back wasn't broken after all. I was wrong. Jim would never walk again.

Cherylene touched me gently on my arm. 'I think we should lock the shop.'

I padlocked the shop door and walked over to an elderly couple who were sitting patiently beside their hire car. 'I'm really sorry. I can't serve you right now. Do you have enough fuel to get to Mount Barnett?'

'Yes, dear', the lady said. 'We're fine just sitting here. Can we do anything?'

I looked around. There was an air of calm now. Everyone was waiting for help to arrive. I felt like I was the only one who knew it wasn't coming soon. 'I think we're okay.'

At one point, someone shouted, 'The Flying Doctors are here!' and we all looked up at a small plane glinting in the clear blue sky. I knew that wasn't right. Although the community had been asking for an airstrip for more than twenty years, there was still no landing strip anywhere near Imintji. Funding for the project had been approved years ago, but the plan had been halted by a dispute with the cattle station about land ownership. Ironically, the proposed location of the airstrip was pretty much exactly where the helicopter now lay.

Matt and I watched the plane circle above us. 'I think it's ours', he said, embarrassed. The ABC was shooting aerial footage of the mangled helicopter for that night's news bulletin.

We opened the shop to give everyone lunch. We emptied the pie drawer and handed them out with cold drinks.

It was after two o'clock and James was now meant to be driving back to Mount Barnett to pick up the kids. I rang the school. 'There's been an accident …'

'It's okay, we've heard. The kids know that none of their parents have been hurt. Gary will drive them back.'

I hadn't even thought about the kids finding out. Oscar and Dylan had already been in the helicopter twice. What if … I refused to think about that, I just stopped that thought, told it to get right out of my head and never come back.

The day got hotter and quieter. Cars pulled in occasionally, slowing down as the drivers realised that something wasn't right. I moved them along, not letting them get out of their vehicles. I didn't notice the elderly couple leave, but they returned the next day and told us their son had been badly hurt in a car accident in a remote area a few years ago. They had been thinking of him as they sat and watched us bustling around our friends.

The school's dusty troop carrier arrived at three o'clock. Normally the kids exploded out of the bus, all legs and arms and bare feet pounding the red dirt as they scattered and ran for home. Today they climbed out slowly, checking out the scene with wide eyes. Their parents were there to meet them and walk them quickly into the community, away from the chaos. We grabbed our boys and hugged them and tried to explain. 'Jim and Stan and Jenny are going to be all right. There's a big helicopter coming to take them to hospital very soon. We don't want you to worry. It's all going to be fine.'

And, being kids, they believed us. Minutes later, my heart jumped as I saw them kicking a football in the garden, just metres from where Stan and Jodie were lying on the grass in neck braces. I bundled them into the caravan, turned on the air conditioning and the tiny portable television, and told them to stay put.

Finally, just before five o'clock, the biggest helicopter I had ever seen flew in from Derby. The sound of the giant rotors beating the air was deafening. As it landed beside the store, the noise and swirling red dust were exhilarating and wonderful. The cavalry had finally arrived.

The doctor checked out Jim first, and then helped six men to lift him onto a stretcher and manoeuvre him into the back of the helicopter. When I said, 'The others are out the back', she smiled at me.

'I'm afraid we've only got room for one. The Flying Doctor is coming for the others.'

Jim took all the adrenalin with him when he left. I saw the exhaustion in James's grey face and realised how tired I was too. The ambulance went back to the bike ride. The bus driver said he should get his tour group going. We thanked them for their help and I opened the store to give them food and drink, but they all insisted on paying. Within minutes of opening up, the store was full. The whole community had been waiting patiently for me to open up so they could shop for dinner.

Llane came in to say the Flying Doctors would be landing at the airstrip at Mount Barnett later that night. She had to drive Stan, Jenny and Jodie there in her troop carrier. 'We'll have to get going before it gets dark. I don't want to hit a bloody bull on the way back.'

As we helped Stan climb into the troopie, he looked old and tired and scared. Jenny was angry now. She was furious that they had to undergo a two-hour drive on a corrugated dirt road at dusk. Jodie was distraught, unable to do anything but sob quietly and moan when she had to move. They were all terrified at the prospect of flying in a light plane in the dark over some of the remotest areas in the country. I felt awful for them.

The police left too. Because there were no fatalities, the helicopter company could investigate the crash itself. We wondered about the wisdom of that decision a few weeks later when another Robinson R44 helicopter crashed in similar circumstances in Queensland. And again later that year, when the one we had gone in fell out of the sky over the Bungle Bungles, killing everyone on board.

In the days ahead, the community tried to stop sightseers driving off the road into the scrub to photograph the crash site and souvenir pieces of the wreckage. The carcass of the helicopter lay in the scrub, next to a small tree it had sliced in two on its way down. Its black skids pointed up in the air, like the legs of a dead bug. Glass from the broken cockpit window glinted in the long dry grass. A couple of weeks after the crash, the wreck was hoisted clumsily onto the back of a flatbed truck, tied down with orange straps, and driven off down the Gibb. In an ugly moment, it sailed past Stan and Jenny as they were travelling from Broome back to Derby.

But that night, when everyone had finally gone, and we were the only ones left, the Kimberley turned on a sunset that made my heart soar. We sat on the grass outside our van, eating microwaved pizza and drinking Coke from the bottle. As the first stars popped out of the darkening sky, something in my chest loosened and I felt giddy.

'I guess we have to run the shop now.'

Chapter Seventeen

After that dramatic start, the next few months of our lives fell into an easy routine. We woke early and had a quick breakfast in the tiny caravan. The boys would crawl out of their beds in the striped canvas annexe, all yawns and morning hair, and slump on the floral-covered foam cushions surrounding the laminex table waiting for their juice and cereal. After his cup of tea James would go and start up the new orange bus that had arrived from Derby. Our boys were the first ones on board and then the bus cruised slowly through the community, stopping outside the houses where school-aged kids live. Sometimes, by the time James had done a full circuit of Imintji and turned north onto the Gibb River Road, the bus would be nearly full of sleepy children. They would stumble out of their houses, wrapped in blankets or carrying still-sleeping younger siblings. Other days, Oscar and Dylan were his only passengers.

The road had straight sections of smooth red dirt, stretches covered in uneven white rocks that made the bus shudder and shake, thousands of corrugations and steep creek crossings. It passed the turn-off to the station where we thought we would be working, wound up the ancient hills of the Phillips Range, down a sealed section to Adcock Gorge, went past Galvans Gorge where we had seen our first Wandjina, through one final river crossing and turned right into the community of Kupungarri at Mount Barnett. Sometimes there were cattle on the road – ghostly pale Brahmans, with their distinctive humps, that would amble slowly off to the side, and their skittish, gangly calves, which couldn't be trusted not to get spooked and run towards the bus. James knew every pothole, every sharp turn and every place where the smoothest ride could be found by steering the bus over to the far side of the road.

School started at eight o'clock and the drive took nearly an hour. James liked to get there early so that he could use the school's kitchen to heat up baked beans or throw together a big bowl of cereal for the kids who hadn't had a chance to eat breakfast. When the bell went and everyone disappeared into one of the three classrooms, he spent the rest of the day cleaning the bathrooms, vacuuming the rooms and gardening. The schoolyard was blessed with huge trees that gave plenty of welcome shade, but they constantly dropped their leaves. He'd rake and sweep, gather up the debris into a wheelbarrow, transfer load after load to the 44-gallon steel drum behind the school and then set it alight.

My day at Imintji started at seven o'clock in the shop, where I was back to being an assistant. Stan and Jenny had returned to work just ten days after the accident. I cleaned the toilets, helped Stan restock the shelves and fridge and freezer, loaded up the pie warmer and made rolls and sandwiches to sell during the day.

At half past seven every morning, Nev, the mechanic who ran the workshop next to the store, would ride past. Nev had been away when we arrived.

'Guess I'll meet him soon then', I'd said, the day that Kevin told me he was back.

At that exact moment, a quad bike rumbled past the store. A man who looked about James's age was riding it, and an old yellow dog sat majestically in a milk crate attached at the back. Nev was dressed in fading dusty shorts that came about halfway up his sturdy freckled thighs and an ancient blue singlet that hung off him like a butcher's apron. He waved a roll of toilet paper at me and grinned happily.

'Yeeeee-harrrrr!' he cried as he sailed past, on the way to the toilet block I had just cleaned and hosed out. Kevin was bent over beside me, giggling like a girl.

'Yep, that's Nev', he wheezed. 'Mornin' routine. Drives Jenny nuts.' He lost the power of speech, flapped a hand at me, got in his ute and drove off, still shaking his head and wiping his eyes.

Sometimes, as I waited for the first tourists to arrive, I'd make a cup of tea and sit on the wide wooden verandah of the store to enjoy the gentle warm air and the view. If a phone order came in from one of the outstations, I'd pack it up and get it ready to hand over to whoever was driving through to deliver it. I was taken aback the first time Stan showed me the envelopes that contained the keycards and PINs that we used to get payment for these orders, but we were careful to keep copies of all the orders and receipts and, although it relied on a huge amount of trust, the system seemed to work.

Most mornings, Jenny would cook up huge batches of homemade pies – kangaroo was the biggest seller – and bake cakes and slices in the kitchen of her house. Stan spent a lot of time organising the stock and working the diesel pump whenever a vehicle drove in. As the day warmed up, I served customers, chatted to the tourists about their trips, answered questions about the best places to visit, and made endless rounds of toasted sandwiches, coffees and milkshakes.

In the afternoon, Jenny and I would make up school lunches for the next day and then I'd take over from Stan on the fuel pump so he could start putting together that week's order for the store from the suppliers in Broome and Derby. That was my favourite job. It was hot and dusty out there, but I loved looking up at the escarpment behind the community and letting my mind soar into the distance. I felt alive and free and incredibly lucky to live somewhere so beautiful.

When we locked up at five o'clock, Jenny went back to her house to make dinner, Stan counted the day's takings, and I swept and mopped the floors in readiness for the next day. Most afternoons James and half of Imintji's kids would already be down at the local creek. Sometimes, if no-one could be bothered to walk, James would load them up on the roof of our car, six at a time, and drive slowly past the store, down the road and through the creek crossing while the kids shouted and waved at the tourists. We borrowed inflated inner tubes from Nev and floated in the warm, brown water amongst the water lilies, watching the older children swing off a fraying rope tied to an overhanging limb and splash into the water.

On my days off we drove to Bell Gorge and spent the day in the cool fresh water. Once we took a couple of the Imintji girls with us. At the top of the waterfall we started to cross the creek with our load of snacks, drinks, books and inflated inner tubes. One of the girls, Dellie, looked confused.

'Where you going?' she asked.

'Over here', James explained. 'So we can get down there', and he pointed to the pool below, where we planned to spend the day.

She laughed. 'Why this way? We can jump.'

Oscar's ears pricked up and he looked at her with awe.

'Can we?'

'Yeah. We do it all the time. We go from that ledge down there.' She pointed to a large flat ledge in the cliff wall, about two metres below the point where the water rushed over the edge and fell straight down. 'My brother, he jumps from right up the top. Runs straight past the tourists and just keeps going. They all scared for him. Sometimes they take photos.'

They did, too. We saw one months later at the Kununurra visitor centre. He had been snapped in mid-air, a gangly silhouette hanging above the waterfall. It was all I could do to stop myself unpinning it from the corkboard and stealing it.

Dylan and I walked down as usual, carrying the picnic, but James and Oscar jumped with Dellie that day and every single time afterwards.

As much as I loved the store and my job, it was soon obvious that Stan and Jenny had come back to work too soon. They were still suffering, not just from their injuries but also from shock. Stan had damaged his neck and he moved slowly and stiffly. One morning I watched his awkward gait as he walked along the short path from their house to the store and realised he looked much older than his years. Jenny had constant pain in her arm and shoulder, but the hospital had given her the all clear and told her the pain was purely in her head.

A bigger problem was that, while Jenny was processing what had happened to them by talking about it, Stan refused to discuss the accident. He just wanted to keep doing exactly what he had been doing before he had fallen out of a clear blue sky and landed on the red dirt in a pile of twisted metal. When the doorbell tinkled, he would go out and stand behind the counter and Jenny and I would hear him chat with the customers, just like he always had. He offered friendly advice and laughed with them about what a beautiful oasis he and Jenny had created 'all the way out here'. When he came back to the kitchen he would go silent again, turning his back stiffly on us to peck slowly at the computer's keyboard.

Only once did I see him falter behind the counter. Two women came in to look around the store while their husbands debated the price of diesel and decided whether or not to take their chances on fuel being cheaper at Mount Barnett. James checked the prices at Mount Barnett every day so Stan could set his a few cents lower, but if I tried to tell that to men like this their faces would close up and they would ignore me, convinced that I was trying to rip them off. As I waited behind Stan, one of the women came up to the counter and smiled knowingly at him, her dyed-too-bright red hair swinging.

'I heard you had a helicopter crash here', she said, a little too eagerly.

'Hmmmm', Stan murmured, looking down at the till.

'That must have been exciting!'

He turned around to reorganise the dusty souvenirs on the shelf behind him, which hadn't been touched once since my arrival, then mumbled something to me and walked out to the kitchen.

I glared at her. 'He was on that helicopter', I hissed.

The men outside gestured impatiently at the locked pump. I grabbed the key and shouted to Stan that I was going to do fuel. As Stan emerged reluctantly from the doorway, she trilled, 'I heard you all died!'

I wanted to go back in and punch her hard in the face.

As the weather improved and more and more tourists came in, another couple were hired to help out. They were closer in age and personality to Stan and Jenny and we often heard them laughing and drinking together in the evenings. Jenny seemed relaxed and happy around them, in a way she certainly wasn't with me. I wasn't too surprised when Stan knocked on the door of our caravan at six o'clock one morning and told me I wasn't needed anymore.

With lots of free time on my hands, I took to visiting Nev's workshop. I answered the phone and chatted to the people who drove in with blown tyres or disturbing rattles in their engine. Sometimes I just went over to escape the claustrophobic heat of the caravan and lie on his couch to read a book. One day he said that he hadn't done a tax return for years because he couldn't get his head around the paperwork. He gestured in the direction of six plastic tubs stuffed with receipts, bank statements, chequebook butts and a few girlie magazines. I spent the next three days sitting on the seagrass matting that covered his concrete floor, sorting documents and making lists of expenses and income while sweat dripped from my nose onto the papers.

Nev had lived at Imintji for years. He'd seen shopkeepers and people like us come and go. He'd learned to live with the land and the people, building up a viable business on the edge of the community and keeping pretty much to himself. When one of the families went into town and left behind a pregnant dog, Jenny asked him to help her break into the house to rescue the dog and her litter. Although he'd told me that in the wet season he sometimes had to shoot starving dogs that were roaming the community and becoming dangerous, he was reluctant to get involved.

'They always know', he explained to me. 'Dogs and cars. It's a connection they have. One bloke left his car with me when he went off to work on the mines. It was stuffed, so it just sat in the grass behind my place. Over the wet, the grass grew so high I couldn't even see it. Then one day a tourist car limped in. God knows what they thought they were doing on that road in the wet season. I didn't think I had the spare they needed, but I remembered the bloke's car was the same model. So I got the part off it, thinking I'd replace it the next time I was in town. Wasn't like the car was going anywhere. But you know, even though there wasn't anyone in the community, I did think twice about it. The very next day, the phone rang. It was the bloke calling from Kununurra. "You been stripping my car for parts, you bastard!"'

In July the Imintji community chartered the school bus to take them to Derby for the annual Boab Festival. On the way into town I got a running commentary from one of the men about the country we were driving through. He told me unlikely stories about clocks nailed to trees so that the stockmen would know what time it was and of plumbed taps in hidden gorges. I was used to being teased. There seemed to be nothing the Imintji mob enjoyed more than telling me unbelievable stories with perfectly straight faces, waiting for me to go along with it before cracking up in hysterics.

'Over there, between those hills, that's where they wanted to put this road. But we said no, you can't do that. What about the elephants, we said. We made them go round instead.'

I raised my eyebrows a little and sat up straighter, shifting the damp weight of the toddler who was asleep on my lap. 'What elephants?'

He threw his head back and laughed, delighted. 'Hey, you mob. Lorna here, she don't know the elephants!'

The laughter spread through the bus. People were turning in their seats, looking back at me and shaking their heads.

'You drive along here all the time and you never seen the elephants?' said one of the young women incredulously.

Someone tapped James on the shoulder and asked him to stop the bus. The young woman climbed out and waved at me to follow. I handed the toddler back to his mother and jumped down. We stood on the side of the road and she pointed to the rolling hills ahead. The road curved, taking a very wide detour around them. I could see why the engineers might have preferred to build the road in a straight line through a convenient gap between the hills right in front of us.

'See?' she asked. And suddenly I did. Two elephants in silhouette, each made up of two hills – one for the body and a smaller one for the head. Behind the larger elephant, on the other side of the gap, a smaller elephant was right on its tail.

'Be wrong to separate a baby from its mother', she said matter-of-factly, heading back into the cooler air of the bus.

Every few weeks, nodding a greeting to the elephants, I drove into Derby to shop. The Snack Stop on the Lennard River, where we had stopped for ice-cream the year before, was halfway between Imintji and Derby. We had introduced ourselves to Robert, who had teased us the year before about the male croc, and I always stopped to have a cup of tea and see if he needed anything in town. Often he did, so on the way back I'd off-load cartons of soft drink or bags of groceries.

One day Robert spoke longingly about a girl who used to help him at the store. 'Lovely girl. She used to come and mind the van for me. Sometimes I need to go into Derby, but I can't leave the place empty.' He looked at me.

'Just ring me, Robert. Any time.'

A few days later he did, his scratchy voice barking over the sat phone. 'Next Tuesday?'

I took Dylan to keep me company and we got to Robert's before eight in the morning. He showed us around the van and gave us our instructions. 'Help yourself to whatever you want, make sure no-one steals anything and don't drink all my beer.'

Not long after he left, a truck pulled up and three young men climbed out and asked for coffee, Coke and pies. Dylan handled the cold drinks and took the money, counting the coins out carefully and checking with me that he had it right. He took the job as seriously as only a seven-year-old could. I dealt with the hot drinks. On the bench beside the kettle was an old tea strainer that Robert had said was to catch stray frogs that might have climbed into the kettle overnight. I was pretty sure he was joking, but I did it anyway, pouring the boiling water carefully through the brown mesh, looking for intruders.

It wasn't even nine o'clock but it was already hot. After breakfast, the men walked down to the muddy waterhole that was all that was left of the river and jumped in for a swim. Dylan went with them and I sat and drank my tea and watched him. Just a year and a half ago he had been a city kid and now he was splashing about in murky brown water with three big Aboriginal blokes. And he also seemed to have completely forgotten that he had seen crocodiles in this river.

In the end, not many people came in. It was September, late in the season, and getting too hot and humid for tourists. When Robert got back, he showed us a tattered book in which he wrote down all the questions that tourists asked him. Dylan read some out loud and Robert crowed his standard responses.

'Do you live here?'

'No, I fly in by helicopter every day from Derby.'

'Do the crocodiles have their babies here?'

'No, there's a special maternity ward for them at the hospital in Broome.'

'Where do you sleep?'

'In the five-star hotel over that hill.'

He actually slept on a stretcher bed beside the caravan: outside, under the stars, unperturbed by mosquitoes or moths or snakes or bugs. He had a colourful crocheted blanket that was tucked in tightly over the mattress. His old dog slept by his side.

'Don't you get lonely?'

'No, because you buggers keep coming in and asking me stupid bloody questions!'

'Why did you put the sticks up there?'

The three of us looked up at the brittle grey twigs lodged in the tropical roof above the van. In a month or two, the rain would start falling and the Lennard River would flow. At its peak, the river rushes through the Napier Range into Windjana Gorge where it has carved out a path that is 100 metres wide with cliffs up to 30 metres high. The water would rise up the bank to flood the spot where we were sitting and keep rising until the roof above us was submerged. The sticks were from last year's wet season: floating debris caught in the corners of the metal roof as the water retreated and reminders that this was a transient, seasonal place.

'Why do you live out here?'

He just looked at me. I knew the answer to that one now.

On our way home, we drove past the surreal black rock formation of Queen Victoria Head, where the road cuts through the Napier Range and creates a perfect silhouette of an imperious face with a truly regal nose pointing up to the sky. From here, the road struggled up steep hills and down through dry creek beds. Whenever the car rounded the high bends, the world dropped down below us and I could see for miles. I had to drag my eyes from the view and concentrate on keeping the car on the road. Most of the track was rocky and corrugated, except where it was sealed at river crossings and the steepest jump-ups. The whole way home, I could hear the shopping Robert had picked up for me crashing around in the back.

Every time I drove that road my heart thumped hard in my chest as the car veered unexpectedly on a patch of loose gravel or thudded into a pothole. But tears always clogged my throat when I got to the lookout at the top of the King Leopold Ranges and looked down at the country I was lucky enough to live in.

One night we went up to the lookout with Nev to watch the sun set over the escarpment behind Imintji. Bushfires were burning in the national park below us and, as it grew darker, the line of fire shone brightly. On the top of the range, I could make out a dark crimson glow. I watched as it grew brighter, wondering if this was another fire that we should be worried about, when a huge red orb suddenly glided over the escarpment. I gasped. It was massive and terrifying and beautiful.

'Now there's a Kimberley moon', said Nev.

Chapter Eighteen

The dry season was retreating and it was getting hotter and more humid every day. The swimming hole at the creek was warm and sluggish and was becoming less and less inviting. We'd already seen the first snake of the season and I was getting worried about the boys. They were still sleeping in the caravan's rotting canvas annexe and woke up most mornings with new mosquito bites on their faces and necks.

Most of the families had gone into town for a funeral and weeks later none of them had returned. Oscar and Dylan were banned from wandering around the community without an adult – the stray dogs were becoming more and more aggressive – and they were getting bored and grumpy. Bell Gorge was about to close for the wet season and the novelty of living on the Gibb was wearing thin.

The problem was that a few months earlier James and I had decided that we weren't going home at the end of this second year of our trip. We still couldn't think of a good reason to go back, and we had also really wanted to experience a Kimberley wet season. But now I couldn't imagine spending the next six months in this caravan. There had already been one big dump of rain and it had poured in the roof and into the domed plastic light fittings, filling them with rusty water. I had no idea how we would get through months of torrential rain and oppressive heat with only a tiny van for all four of us to hide in. The temperature was regularly hitting 40°C and humidity was up around 90 per cent.

When the September school holidays arrived we bolted for Broome, relieved to have a fortnight's break from the increasingly claustrophobic atmosphere of Imintji. We were looking forward to swimming at Cable Beach and visiting our Scottish friends, Linda and Andy. Broome was also a chance to shop for new clothes and books – maybe even go to a restaurant and see a movie or two. We'd been away from Melbourne for more than 18 months and, although we'd booked flights to go back home for Christmas, we were in desperate need of some creature comforts and friendly faces.

First, though, we decided to spend a few days camping at Middle Lagoon again, and also have a look at Cape Leveque. We planned our drive up the Dampier Peninsula on a weekday this time so that we could drop into Lombadina. Twelve kilometres from the tip of the peninsula we turned left off the main road and followed the signs into the community. After paying the $10 visitor fee at the office we parked the car and went exploring on foot. The community's main buildings – a cool, open-sided church with a paperbark roof, an elevated building that was used as a workshop and craft store, a garage and workshop, a health clinic, an old bakery, a tiny store and a primary school – sat around a neatly mown oval that was dotted with trees. Picnic benches sat outside the store in the shade of a large gum tree, and a concrete basketball court was cracking in the bright sunlight. As we wandered around, I thought it looked a bit like an outback version of a traditional English village green.

Lombadina was set up in the early 1900s as an outpost of the larger Catholic mission at Beagle Bay, 60 kilometres south. The Sisters of St John of God ran the mission and its school until 1968 and the church was built from local materials in 1932. Lombadina and its close neighbour, Djarindjin, are now both self-governing and independent communities. The school, church, cemetery and health centres are shared resources. Lombadina is often held up as an example of an Indigenous community that has built up a successful and sustainable industry around cultural tourism. Visitors can stay in cabins and go on tours with local community members – mud-crabbing, kayaking, fishing and whale watching – learn about the history and culture of the country, eat bush tucker or take a drive to see ancient fossilised human footprints preserved in the nearby rocks.

In the store, as I was paying for a huge freshly baked loaf of crusty white bread, still warm in its white paper bag, I saw a note stuck on the door. 'Wanted: A couple to run the store and do general maintenance work. Accommodation supplied. Apply at the office.'

We took our bread and drove along a track over the sand dunes to the beach. Dunes lined the 8-kilometre length of the gently curved bay. Red cliffs in the distance gave way to white sand that slid into clear turquoise water. Apart from a few vehicle tracks and one tiny shelter made of timber and topped with palm fronds, there was no sign of anyone else. We sat on the sand, ripped the fresh bread apart with our hands and washed it down with warm cordial from the car. When the boys went for a swim, James and I stood on the beach and kept an eye out for crocodiles. The woman in the shop had said it was rare to see them in the bay and the glimpse we caught of something dark moving in the waves turned out to be a huge sea turtle. The boys ran in and out of the small waves, splashing and shouting.

'Did you see the job ad in the shop?' I asked James. He nodded slowly, still gazing out to sea.

Ten minutes later we were knocking on the door of the office.

The jobs came with a house. Caroline Sibosado, a stern Aboriginal woman in her sixties who was obviously the boss, offered to show it to us. She walked with us along the red sandy track behind the store to a yellow house beside the cemetery. From the outside, it looked like a tin shed but inside there was a kitchen, a bathroom and three bedrooms. It was fully furnished. It even had an air conditioner and a television.

It seemed rash to apply for the jobs on the spot, so we said we'd think about it and call in a day or two. Caroline walked us back to the office where she fished out an old business card and handed it over without another word.

Back at Middle Lagoon we talked about nothing else all night. I had no qualms at all and the boys were ecstatic. 'We could see the school from the kitchen', Dylan said. 'We could be there in about half a second.'

Oscar had his sights on something else. 'We can have our own rooms.'

James agonised over the decision. He felt a huge responsibility to the community of Imintji and the Wananami school. But most of the Imintji families had left and weren't expected back until the next dry season, which was still six months away. I had no job and no real role to play apart from covering books in the school library.

The next morning I rang the Lombadina office and asked to speak to Caroline.

'Mum's not here. She's gone to town.'

Suddenly terrified that we might miss out, I gabbled something about having been in the day before and the jobs and looking at the house and really wanting to apply.

'Oh, yeah, she mentioned you. When do you want to start?'

We moved all our stuff into the yellow house a week later.

James surprised the boys when we arrived with a secret purchase he had made in Broome. They were ecstatic about the PlayStation, but they didn't want to play with it right away. Instead, they each went into their own separate room, closed the doors and didn't come out for hours.

Life at Lombadina had a new, more relaxed, routine. The boys now left home just before eight o'clock, walking in bare feet across the cemetery to the school. James and I wandered down to the office where I collected the shop keys and he hung around waiting for someone to decide what he had to do that day.

The office was the heart of the community and Lombadina, we had been told, was the jewel in the crown of the Indigenous communities in the Kimberley. When people found out that we lived there, they wanted to know what made it so different. As far as we could tell, the secret ingredient was the Sibosado family.

Caroline and her husband, Basil, had set up one of the first Indigenous tourism ventures on the Dampier Peninsula. Their aim was self-sufficiency, and no-one was allowed to live in Lombadina if they didn't work. Their sons and daughters-in-law ran the office, the workshop, the tourism business and the employment office, and had road maintenance contracts with the local shire. They had just built a new conference centre and there were plans to grow commercial crops of a local fruit, gubinge, which has the world's highest known concentrations of vitamin C.

We weren't the only non-Indigenous people working at Lombadina – two older couples cleaned the tourist accommodation, and the current baker was a white-haired man who barely spoke a word to me for weeks. But everyone else was related to the Sibosado family.

By the time I opened the store, it was usually about a quarter past eight. In the morning, most of the customers were people who had driven from other communities or bush camps to visit the clinic. Sometimes there would be a few people sitting on the old metal school chairs outside but, unless they were tourists, no-one ever minded that I was late. We were all on Kimberley time.

After an initial flurry of purchases of iced coffee and smokes, the shop would be empty again. I filled the rusty pie warmer with pies and sausage rolls, turning it up to make sure the food was ready for smoko, then put on a thick jumper to go into the fridge to restock the drinks.

Three times a week, the baker stoked up the wood-fired oven next door and brought in trays of warm loaves in white paper bags. The loaves were huge, with crusts that varied from pale yellow to charcoal, and so soft that it was impossible to slice them neatly. Everyone in the community had a regular order and sometimes tourists who had worked out the system would ring and order the day before. I wrote names on the bags and then worked out how many were left to sell. On my first day, I had been told that the most important parts of my job were to make sure that everyone in the community got their bread and that the shop never ran out of Coke or Winfield Blue cigarettes.

One of the local women, Audrey, helped me in the store. Every day she came to work in one of a collection of baseball caps that she wore to keep her long grey hair out of her failing eyes. She had been waiting for over two years for an operation to remove the cataracts and she had to peer closely at the labels on the tins she was stacking to see what they held.

At first, when Audrey and I sat together outside the store, I would fill the space between us with small talk, irrelevant chatter and intrusive questions. Audrey just looked past me, into the distance. If I pressed her for a response she would mumble, 'Don't know 'bout that', before moving away. When it finally dawned on me that Audrey never answered any of my questions, I stopped asking. Slowly, I learned to let a thought float through my mind without having to speak it out loud.

One afternoon a battered, red Volvo pulled up outside the store. A young man came in and after I served him I wandered outside. Bruce Wiggan, the man with the cowboy hat and plaits whom we had met at Ardyaloon the year before, was sitting next to Audrey.

'You the new shop lady?' he asked.

'Yep.' I sat beside him. 'We've met before, actually. Last year.'

He looked me up and down and smiled. 'I remember you. I always remember the pretty ladies!'

I tried to catch Audrey's eye but she ignored me.

'I was with my husband and my kids. You said you'd dreamed about us. Before you met us.'

His grin grew wider. 'I still dreaming you! I dreamed about you last night. You and me. That was one nice dream!'

I shook my head, but I couldn't help smiling. I knew he was teasing me, but a part of me also really believed that he had dreamed us. I didn't think it was a coincidence that I was back here meeting Bruce again. I had also finally met Roma from Chile Creek. She had come into the shop to introduce herself and make sure I knew about her bread order. I still had that Chile Creek brochure, now torn and dirty, tucked into one of my books of maps. Every time I looked at it I remembered picking it up at Iga Warta, just over a year and a half ago.

'Come over anytime', Roma had said and, weirdly, that invitation also felt inevitable.

Despite being a lifelong atheist and sceptic, I had lately accepted – quite easily – many more inexplicable events than I would have believed possible. I had mentioned to Nev once that we had been in places where I had felt incredibly uncomfortable and unwelcome. In Cape York, we had camped on a beautiful beach lined with coconut palms with crystal clear water and white sand. I hated it. I was on edge the whole time and I couldn't eat or sleep for the three

nights we were there. James and the boys couldn't understand what
my problem was.

'Probably men's country', said Nev in such a matter-of-fact way
that it immediately made perfect sense to me.

At Lombadina, we had been told which areas we shouldn't go
near. I had also been warned about nearby law grounds and told that
the boys shouldn't play there. Before we left Melbourne, I would have
agreed that there were some places that had great cultural significance
and had to be respected, but now I took these warnings as seriously as
if I had been told not to let the boys run out onto a six-lane highway.

Oscar and Dylan were having their own cultural learning expe-
riences over at the school. Towards the end of our first week in
Lombadina, one of the Aboriginal teacher aides came into the store.
She leaned towards me as I worked out the cost of her purchases.

'Where you lot from?' she asked.

'Down south. Melbourne.'

She paused. 'So where've you been then?'

'At Imintji, on the Gibb. We were there for six months.'

She smiled triumphantly. 'I knew it! The minute I met them I
said to myself, those little white boys, they been around Aboriginal
people a lot.'

I was a bit embarrassed. 'It was the Kriol, wasn't it?'

A few months earlier I had been helping out in the library of the
Wananami school, where the shelves were labelled both in English
and the local dialect, Kriol, and the fiction collection was called 'Liar
Stories'. I thought I heard Dylan speaking in the lilting rhythm of the
local kids so I went outside to check it was him. Standing beside the
principal on the wide shaded verandah, I had cringed a little. 'He's
picked the accent up pretty quickly', I said apologetically.

Gary glanced at me with his usual serious look. 'It's a good thing.
It means he's settling in. Some white kids never do that; they hold
back, don't get involved.'

At Lombadina, where they weren't the only non-Indigenous
children, Oscar and Dylan's Kriol disappeared pretty quickly, although

I often heard Dylan using it as he played outside our house. He never spoke it with the Sibosado kids, though. They all spoke the Standard Australian English that was taught as a second language at school.

The boys also had to come to terms with the religion that was woven through the entire curriculum. James and I weren't at all religious but this was a Catholic school and the teachers took their role as religious educators very seriously. In art, the kids drew pictures of Jesus; in music, they sang hymns and learned the art of liturgical dance. Word searches asked them to find 'prayer' and 'worship' and the concept of area was taught by getting them to write 'Jesus loves me' in block letters on graph paper and counting the number of squares inside the letters. For the most part our kids ignored it, but one afternoon Oscar had a few questions.

'So, did you learn any Jesus stuff today?' I had asked him over lunch. The community shut down every day from eleven until one o'clock, so we had made that our main meal and ate together at the yellow house.

'Yes, Jesus washed the feet of the twelve apostles. He did it because … ummm …'

'To show them he wasn't better than them?' I suggested.

'Yes, that's it. What's an apostle?'

I struggled to get my definition right. 'Someone who followed Jesus, who believed in what he was saying.'

'So they were his friends?'

'Yes, I guess so.'

'Okay.' He paused, his forehead furrowed. 'So … why did he turn them into rocks then?'

He was thinking of the Twelve Apostles formations on the Great Ocean Road in Victoria. I had to pick James up off the floor, at the same time assuring Oscar that his dad wasn't *really* laughing at him.

The busiest days in the shop were 'doctor days', when a doctor flew in from Derby to spend the day in the clinic. The nurses handled most of the medical issues the rest of the time, so it was them whom James went to when he developed a weeping, raised welt on his collarbone that refused to heal. He came into the store an hour later, pale and clammy, with a huge white bandage stuck to his chest.

'She cut it open with a scalpel. She said it's a boil.'

A few weeks later, Dylan complained of a sore knee. All we could see was a tiny red mark but James took him to the clinic anyway. Janice was the nurse on duty that day, and she sent them immediately up to Ardyaloon, where the doctor was running a clinic. Dylan had a boil deep under the skin that was dangerously close to his knee cap. If it couldn't be treated with antibiotics and drawing cream he would have to go to Broome to have it opened surgically.

Boils, usually caused by infections in the hair follicle, were apparently very common in the Kimberley. The humidity made it hard to keep your skin clean and dry, and naturally occurring bacteria could easily find its way down the hair shaft and start causing trouble. More worryingly, enthusiastic treatment of skin infections with antibiotics in the 1980s meant that many Indigenous communities were now home to antibiotic-resistant strains of the bacteria. The recommended treatment now involved lancing and draining the boil. One doctor also told me that, particularly for fair-skinned people, it was possible that increased exposure to sunlight lowered the immune system and made you more susceptible to infections.

The ointment they gave us for Dylan looked like Vegemite and smelled worse. Over the next few days we smeared it on his knee and watched in amazement as a big red lump came up and formed a head, like a huge pimple. It finally burst, spewing out an astonishing amount of foul-smelling yellow pus and blood.

When a painful red lump came up on the side of my knee, I was ready for it. For a week I covered it in the black ointment and tried to draw it out with heat packs, but it got bigger and angrier until I had to give in and go to the clinic. Janice examined it and then asked the other nurse to come in and take a look. They prodded and pushed at it, ignoring my pitiful yelps.

'I think it's compacted', said Janice.

'What does that mean?' I asked.

'It means the head's not going to come up on its own and you're going to have to get it cut out', said the other nurse, with just a hint of glee.

'Here? Now?' I asked, horrified.

'No, I'm not touching that one', said Janice. The other nurse looked a little disappointed. 'You'll have to see the doctor. He'll be here tomorrow.'

The next day the doctor said, 'That's a good one. I could try and give you antibiotics, but the thing with boils is that they're basically a big ball of infection. The antibiotics can't get in and do their stuff. Really, the only way is to cut it out. I have to warn you, though, the local anaesthetic doesn't work. The stuff inside the boil kind of neutralises it. I might be able to give you some pethidine, if that would help.'

'I've never seen anything like it', said James an hour later, after I had entertained the entire clinic, staff and patients alike, with pethidine-fuelled ravings. He had watched the whole procedure with voyeuristic fascination. 'He scooped all this pus out with a thing that looked just like a teaspoon. And now there's a hole in your leg. He put his little finger in to get the last of the pus out and it went in all the way to the second knuckle.'

That weekend, as I lay on the couch with a huge bandage on my leg and a package of codeine by my side, James and the boys built a tree house. It took all of Saturday and most of Sunday but, with the help of a small group of fascinated kids, it was finally finished.

One of the boys' friends was a bit wary. 'Lorna, I don't think this is really very safe.'

'It's a tree house, Sebastian, it's not supposed to be safe.'

It was actually very safe. After securing the platform with solid beams of wood that he bolted to large branches, James had made handrails around all the sides. To get to it, the kids climbed up a series of solid planks of wood, which were securely nailed to the sloping trunk of the tree to form steps. James and Dylan returned the unused wood to the tip and came back with a discarded tyre that made a perfect swing.

The boys and their friends spent hours devising lists of the people who would be allowed in the cubby. As more kids came to look, the rules for membership were loosened until it was declared that all the Lombadina kids had open access – even the girls.

That was Sunday. On Monday afternoon, one of the Lombadina kids raced into the shop.

'Dylan fell out of the tree!'

I rang the office and asked them to find James, locked the shop and started running towards the house. It was hot and the track was covered in deep sand, making it impossible to run fast, and when I heard a high-pitched scream I felt as if I was living out my worst nightmare. James had made it there before me and had already picked Dylan up off the ground and put him in the car. He stopped to pick me up on the way to the clinic. As I jumped into the car, I caught a glimpse of Dylan's arm cradled in his lap and I had to work hard to stop myself from turning away from him.

At the clinic we got a good look at what he'd done. His arm was broken in at least two places. It was shaped like an 'S'.

'That's definitely a trip to Derby', said Janice.

She put a needle into one of Dylan's tiny veins and pumped morphine and fluids into him. The other nurse put a temporary slab of plaster under his broken arm and got him ready for the Royal Flying Doctor evacuation. At five o'clock, Dylan and I were at the airstrip and by six o'clock we were in Derby Hospital.

I had already been told there was no surgeon in Derby or Broome that day. The nurse said that the doctor would probably try to align the bones by manipulation. The X-ray process was horribly painful. I told Dylan he was allowed to say the worst words he knew if it made him feel better, but he wouldn't do it. When the doctor went behind the screen to look at the result, he said some of those words for him. Dylan had broken both bones completely off his wrist and also snapped the end of one of them. The loose bone was floating around at right angles to the others. All the doctor could do was straighten the bones as much as possible to prevent damage to his nerves and muscles and relieve his pain.

The next morning we were sent to Perth with 11 milligrams of Panadol and codeine in a syringe, an envelope of X-rays, the address of the hospital and a taxi voucher. Six hours later, we arrived at Princess Margaret Hospital. When they tried to put us at the back of the triage queue, I lost my temper and demanded to see a doctor. By five o'clock, a team of orthopaedic surgeons had put all of his bones back in the right place, without surgery.

A few days later, the doctors said we could go back to Lombadina. It was James's birthday, but I couldn't call him to tell him the good news. Six houses, including our yellow house, had been cut off when a builder had put a shovel through a Telstra cable and James had been calling us from the public phone box three times a day.

'We'll be home tomorrow', I promised Dylan.

The next day, the doctors on their morning rounds asked what time our flight was. I hadn't been told yet, so I asked the ward clerk. She didn't have any paperwork for us. 'It's up to the patient repatriation scheme in Derby. But it definitely won't be today.'

Dylan started crying. I asked if I could call them.

'There is absolutely no point in that. Parents have tried that before and it makes no difference. You just have to wait.'

She really shouldn't have said that. I rang James and got him onto it. Within an hour he had found out that Derby had referred our case to Broome, but no-one in the Broome office had ever heard of us. He did the 'outraged parent' routine and within half an hour, and despite still having no paperwork, we were booked on the afternoon flight. I wondered what happened to families from remote communities who weren't so confident about taking on the bureaucracy.

I called Linda from Perth Airport and asked if we could stay with them in Broome that night. She was happy to help, promising to pick us up from the airport and have ice-cream, chocolate and lollies on hand for Dylan. He was pleased, but not sure why he was getting so much junk food. I told him that the Scottish tradition of plying children with sugar became compulsory if they were sick. As the plane headed towards the runway, the lady next to us leaned over and offered us her open packet of Columbines.

'Wid ye like a sweetie for take-off, hen?'

Chapter Nineteen

At Christmas we flew home to Melbourne. The Canadians had gone home and we had managed to rent our house out again from February, so we just moved back in while it was empty. We wandered around Fitzroy and bumped into friends and neighbours who were surprised to see us, and then confused when we said we were only home for a month. We stretched out on our couches and watched television. We shopped at the Queen Victoria Market and were stunned at how fresh and cheap everything was.

Soon I couldn't remember why we had decided to go back to Lombadina for another year. I watched the boys as they played with their old friends, learned to ride their new ripsticks around the streets and celebrated their eighth and tenth birthdays in the first week of January with a joint slumber party where no-one went to sleep until the small hours of the morning. I wanted to stay. Life was easy, our friends were happy to see us, the boys could go to school with teachers who weren't overwhelmed by low literacy levels and erratic attendance, I could get back to doing work I was good at and that my clients appreciated and we could just be *normal* again.

James, on the other hand, couldn't wait to leave again. 'It's all so … fake', he said, trying to explain how he felt. What I saw as 'easy', he saw as a manufactured, consumerist lifestyle. 'All we do is *shop*.' And it was true. We were back to being the kind of people who couldn't walk out of our front door without spending $50, except now it was $50 that we really didn't have to spare. And three $50s wouldn't even buy you a thin cardigan from the shop on the corner of our street.

I argued with him for a while, trying to convince him that we could somehow cancel the tenants, retrieve our car and the camper trailer and drive from Broome to Melbourne in time for the school year to start but, even as I spoke, I knew we weren't going to do that. I retreated into a dark place in my mind and refused to talk to him for days on end as I grieved for my city life and wondered if we were making a terrible mistake.

Far too quickly we were back at Lombadina. It was early February and the wet season was meant to be in its final weeks but it was still incredibly hot and humid. On our first day back, Janice took one look at my tear-stained face and gave me a hug, a bottle of multivitamins and a box of antibacterial soap to ward off boils. During our short absence, the yellow house seemed to have shrunk and become horribly filthy and shabby. I spent two days scrubbing the floors, the corrugated iron walls and the kitchen cupboards. I was so determined to clean every inch that I gave myself a mild electric shock by wiping the power points with a wet cloth.

As the humidity retreated, the tourists started to arrive. Lombadina had no camping facilities, so we didn't see many camper trailers or caravans. Families, especially, tended to just drop in for the day to buy fresh bread and ice-creams and hang out at the beach before driving back to their campsites.

Some people, usually older couples, stayed in the accommodation for a few days and went on kayaking and mud-crabbing tours with Robert, Caroline's son. They often liked to chat and after a day or two we would get to know them and invite them to join us for a Friday night campfire on the beach at sunset.

The majority of the tourists came on day trips from Broome. They got on a bus early in the morning, bounced along for 100 kilometres to Beagle Bay, where they got out to look at the church, climbed back on the bus for another 100 kilometres to Ardyaloon, where they got out to look at the trochus hatchery, got back on the bus to have lunch and a swim at Cape Leveque, then boarded it again to visit Lombadina. I was never sure if it was because they were exhausted from their day, or if they were made like this, but they were almost without exception completely devoid of the ability to engage or communicate.

'Hi!' I would call out. 'Does anyone want an ice-cream or a cold drink? We've got fresh bread too. Only three dollars!'

They would glance at me and wander past in their group, listening to their guide telling them about the history of Lombadina, then pile back on the bus to go back to Broome.

Tourists weren't the only people who were easy to classify. Someone had told us that there were four kinds of white people who choose to live in Indigenous communities: mercenaries, missionaries, misfits and malingerers. James and I decided we definitely weren't missionaries, except for a short period at Imintji when we lobbied Stan and Jenny to make cheap school lunches for the kids. We didn't consider ourselves to be mercenaries either, unless a desire for experience could be interpreted that way. We were undoubtedly malingering, though. Every day, we spent the first hour of our two-hour lunch break at the beach, lying semi-naked on the hot sand and jumping in to cool down when we got too sweaty. And I had to admit to a fair proportion of misfit too. I was losing the ability to chat to the tourists. It wasn't them who had changed: I just couldn't be bothered. I was starting to sympathise with Robert at Lennard River and his book of stupid questions. I had compiled my own list in my head.

'How long have you been here?'

'How many people live here?'

'Do you live in the community?' This one always confused me. Did they think I commuted 400 kilometres a day from Broome?

'Why is it so nice here?' The unspoken part of the question was: '… compared to other communities we have seen.'

'Why are *you* working here?' In other words, 'Why is there a white person working in the shop?'

'Where is the church/craft shop/beach/toilet/fuel/bakery?' All were clearly marked on the map they were given at the office. If they didn't have a map, it meant they had driven in without registering, and I wasn't going to help them out with directions.

'Is the beach nice?' Once, this was followed by '… because the beach at Cape Leveque is pretty ordinary.' This was a family from

Sydney who were making their way around the entire country, apparently determined to be unimpressed by any of it.

'Do I really have to drop my tyres to get to the beach?' James and I regularly helped people who were bogged in the soft sand because they had ignored the signs and not reduced their tyre pressure.

'Are the people here nice?' I was once asked this when the shop was full of community members patiently waiting their turn in the queue.

'Yes', I had replied. 'Except for Alphonse over there who is a bit of a mongrel.'

'Do you sell beer?' No, we didn't. Not all of the communities on the Dampier Peninsula were officially dry, but there was nowhere to legally buy takeaway alcohol north of Broome.

'Is there anywhere I can buy beer?' No.

'Can I get takeaway beer from the restaurant at Cape Leveque?' NO!

Sometimes I helped out in the office, where there was always someone who got annoyed at having to pay a $10 fee for access to the community and the beach.

'I think that's ridiculous', she – it always seemed to be a woman – would say. 'It's not like you have to pay to come and drive down my street.'

'Fair enough', I wanted to answer. 'But your street is maintained by your council. You don't have to keep the roads graded so that residents can get around and the supply truck can get in to deliver food. And you probably don't have tourists refusing to let their tyres down when they drive on the road to the beach, which trashes the track and means the next lot of tourists get bogged and have to get towed back out and then you have to grade it again. And I'm guessing that your street is pretty much the same as thousands of other streets in the country and *you* are the one who just drove for two hours from Broome to visit this community.'

One afternoon a couple arrived in a shiny black Hummer. They had rung a few days earlier and paid a deposit for three nights in one of the two new motel-style units. When they checked in and took the key, the woman said she would pay the balance after they had looked at the accommodation. Caroline apparently knew what was coming, because she rolled her eyes and retreated to the very back of the office. The woman came back in with a sad look on her face.

'I'm sorry. I really don't think we can stay there.'

'What's wrong?' I asked, reaching for the phone to check if the unit had been cleaned.

'Well, dear, it doesn't even have a TV!'

I managed not to laugh. 'Most people come here for the outdoor stuff. It is kind of remote.'

'But what do you expect us to do at night? Sit and look at each other?'

'Play cards?' I suggested. She glared at me.

Caroline was still pretending to be deaf so I rang her daughter-in-law for help.

'Tell them to get fucked.'

I translated: 'I'm sorry but we are fully booked this week and I can't refund your deposit.'

They left to drive the Hummer all the way back to Broome. When Robert came in I told him what had just happened.

'Why didn't you put them in the other unit?' he asked. I looked at him, confused. 'You know, the one that has the telly.'

One Saturday afternoon, Oscar's best friend, Jumat, knocked on the door. He was carrying a paper plate loaded with big chunks of dark-red barbecued meat.

'Dad thought you might like to try some dugong.'

'What does it taste like?' said Dylan warily.

'Pretty much like beef.'

It did too, although after chewing on a rubbery slab of pale green fat for a while I had to admit defeat and drop it in the bin. Jumat didn't seem to mind. He didn't eat the fat either. Later, Jumat's father gave

Oscar and Dylan the dugong's tusks. They were yellow and stained, with small cracks running along their curved length, but we wrapped them up and put them away safely to take home with us.

Dugong wasn't the first endangered animal we had eaten. A few weeks earlier, we had been invited to a ceremony on the beach. As part of the celebration, the Bardi rangers had caught and cooked two sea turtles, upside down and still in their shells. There was a lot of shuffling feet and shaking heads as the turtles baked. There was a difference of opinion between the communities on the Dampier Peninsula about how to cook turtle. In Djarindjin, they really liked the green fat that sits in a thick layer between the meat and the shell, but the Bardi mob preferred their turtle well-done. People were standing around fuming as the turtles were cooked … and cooked … and cooked. A perfectly good turtle had been charred to a crisp. There wasn't a piece of green fat to be seen anywhere.

A fortnight later it was the July school holidays and we'd decided to visit Nev. As we drove up the Gibb back towards Imintji, we realised we looked exactly like regular tourists. We had the camper trailer, the kids in the back with their faces stuck in books, and Victorian number plates on the car. We agreed not to tell people how long we had been away from home – we didn't want to sound like show-offs – but we only lasted an average of three minutes before one of us said something like 'We left Melbourne two years ago' or 'We live at Lombadina'.

We camped behind Nev's workshop at Imintji, caught up with friends, climbed to the top of the escarpment and spent a glorious day back at Bell Gorge, our favourite spot in the world. One afternoon Nev took us to one of his favourite places. We drove behind him, off the Gibb River Road, over a wire fence and along a narrow track to a huge waterhole that dropped down at the end of a stretch of flat, red rock. A sandy beach sloped gently into the clear, green water. The boys gathered wood and Nev built a fire in the sand and scooped water from the river in his billy to make tea. On the other side of the pool, the rock folded and curved around the water. We swam across to explore the ledges and caves and Nev showed us where figures had been carved into the rock wall.

'It's a men's place', he said. 'The elders used to bring the young fellas here and teach them the old stories.' He looked at me. 'You shouldn't really be here, but we won't stay long.'

For the next few hours we swam, lay on the hot sand and chewed on beef ribs that Nev cooked on the coals. For most of the day, the sky was the usual bright blue of the dry season. Wisps of cloud floated above us. As the sun began its downward arc, the clouds became puffy and more solid, like balls of cotton wool. A few of them joined up and started to look quite substantial. Within an hour, there were definitely more.

'Do you think it's going to rain?' I asked Nev.

'Dunno. Pretty unusual for this time of year. We should think about getting back, though. Don't want to get caught out if it does.'

As we packed up the debris of our lazy day, a large cloud formed above us.

'Oh, yeah', said Nev. 'Time to go. We've pissed the spirits off. Look at that!'

I looked up just in time to see the distinctive face of a Wandjina forming in the cloud towering over the waterhole. More puffs of white scudded across the sky and joined up with it.

'Never seen one that good before', said Nev.

Back on the main road a few heavy drops of rain fell, bouncing on the red dirt in front of us and throwing up dust before sinking into the track and disappearing. By the time we were back at Imintji the sky was clear again.

When we got back to Lombadina, the humpback whales had arrived on their annual migration. We had spotted a few on the horizon from the beach, but I was desperate to get out in a boat and see them up close. I dropped hints for weeks until Robert said he'd take us out on the boat. He wanted to go fishing, but we could have a look for whales first.

Before the boat had even reached the reef we could see them. One humpback was jumping, splashing and spouting as if it was inviting us to come and play, and a group of three whales was further to sea. Robert cruised slowly towards the group, saying that if we approached slowly they were less likely to swim off. As we got closer, they moved towards us. Soon they were so close that we could see them clearly under the water.

I raced around the boat to see them better. Robert directed me from the cabin. 'They're out the front now! Over there, there they are! Just to the left, look, they're about to come up!'

Up they came. One, two, three massive whales, blowing and splashing, rolling over and waving a fin in the air then sinking under the surface like synchronised swimmers. I tried to take photos but when I was looking through the lens I got confused about where they were. When I looked up from the camera, it was like a slap in the face. There was one right in front of me. I looked straight into a massive eye that was most definitely looking right back at me.

After 10 frenzied minutes of doing battle with my camera the whales submerged and didn't reappear. 'I reckon that's it', Robert said, getting ready to move on to a good fishing spot.

I slumped down, exhausted and exhilarated. Suddenly, just metres from where I was sitting, two whales rose up and blasted water, snot and foul-smelling air straight at us. I put my camera down and watched from the side of the boat. And, as if they had been waiting for my full attention, the real show started. They flashed their white bellies; they swam under the boat and popped up again on the other side; they pretended to leave and then dived, turned, and emerged from the water heading right towards us. Eventually they lined up beside the boat and flipped their tails in unison. When they left, they just melted into the water, blowing a couple of times from a distance as they headed back out to sea.

At the end of July, Oscar went back to Melbourne with five other boys from the Lombadina school. The teachers put together bags of warm second-hand clothes for the boys: socks, jumpers, jeans, shoes – all items that they had never needed before. Some of the kids hadn't been further from home than Broome. They had never seen high-rise buildings, trains or even traffic lights. They had spent their lives in a community where they were related in some way to just about everyone they knew.

The boys were billeted in pairs with families from a private school in the eastern suburbs. Some of them stayed in homes with indoor swimming pools and tennis courts in the garden. One of the boys told his parents later that he had lived in a castle. With its basketball courts, science labs and expansive grounds, the school was a huge culture shock as well.

They rode trams, went to a football match at the MCG and met the players afterwards, and went to Mount Buller. It was the first time any of the Lombadina boys had seen snow. In the photos of their first moments on the mountain they looked miserable. Rugged up in beanies, scarves, jumpers and long pants, they struggled to walk in the heavy ski boots. All the boys were used to being barefoot. At Lombadina, to their coach's frustration, they had refused to wear the football boots that were donated to the local team by sporting charities. He told them that if they wanted to have a chance at attending the Clontarf Academy in Broome, which aimed to engage young Indigenous men in school through football, they had to get used to the boots. It didn't work. The donated footy boots were always left in the box, still tied together in pairs by their laces. But by the end of their short ski lesson, they all had wide grins as they slid down the mountain, legs and arms held wide. When they got home, they said it was the best part of the trip.

In September, the Melbourne school sent up a group of students to visit Lombadina in return. I asked one of the teachers if they would like us to billet some of the visitors. She looked at me a little strangely, and said no, they would be staying in the tourist accommodation.

The boys from Melbourne did all the things the tourists did: mud-crabbing, kayaking, searching for oysters on the rocks, swimming and spear fishing. On their last night, we joined them for a barbecue at Cape Leveque. I got into conversation with a teacher who was praising one of the Djarindjin boys for how much he had matured since their visit the year before.

'He's a great kid', he said.

'Do you think any of them will end up at your school?' I asked. The school promoted itself as providing scholarships and opportunities for Indigenous children from remote areas. They were 'building relationships' with this community.

'Well,' he said carefully, 'there are basic academic standards that we have to consider. There'd be no point putting these kids in a situation where they would be completely out of their depth.'

'So you wouldn't take any of them?'

'No, I don't really think so.'

'Who does get the scholarships then?'

He thought for a moment. 'I think there's a young boy from Arnhem Land. We're doing some testing on him. We'll see how that goes.'

I looked around at the boys. They were climbing over rocks to get to the beach, jumping from boulders that were glowing in the light of the setting sun and landing with a thud on the soft, yellow sand. For most of them, their futures were mapped out already. The white kids, including our boys, would definitely finish secondary school, probably move on to university, get jobs of one kind or another, earn money, stay fairly healthy throughout their lives and make their own choices about how to live their lives.

Many of the others might never finish school, remain semi-literate, have limited access to further education or training and live their lives hamstrung by poverty, illness and perhaps incarceration by the time they were in their twenties.

'It doesn't seem fair, does it?' I said.

He shrugged and turned away.

This year, the dry season seemed to fly past too quickly. By early September, the clouds were gathering, the humidity was rising and the tourists disappeared. Some days no-one came into the store for hours. I had planned to do a big spring clean when things quietened down but the heat and humidity drained all my energy and it was as much as I could do to sweep the cobwebs from the corners and mop the floors. Audrey and I spent hours sitting outside the shop, trying to catch a breeze. I would look at the clouds gathering above us and ask her if she thought it would rain soon.

'No, rain long time yet.'

The sea was off-limits because of stingers but the water table rose and a freshwater lagoon formed behind the first line of sand dunes. For a week or two it was lovely to sit in at the end of the day, despite the fact that it was very warm. After a while the water became stagnant and Janice told us to make sure not to put our heads under.

'I call it Conjunctivitis Lake', she said.

I had taken to jogging along the beach in the morning. I had to go well before sunrise because as soon as the sun peeked over the dunes it became too hot to do anything much at all. One morning Robert came into the shop and asked if I'd been running that day.

'Did you see the crocodile tracks?' he asked.

I shook my head. 'Stop teasing me.'

This time he was serious. 'I can't believe you didn't see them. I reckon it must have been about twelve foot long. Go have a look.'

James and I drove to the beach at lunchtime. We found the first tracks right near the top of a dune – the crocodile had slid into the lagoon at about the spot where we had been swimming just a few weeks before. Either it had come out of the sea at high tide or the tracks it had made had been swept away by the sea. About half a kilometre along the beach, the tracks emerged from the skanky water, crossed the sand and disappeared back into the ocean.

My morning footprints crossed the line of deep claw marks. I couldn't believe I had missed them either.

'Unless', said James, 'the tracks weren't there when you were running.'

After that I stopped going for my early morning runs. It was getting too hot anyway.

We had now been away for more than two and a half years and we were ready to go home. Oscar was about to finish Grade 5 and we wanted him to spend his last year of primary school catching up on anything he might have missed out on, so he wouldn't be behind when he started secondary school. We had used up all of our savings, and I was worried about being out of the workforce any longer.

On our last day at Lombadina we spent the morning mud-crabbing with Robert, and then boiled up the crabs and ate them as we watched the AFL Grand Final on the verandah of the yellow house.

Audrey came over for a beer and a crab sandwich, as did the new shopkeeper and maintenance man and their two young daughters. Like us, they had been travelling for a while and were eager to stop and experience life in an Indigenous community. They had asked us for advice, but we hadn't been able to think of much to say. They'd work it out for themselves.

When the woman had come into the shop a few days before to learn how to run the store, she had bombarded me with questions. I couldn't answer her properly because she constantly interrupted me. She was overflowing with comments and ideas and suggestions. She would ask a question and then begin to answer it herself, as if every thought that ran through her head also came out of her mouth. It was like walking into a wall of noise. She finally left, announcing that she was even more confused now than she had been before our handover.

I had plonked down beside Audrey, who had retreated outside long before. The woman had exhausted me with all her questions and chatter.

'White people talk a lot, don't they?' I said.

Audrey barely glanced at me, but I had learned to read a lot into those small movements of hers, and I was horrified.

'No! Do I still talk too much, too? Do I, Audrey?'

She looked away, not wanting to offend. 'Sometimes.'

But now, as we all sat together on the verandah, Audrey had a suggestion for them. 'You bring me fish', she said, waving her stubby at them. 'James, he bring me fish all the time. Lots of fish. Big beautiful fish. He's a good man. And Lorna! Lorna, I miss you!'

It was the longest speech I had heard her give all year.

'You always said you'd take us fishing', I said.

She looked at me with a sharp glint in her eye. She might have had a few beers but she wasn't going to let that one through. 'Ah, but you on *my* country here. When you go fishing I say to the spirits, you welcome them. And James, he gets big fish. Beautiful fish! My country ...'

We left the Kimberley by driving out along the Gibb River Road past Imintji. On our final night, we sat at the lookout with Nev and watched a thunderstorm brewing around us. Lightning cracked and lit up the sky in all directions. The air felt charged and alive and I knew this wouldn't be the last time I would stand here and look down across the country. Outside Kununurra, we stopped at the last boab tree and collected a box-load of fallen nuts. We had no real plans for them but I couldn't bear to leave the Kimberley without taking a little piece of it home. We kicked the footy over the border and left Western Australia behind. Now we really were tourists again.

Chapter Twenty

This time we drove from Kununurra to Katherine in a single day. At Nitmiluk National Park campground there was a landscaped swimming pool, bar and restaurant, but the spots for caravans and tents looked like a shopping centre car park. White lines marked the edges of each site and power poles sat between each one like parking meters. As the sun set, a middle-aged couple in purple polyester jumpsuits set up a keyboard and amplifier and treated the campers to live lounge music by the pool. We played canasta and sang along to 'The girl from Ipanema'. It was the most bizarre evening we had ever spent in a national park.

That night the temperature didn't drop below 32°C. We got up early and spent the day canoeing along the cool, wide river that flowed between the high sandstone cliffs of Katherine Gorge. We took our time, stopping and swimming at the sandy beaches at the base of the cliffs. When it got too hot to be outside, we hid in the Interpretive Centre and did some half-hearted schoolwork. By this point, school consisted of a couple of pages out of an old maths book for Dylan, some random maths problems that I made up for Oscar and a quiz that James created from information in the centre's displays.

Kakadu was next. We had met lots of travellers who dismissed Kakadu as overrated and didn't go there. I couldn't work out why – it was stunning and, surprisingly, still free to visit. The heat and humidity of the build-up was oppressive, though, and made everything difficult. Sleeping was hard and it was even exhausting to walk the short circuit of the rock art galleries at Ubirr. We stumbled along the sandy path and huddled in the shade of overhanging rocks, wondering about the artists who had seen and drawn those early European ships on the northern coast of Australia. We stayed in Kakadu as long as we could before the heat got to us and we had to slink back to Darwin and recover in Nannette's air-conditioned flat.

Travelling south again, we stopped for a swim at Mataranka, 107 kilometres south of Katherine, where I had met up with James and the boys two years earlier after my short trip back to Melbourne to work. The flying foxes had arrived too. Estimates put the population at this time of year at a quarter of a million. A warm, musky smell hung unpleasantly in the air when we got out of the car and grew stronger as we walked along the boardwalk to the hot springs. Dylan jumped straight into the water but Oscar hung back. He was fussing around, finding a dry spot to put his towel and playing with his goggles, but I knew he was just reluctant to get in. The smell was getting to him. I was feeling a little nauseous too but I slid in. The water was too warm to be refreshing and it felt sticky on my skin.

James and I were huddling at the edge of the springs when the English girl we were chatting to said, 'Oh, that's a good idea, they've put the sprinklers on.'

We looked up and saw a steady stream of drops falling from the trees above.

'No', James said. 'That's bat piss.' We dried off quickly and left. It was half an hour before any of us could face eating lunch.

Fifty kilometres out of Tennant Creek and 1500 kilometres from the east coast, with the temperature outside hovering at around 40°C, the car's air conditioning belt finally snapped. We wound down the windows and dust blasted our faces and hot air swirled around us as we drove. Just when we couldn't feel any sorrier for ourselves, we saw something shimmering on the bitumen in front of us. A man was walking along the highway with two camels towing a broken-down car that had an Imintji Store sticker on its back window. We stopped and shared our cans of cold lemonade with him, gave him our last bottle of iced water and drove on with a better attitude.

In Richmond, back on the Queensland dinosaur trail, we went to a local country race meeting on Melbourne Cup Day. The next day we drove through Muttaburra. It was a strange little town, tiny and seemingly completely deserted except for the dark green plaster statue of the muttaburrasaurus dinosaur it was named for. At Barcaldine we stood beneath the new architectural structure that protects the now-dead Tree of Knowledge. I tried to explain to the kids about the 1891 shearers' strike and the formation of the Australian Labor Party but they weren't listening. In Rubyvale we spent an hour fossicking for sapphires using a bag of bought dirt that had been laced with small gems, before deciding it wasn't really for us.

It was around about then that it occurred to me that our extended journey of discovery and adventure might have killed off the boys' curiosity.

'Hey, let's go look for dinosaur fossils!'

'No.'

'How about we hire a canoe, paddle out on the dam and catch some fish?'

'Nuh.'

'What if we find some natural ochre and paint our faces with it? Pan for gold? Make damper?'

'You go. We're reading our books.'

I found myself having one-sided conversations with them as they gazed blankly into space or read, for the fifth or sixth time, a torn and stained novel they had found on the floor of the car.

Forty-four days after leaving Lombadina we made it to the ocean. At a caravan park on Coolum Beach on Queensland's Sunshine Coast, we wedged our camper trailer into the tiny east-coast-sized space and tried not to spread past over the painted border onto the neighbouring site. James celebrated his birthday by doing his first skydive. He was the only person jumping: Friday the thirteenth wasn't the most popular day to attach yourself to a stranger and fall out of a very small plane at 10,000 feet.

On the Gold Coast, we visited Tim and Sue again. When I rang to let them know we were passing through their neighbourhood again, Sue had warned me that Tim had not been well. He had recently been diagnosed with a particularly nasty form of cancer, which he was actively fighting with both mainstream treatments and alternative therapies that he had researched thoroughly himself.

Despite that, Tim had lost none of his energy or enthusiasm for the surf. He gave Oscar and Dylan their first surfing lesson at the local beach and Oscar reciprocated by teaching Tim and Kirralee how to ride a ripstick. We spent a day on their boat, cruising the canals behind the Gold Coast. Kirralee showed the boys how to catch worms, sucking them up from the mud with a homemade pump and grabbing the wriggling creatures before they could bury themselves again. Oscar and Dylan were reluctant to handle the worms, but were more than happy to squirt mud over her and themselves.

Kirralee also showed us a school project she had done, documenting Dylan's trip on the Royal Flying Doctor plane from Lombadina when he broke his arm. She had used it to demonstrate the vast distances in Australia and explain how different it was to the city, where hospitals were conveniently nearby.

We left them armed with advice about camping spots further down the coast and headed to Byron Bay. After the obligatory visit to the most easterly point of the mainland, the lighthouse at Cape Byron, we drove on through Byron to the caravan park at Broken Head. It was a quiet and pretty spot, nestled between the rainforest and the beach, and unusually hilly for a camping ground.

Tim and Sue had told us that earlier in the year they had been greeted there by a man who, noticing the pushbikes on their camper, had said, 'You're not taking those off, are you? No bikes allowed here.'

It may have been the same man who said to Oscar, three minutes after we arrived, 'No riding your ripstick here. That's an absolute no-no.' He pointed to a mark on the wall of the amenities block. 'That was a kid on a skateboard made that.'

Oscar and I examined what was obviously a bicycle tyre mark but we put his ripstick away anyway. Ten minutes later, as the boys were sitting, dangling their legs in the low limbs of a very sturdy tree, the office door flew open.

'GET OFF THAT TREE!'

They climbed down and wandered over to the grassy lawn next to our site and started wrestling. A woman walking past glared at them.

'Do you *have* to do that?'

None of us took any offence: we just chalked it up to being back on the east coast and surrounded by uptight city folk. I did stop Dylan from chasing the bush turkeys with a stick, though. I had to make sure we were complying with the laminated signs in the laundry, which explained that their incessant scavenging for chocolate biscuits and chips was part of the bird's natural foraging behaviour that we should learn to live with. Another camper confessed to me that her father, enraged at the loss of a brand-new box of breakfast cereal, had flung a tent peg at one of the turkeys. To the horror of his entire family, he not only hit the bird but killed it stone dead. They hid the body in the scrub and dragged it up the hill later that night to conceal the crime.

With only a couple of months to go before our trip ended, James and I had started to think about work. A friend had emailed him about a full-time, permanent job that had just been advertised. It was in James's field, started at the beginning of the year and – the real kicker – was only ten minutes walk from our house. We spent an evening huddled around the laptop writing up a resume and an application letter. Inspired, I emailed an organisation I had worked for in the past, asking if they thought there might be any work for me the following year. At the time it felt like a dress rehearsal for real life but a few days later James was asked to fly to Melbourne for an interview. He bought a pair of decent pants and a nice shirt and booked the cheapest flight we could find. He was gone for forty-eight hours and when he got back he thought it had been a complete waste of time.

At Nambucca Heads, 285 kilometres south of Byron Bay, we discovered that the rock wall that served as a breakwater had been turned into a community art project. Anyone could paint whatever they wanted on the rocks. People had documented their holidays or their family or their special interests. We chose a large flat rock, painted a wonky map of Australia on it and marked out the route of our travels. We colour-coded the years and painted our names around the edge of the continent.

'We've been almost *everywhere*', said Dylan.

We stood back and looked. The map was circled and criss-crossed with red, blue and yellow lines. 'Not Tasmania, though', he said, spotting an empty bit.

With only a week left before we were meant to be in Sydney we decided to do some proper camping at Myall Lakes, just an hour north of Newcastle. We were astonished at how beautiful this part of the coast was, and how wild and isolated it felt. The freshwater lakes were protected from the Pacific Ocean by a stretch of huge sand dunes. On the ocean side of the dunes, waves crashed onto empty white beaches that stretched as far as we could see. One morning, as I was sitting at the base of a sand dune and watching the ocean, a squadron of fighter jets from the nearby Williamtown Air Force base roared over a dune and flew directly above me. The sound was deafening and my heart pounded in my chest for minutes after the jets had disappeared from sight. The contrast between the complete isolation of the beach and the sight and sound of the planes was extreme and disturbing.

On the other side of the dunes, the campsite by the lake was quiet and sedate, at least when we first arrived. Every evening, though, a stream of cars drove in and parked close to the water. Entire families piled out, hauling chairs, buckets, torches and long green nets attached to sturdy poles. In groups of three or four, mostly men, they waded into the lake, carrying the nets with them, and disappeared into the dark. We watched with the women and children, slapping at mosquitoes as they bit through our long pants and sleeves. Voices floated over the black water and sometimes we spotted the twinkle of a torch, much further out than we had expected.

An hour or so later, they came back in, their nets heavy with tiny freshwater prawns. Most of the catch went straight into large white buckets that were weighed immediately on rusty old bathroom scales. The results were shouted loudly, to cheers or jeers, then the buckets were heaved back into the cars. A few of the older men had set up camp by the lake for a few weeks. They tipped their prawns straight into big silver vats that were perched on gas rings and filled with heavily salted boiling water. When the prawns were cooked, they were bagged up and put into a chest freezer that hummed busily all night.

As we were packing up, one of the men brought us a bag of prawns that they had caught and cooked the night before. They were small and tightly curled but they tasted sweet and salty and we ate them faster than I could peel them.

Still reluctant to drive into Sydney, we detoured to the Blue Mountains. On the advice of a ranger, we camped at Burralow Swamp on the eastern side of the Blue Mountains National Park. The campground was basically a paddock. It was a barren stretch of dead grass, swarming with flies and one of the most unattractive places we had ever set up our tent, but that night we walked along a rough bush track to a tiny waterfall that was shimmering with glow-worms and fire flies. We sat for an hour watching them twinkling in the air around us before stumbling back to camp in the dark, listening to howling dogs in the distance.

The next day, a different ranger warned against walking around in the bush in the evening. 'We're having to shoot feral dogs', she said. 'They've started hooking up and travelling in packs.'

Finally we arrived at the caravan park in Sydney, filthy and foul-smelling. We deposited three huge loads of washing in the machines, and had four hot and indecently long showers. When we were clean, we rang all our Sydney friends and organised to meet up with them for dinners and barbecues.

The next day, as we were happily wandering around Circular Quay in clean clothes, James's phone rang.

'That'll be them telling me I don't have the job', he said, looking at the caller ID.

As he listened, he gave us a big grin and stuck his thumb in the air. The Manly ferry hooted its congratulations and Dylan ran to James and clutched his leg, shouting, 'Dad's got a job! Dad's got a job!' People walking past smiled at us and James flapped his arms, trying to quiet us down so that he could hear what his new boss was telling him. Yes, he had the job and yes, they understood he couldn't start until early February. They would send him his contract that day.

Stunned, we bought ice-cream cones to celebrate and sat on the grass and watched the yachts float on the harbour.

'I feel like it's all over', said James. All of a sudden, despite the bright sunshine and the million-dollar view, his shoulders sagged. 'I don't think I'm ready to go back.'

'We've still got to go around Tasmania, though', said Dylan.

After a week in Sydney, we had a family Christmas with James's cousins in Wagga Wagga and spent three days overloading our brains in the museums and galleries of Canberra. On New Year's Eve, we didn't even make it to midnight, falling asleep on a friend's couch as the kids watched television and ate chips and chocolate in peace. The next day, we stood at the lookout at the base of Mount Kosciuszko: just six kilometres to the highest mountain in Australia. It was late in the day, we had no food or water, everyone was in shorts and t-shirts and a storm was coming in. Normally all that would have been irrelevant, but we must have been tired because we decided not to do the walk.

We had a few reasons for spending the last three weeks of our journey in Tasmania. The first was the weather: James would only agree to go that far south in the middle of summer. Secondly, we knew that the closer we got to Melbourne the sadder we would be about our trip ending. If we could put Bass Strait between us and home for as long as possible, we were more likely to finish on a high note.

Then there was the third thing. We hadn't actually done any research, but we were pretty sure there had to be a sign somewhere on the south coast that said it was the southernmost point of the continent. We needed a photograph of the four of us standing next to it.

When we drove off the ferry, dawn revealed Devonport to be cold, wet, grey and closed. The clouds seemed to hang just metres above us. We had booked into a caravan park, but we drove past to check it out and couldn't imagine what we would do on a small patch of gravel for a whole day.

James did what he had been doing for nearly three years when things weren't working out. He drove. 'We'll go and have a look at Launceston.'

I was on map duty. Out of habit, I didn't bother to look at it until we had been driving for nearly an hour and we nearly missed the turn-off to Launceston. By nine o'clock we had found a caravan park and were all set up. By midday, the sun was shining and we were swimming at Cataract Gorge.

We had gone into a ballot for camping spots in Freycinet National Park and they had given us four nights at the campground at Coles Bay at the northern edge of the park, close to the small fishing town of the same name that serviced the area. On the first day we had planned to walk to Wineglass Bay but the weather had turned hot and very windy so all the walks were closed. We settled in for a day in the tent. Two hours later, Oscar started vomiting. By the end of the day all three of my men were sick, lying around the tent refusing to eat and requesting jugs of cold water. Finally, on our last day there, we managed the 12-kilometre trek up and over the pink and grey granite mountains to Wineglass Bay and then back down and across a narrow isthmus to Hazards Beach.

At Wineglass Bay, a perfectly curved beach of pure white sand, I realised I had forgotten to pack my bathers so we walked down the beach to get away from the other hikers. On the way we noticed some dead bluebottles washed up on the sand, presumably as a result of the strong winds over the last few days. I stripped off and jumped into the sea. Safely submerged, with only my head poking up, I looked around me. The water was covered in a soft, pale blue foam and the tingling sensation from the cold water wasn't wearing off as quickly as it usually did. In fact, my face felt as if there were tiny needles sticking into it. My arms jerked as little electric shocks went off just under my skin. I looked more closely at the foam. Apart from the colour, it looked a bit like frog spawn. Tiny blue globules floated on the surface, clumping together and rushing in and out on the waves, collecting in drifts on the sand.

It dawned on me that I was swimming in mashed bluebottles. The stings spread down to my stomach and legs. To get out I had to stand up and risk getting covered in even more of them. But there was no option. I raced out of the water, trading modesty for speed, and danced around on the sand naked, yelping as the stings fired tiny shots of pain all over me. It took several hours for the sensation to fade.

The next day we drove to Hobart. We hadn't expected it to be hard to find a campsite but everywhere was either booked out or only had gravel sites that were designed for caravans and motorhomes. I flicked through one of the tourist booklets lying in the pile under my feet in the car and booked us a room in a youth hostel. My timing was perfect. The gastroenteritis I thought I had escaped caught up with me and I spent most of the night curled up in the shared bathroom, hugging the toilet.

When I recovered we moved on to Port Arthur and were relieved to find a beautiful campground that allowed campfires. Port Arthur's historical sites were imaginatively presented and, as it was the summer holidays, there were heaps of things to do. We went to a series of open-air plays that dramatised stories of convict life, spent time at the archaeological dig looking at broken tools and old household items, took a harbour cruise, found out about the boys' prison at Point Puer and played quoits on the green lawns. We had decided before we arrived that we wouldn't talk to the boys about what had happened here in 1996, but we banned their favourite game – shooting each other with sticks – for the duration of our visit. On the way out of the site on our last day, Oscar stumbled across the plaque outside the memorial garden that briefly explained the events of that day.

He read it, silently, then looked over at me. I was sitting on the edge of the reflection pool, preparing myself for his questions about how something so evil could happen in this world.

'I get it', he said quietly and put out his hand.

We held hands all the way back to the caravan park. I knew that there was a lot of debate amongst families travelling in Tasmania about whether or not to visit Port Arthur. I was very glad that we had. That day I caught a glimpse of the adult my son would soon become, and I loved what I had seen.

The three weeks in Tasmania flew past and soon we were reluctantly counting down the sleeps until the end of our trip. A few nights before we left, I made everyone sit down and write a list of the best things that we had done on our trip. I read out the suggestions and we voted for our favourite. In third place, below 'Living at Lombadina' and 'The helicopter ride at Mitchell Falls', was 'Leaving in the first place'. I looked at the list for a long time, remembering the night that James and I had decided to go on this crazy adventure. The boys had only been two and four back then. They were nine and eleven now, and I wondered how the past three years had changed them, and if we would ever have any regrets about what we had done.

We sailed out of Devonport at dawn and sailed back across Bass Strait to Melbourne, back to our home, our friends, the boys' school and a new job for James. By late afternoon we were in our street in Fitzroy, looking for somewhere to park our dirty big LandCruiser and even filthier camper trailer. It was all over.

Chapter Twenty-one

After being away from home for 1000 days, driving 90,000 kilometres and setting up our camp nearly 200 times, it was lovely to be home. The joy of having a dishwasher and a big fridge and a washing machine and hot water on tap and shops around the corner and all our old books on the shelves and friends right around the corner was overwhelming at first, but quickly it just felt normal.

James started his new job. It was the first real nine-to-five job he'd had for years and he was struggling a bit with that, but it was important that one of us had a regular income. The work wasn't physically hard, but he sometimes lost the strength in his hands for weeks at a time. It was a remnant of the Ross River Fever he had contracted at Mission Beach. I decided to work from home because neither of us could bear to think of the kids coming home to an empty house at the end of the day. It was meant to be a temporary arrangement, but I found that I enjoyed the quiet and solitude during the day and I was in no hurry to move into a studio or office.

For the first few nights, the boys crawled into bed with us and we all slept together in a queen-size bed that felt a lot smaller than it had three years before. The room they shared, despite being right next to ours, was too far away from us for their comfort. Oscar also refused to be left alone in the house.

'There's spirits here. In our house. And I don't like them.'

I laughed the first time he said that. 'You had too much of that talk at Lombadina, I think.'

Spirits had played a big part in the stories that the older Aboriginal people had told the kids when they came into the classroom to teach them about their culture and country and language. I remembered one in particular: the old lady who lived in the mangroves.

'She's got really, really long … boobies', Dylan had told me, embarrassed. 'You know, with milk, like for babies. And she catches the kids who go in there and she makes them drink the milk and they go to sleep. Forever and ever.'

It made perfect sense to me. You didn't want kids messing about on their own in the mangroves where crocodiles could be lurking. As a cautionary tale, that one would definitely do the trick.

I wasn't immune to the spirits either. In the first few months of being home, I followed Sue's lead and filled our house with reminders of our adventures. I printed out photographs, bought frames and put them up all around the house. I had the dugong tusks, which Jumat's father had given the boys in Lombadina, polished, capped with silver and strung on black leather thongs. I got the canvases we bought in Lockhart River stretched and hung those too. But my favourite art-work was a Wandjina that I had bought on impulse at the Mowanjum Art and Culture Centre on one of my trips from Imintji to Derby. Painted in dark red ochre on a solid black background, the Wandjina had transfixed me with his star-shaped eyes when I unrolled the canvas that day. Now he looked down solemnly at me from the top of the stairs, reminding me of a day when clouds had gathered in the sky because I had spent too long in a place I shouldn't have been.

Three of the Sibosado girls were starting at a boarding school in Melbourne and Robert had flown down with them. When he came for dinner, I told him about Oscar's spirits.

He listened carefully as Oscar described how he felt. 'Oscar, the thing is, there's spirits everywhere. You have to tell them who's the boss. Don't let them mess with you.'

Oscar nodded and wandered off. I shook my head at Robert. 'That's not what you were meant to say.'

'It's the truth, though', he said. And he was right. Oscar made peace with the spirits and grew comfortable with being in the house again.

That wasn't the only incident that brought home to me how much we had changed while we had been away. A few weeks after we got back, coinciding with the third anniversary of the day we originally left Melbourne, we had a barbecue to welcome ourselves home. I had bought a couple of boxes of soft drink, but that afternoon I heard nearly all of our friends telling their active, healthily skinny kids to find the non-existent sugar-free drinks. I could laugh that off, but it was trickier when someone said they were worried about the standard of education at our local school. I wanted to shake them and tell them that – in this country – some kids were lucky to come out of school with basic literacy and numeracy skills. All of the schools near us had resources, great teachers and fantastic outcomes for all their students.

Four days after arriving home, but not without an argument about why they had to wear shoes and sunhats, Oscar and Dylan went back to their old school. Dylan had a warm welcome from his class. One of his friends had even saved a seat for him when they set up their new room before the summer holidays. They were excited to have him back and he was inundated with invitations for sleepovers and movie dates. He was happy at school and talked a lot about what they did each day. I was surprised when, months later, his teacher said she was pleased he was finally getting used to being in a regular classroom again.

'I thought he was fine', I said.

'He is. It's just that sometimes he just … wanders off in the middle of a lesson. He's not at all rude about it. He just goes and sits in the corner and reads a book.'

This was exactly what Dylan had been encouraged to do for nearly two years. When lessons were pitched at a level that was far below what he was capable of, his teachers had told him to 'go and read a book'. It was a hard habit to break and he still disappears into a book at every opportunity and carries his Kindle wherever he goes.

Oscar's re-entry to school was trickier. The boys in his class closed ranks on him. His teacher said that they had a difficult time the year before, and had been bullied by the older boys. Now that they were the oldest kids in the school, they were repeating that behaviour. Oscar was an outsider, so he was the easiest to exclude.

It took us a while to work out what was happening. When we did, I was more upset and angry about it than Oscar was. One day, when Oscar was talking about Jumat, one of the boys called him a liar. He said Oscar hadn't really lived with Aboriginal people and didn't have any Aboriginal friends.

'But that doesn't make sense', I said to Oscar when he told me.

He shrugged. 'I think he's just a bit jealous. He's used to being the one who's done stuff other people haven't.'

'Do you want to take some photos to school to show them you aren't lying?'

'Not really. It doesn't really bother me.'

It bothered me. It bothered me a lot. That year Oscar taught me a lot about bravery and self-belief. He had such a strong sense of who he was that it couldn't be easily shaken. When things got worse I offered to take him out of school and homeschool him but he wouldn't consider it.

In the middle of the year Oscar surprised himself, us, and his teacher when he was shortlisted for a program for students with academic potential at a nearby secondary school. In the interview he spoke about his time in Imintji and Lombadina in a very mature and serious manner. Although his left leg was jiggling furiously and he kept licking his lips, he told the principal what it was like being in a class surrounded by children who mostly had very basic reading and writing skills. His nerves were obvious, but he was calm and confident. I was impressed. So was the principal, and a few days later a letter came offering him a place.

The relief I felt when we opened that letter surprised me. I'd spent three years telling everyone, including myself, that my sons were learning just as much from their experiences as they would have if we had kept them in a regular school. I had always believed that education was as much, if not more, about a child's home life and their relationship with the people around them as it was about what happened in the classroom. I'd even said things like, 'Kids would learn at the bottom of the well if they had access to books and parents who answered their questions.' Yet I had been harbouring a fear that I'd been wrong, that we might have ruined their future by dragging them around the country with us and ignoring their schoolwork for months on end.

We will never know with any certainty how those few unconventional years in childhood will play out in their adult life. When older people we'd met on the road said they had taken their children on similar trips, I'd always asked if they could see echoes of that in their kids as they grew up. Every one of them had said yes. Some spoke of adult children who were working in developing countries, helping to alleviate poverty. Others had returned to live in Indigenous communities or were still travelling around the world, not ready to settle down yet. All of them spoke about seeing in their children an appreciation of what they had experienced and a lack of interest in material goods.

Despite that, we only ever met a handful of other families doing the same thing. Of those, Sue and Tim were special and we stayed in touch when we returned to Melbourne. Like us, they never had any regrets about their decision to take their kids out of school and travel. A few years after their return, Sue told me she could definitely see changes in Troy and Kirralee. 'Both of them have terrific communication skills', she said. She attributed this directly to the months of camping. 'If they didn't speak to the people in the camp next to us, they would have had to play on their own in the dirt.' As soon as she said that, I realised that Oscar and Dylan were very similar. While some of their friends have trouble making eye contact with adults, let alone conversation, Oscar and Dylan have no trouble chatting with whoever is around them.

Sue said of her kids, 'Their rooms aren't filled with rubbish. Kirralee says, "It's just *stuff*."' I laughed when she told me that, and told her that when we eventually got around to giving the boys their own rooms I had given them both some money to furnish and decorate their new space. Oscar had looked confused and said, 'But I don't want anything' and gave it back. Sue also said that when they were travelling, dealing with the inevitable vehicle breakdowns and plans that went awry, they all learned that sometimes, to get where you want to go, you have to be strong. 'They have no fear now', she told me.

Sue, Troy and Kirralee have had to be very strong. Tim fought hard but the cancer eventually won and they lost him, far too young. They hold tight to the memories of their months on the road in their campervan. 'It was a very precious time.'

On one of the very last days of our trip, we worked out from our maps that the closest you could get to South East Cape, Tasmania, which is the most southerly point of Australia, was somewhere called Cockle Creek. When we got there the rangers said that there wasn't a track that went the whole way to the cape. We decided to try anyway. It was cloudy and drizzling as we walked out along a boardwalk that stretched, long and pale and straight, over the boggy grassland towards the sea.

Two hours later we sat on a sloping rock ledge above the Southern Ocean and looked at the southernmost point of the continent. It was just a few kilometres away, across a wild stretch of sea and jagged rocks to our right. How many other people have been to all these points of Australia, we wondered. Propping our camera up on the ground with sticks, we set the timer and posed for a slightly crooked picture of ourselves with South East Cape behind us.

We were at the end of our journey. Every step from here would be taking us home to our old lives. But I suspected none of us would ever be quite the same again.

Acknowledgements

Most of the first draft of this book was written at a long wooden table in a house on the edge of the Macedon Ranges, courtesy of Writers Victoria and a Writing @ Rosebank Fellowship. A later draft was knocked into shape in a cubicle provided by a Wheeler Centre Hot Desk Fellowship and the Readings Foundation. I cannot thank enough all those who played a part in offering me those opportunities.

Many of my fellow students in RMIT's Professional Writing and Editing course read extracts (and sometimes entire drafts) of this manuscript and offered advice and encouragement, as did James Shuter, Nannette Hunter, Tanya Hunter and Leonie Starnawski. Zora Sanders, who published two of my essays in *Meanjin*, will probably never know how much that helped.

Thank you to Melissa Kayser and Lauren Whybrow from Hardie Grant Explore for taking a chance on a travel memoir and for finding Martine Lleonart to help turn the manuscript into a book.

But well before all that, long before I even imagined that I could ever write a book, there was the wonderfully generous Tony Birch and the writing group that came out of his classes. I owe a huge debt of gratitude to Andrea Frost and Sophie Torney for always having faith in me and not being afraid to dish out some tough love when it all got too hard.

To James and Oscar and Dylan, thank you for not complaining when I locked myself away for months to share our stories and secrets with the world. Thank you also for being the best travelling companions I could have asked for. May we always travel well together.

<u>Day 1</u> : 28 February 2007
Port Campbell Caravan Park

This is 'The Most Important Thing We Have'

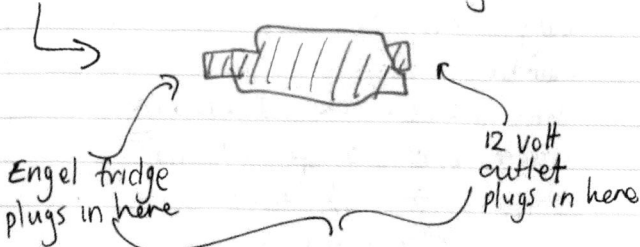

⤷ →

Engel fridge
plugs in here

12 volt
outlet
plugs in here

= Fridge in kitchen, not car

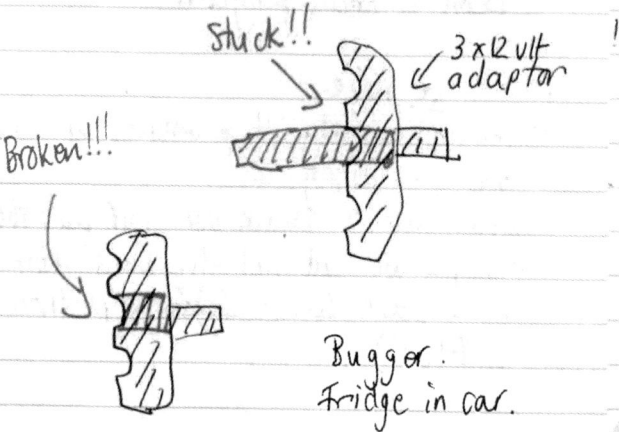

Stuck!!

3 x 12 vlt
adaptor

Broken!!!

Bugger.
Fridge in car.

Day 1: The Most Important Thing We Have

Top About to head over the West Gate Bridge on the first day of the trip
Bottom Camping at Princess Margaret Rose caves in Lower Glenelg
National Park, Victoria

Baloo = please come
DUMBRUH = home
Bolongdyidan
                Abee = brother

Jabarra = emu
Djuruk = swimming
  Djunk laboon = swimming in water
Loor = tree snake

Dujugoodie = short neck turtle

Maranggi = sun

Ulingi = rain

Ludgarrie = boab

Jungi = ant pit

Uran = tree

Yandall = crocodile

ne gotten in dgargeh

mangat = goanna
minjal = to eat
mungarri = food

ara booma = sit down

bedyia = see you

woolwoolma = sleep

eagle hawk = warana

oorra = ground

Dayo = barramundi

Damboo = camp
Nahloo = family
windjiangon = fire

Left top Successful fishing at Steep Point, Western Australia *Left middle* Waiting for the *Ghan* to pass *Left bottom* Oscar and Dylan at the Imintji Store, Western Australia *Above* Language lessons at Wananami School, Mount Barnett, Western Australia

NOTES	melb mileage	litres	$/litre	COST
28.2	193,310	Fill tank (63)	$117·50	$74·15
4·3 Port Fairy	193,700	Fill tank (73)	123·9	$87·12
15·3 Kingston	174.353	Fill tank (108)	$129·9	132·00
22·3 Adelaide	195,130	Fill r can (123)	$119·5	$145·00
25·3 Snowtown	195,963	Fill r can (127)	$124·9	$167·00
29·3 Wilpena		Fill tank	$129 —	$88·00
31·3 Maree	196,877	84 Lt.	140·0	$117·20
3·4 Oodnadatta	197,638	85	158	$134 —
6·4 Erldunda	197,853	94	157	$146·69
10·4 Yulara	198,803	80	157·9	$126·38
12·4 Kings Canyon	199,216		164	$129·00
20·4 Alice	199,877	106	135·9	$140·65
23·4 Kulgera	200,382	78	162	$130·00
24·4 Coober Pedy	200,917	100	137·9	137·90
		100		
	202071	100		
2·5 Ceduna	202592	80	129·5	$113
2·5 Nundoo	202743	30	129·9	$39
3·5 Mundrabilla	203181	92	139·9	$129
4·5 Norseman	203838	117	136·9	$160 (5·5)
7·5 Kalgoorlie	204109	43	123·9	$54
7·5 Esperance	204509		127·9	$80
12·5 Esperance	204841		125·9	$62·13
13·5 Hyden	205242	72	141·0	$105·40
14·5 Denmark	205843	106	133·9	$142
22·5 Pemberton	206411	87	139	$

Keeping track of mileage and fuel costs

NOTES	Camp	Cost	$40/night
28.2 - 3.3	Port Cambell	$134	≈ $33
4.3 - 5.3	Port Fairy	$52	$26
6.3 — 11.3	PMR Caves	$84	$14
12.3 - 15.3	Robe	$164	$41
16.3 - 17.3	Port Willunga	—	
18.3 - 21.3	Adelaide	$115	$38 (-10%)
22.3 - 24.3	~~Wilportia~~ Innes	$31	$10.
25.3 - 28.3	Wilsons	$130	$30
29.3 - 30.3	Arkaroola	$56	$28
31.3	Mulroena	$2	$2
31.4	Halligans	$11	$11
2.4	Oodnadatta	$27.50	$27.50
3 - 4.4	Dalhousie Springs	$22.50	$22.50 (pd 1 night)
5.4	Erldunda	$28	28
6 - 9.4	Yulara	$170	$42.50
10.11.+	King Creek	$80	$40
12 - 13.4	Palm Valley	$30.80	$15.40
14 - 16.4	Ormiston Gorge	$46.20	$15.40
17 - 22.4	Alice Springs	$210 -	$43.00 (-10%)
29.4 - 1.5	~~Re~~ Streaky Bay	~~78~~ $76	$28 -10%.
2.5	~~Sand~~ Eucla	$12	$12
3.5	Norseman	$30	$30
4 - 6.5	Kalgoorlie	$100	$32
7 - 11.5	Lucky Bay	$15	$9
12.5	Wave Rock	$31	$31
13 - 15.5	Cheynes Beach	$100	$33
16 - 18.5	Peaceful Bay	$72	$24

Keeping track of camping costs

Above top Boating in Chamberlain Gorge, Western Australia *Above middle* The track to Lorella Springs in the Gulf Country, Queensland *Above* Crossing the King Edward River in the Kimberley, Western Australia *Right top* Kicking the footy from the Northern Territory into Queensland *Right middle* At 'The Tip' – the top of Cape York *Right bottom* Dylan being loaded onto the Royal Flying Doctor Service plane, Lombadina, Western Australia

Following in Eyre's Footsteps.

EDWARD JOHN EYRE
1841

This is to commemorate that

crossed the Australian Continent on the Eyre Highway
following in the footsteps of Edward John Eyre, reaching
Norseman W.A. on the   day of

Certified by:

Western Australian Tourism Commission

Following in Eyre's Footsteps.

EDWARD JOHN EYRE
1841

This is to commemorate that

crossed the Australian Continent on the Eyre Highway
following in the footsteps of Edward John Eyre, reaching
Norseman W.A. on the   day of

Certified by:

Western Australian Tourism Commission

Certificates for crossing
the Nullarbor

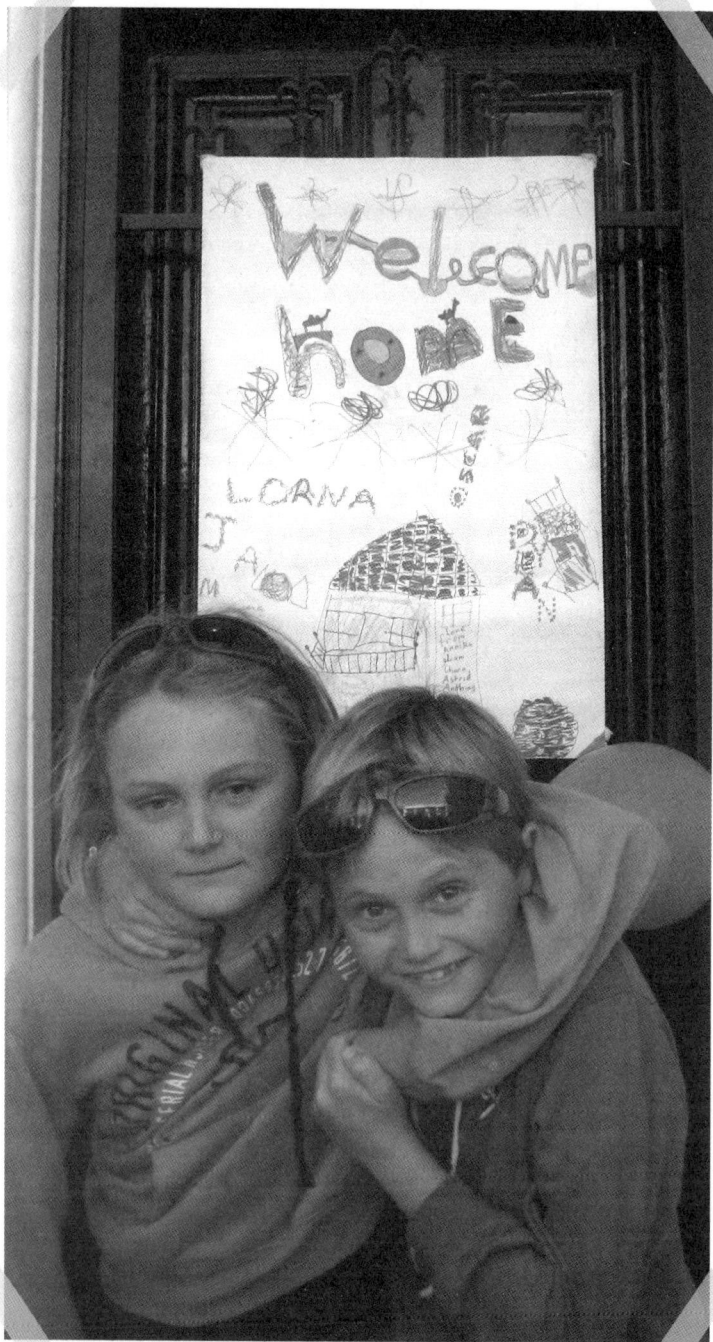

Back home after three years on the road